Access to Power

A Radical Approach for

Changing Your Life

ACCESS TO POWER
A RADICAL APPROACH FOR
CHANGING YOUR LIFE

Julia Kelliher

with

Julia Carol

Paula Elliott

Marybeth Paul

Glenn Smith

Nancy Shanteau

Spring Street Press
2014

Cover art :: *Voyage* by Katherine Smith-Schad

Cover design :: Maxima Kahn

Authors' photograph :: Simon Weller

ISBN :: 978-0-9916006-0-1

Spring Street Press
P.O. Box 2563
Grass Valley, CA 95945

For everyone who longs to be heard.
For Justine, my mother,
who had a lot to say and never wrote her book,
and for Estrella, who despite great obstacles,
brings her voice into the world.

Acknowledgments

We all want to thank our clients, teachers, and significant intimates: friends, lovers, parents, children, extended family, and community. We thank you for your patience, excitement, steady enthusiasm, and emotional support for the work it took to bring this book into the world. There are so many unseen helpers who have made this moment possible—to paraphrase Robert Hall, *How did we ever deserve these blessings?*[1] We are grateful for the random miracle of synchronicity—a potent coming together of teachers and teachings in this small, beautiful place: Nevada City, California.

We thank our family members and friends who supported us through the long years, meetings, weekends spent writing, and the many times we were "in the book." Julia Kelliher thanks Glenn Smith, Stephen, Willow, Shawna, and Jeffrey Hein. Julia Carol is very thankful for the help and support of Roland Juli, Yvonne Devine, Laura Cooksey, Anika Luskin, and Alex. Paula Elliott dedicates her writing in this book to Barbara and Bob Elliott and thanks Harvey, Nick, and Molly Katzman for practicing and embodying the work. Marybeth Paul thanks Nory Fussell, Florence Adler, and Edward Paul, her sister Bev, brother Ed, sister-in-law Dawn, and her children Jamie and Emily Lohmeyer. Nancy Shanteau thanks Geri, John, and Mark Shanteau, Sage Moore, and her dog Gandhi as well as faithful daycare providers Elise and Paul Thompson. Glenn Smith thanks Julia Kelliher, his mother Janice Smith, and all the rest of his amazing teachers in life, music, Radical Therapy, Lomi, and various modes of bodywork. It takes a village to make writing a book possible.

We thank the artists who contributed to this book: Katherine Schad-Smith, Simon Weller, Laurence and Barbara Brauer, Marjorie Woodall, Maxima Kahn, and Molly Fisk. Key thinkers who influenced the theoretical development of Skills for Change include Jennifer Cohen and Mimi Mills. We got important feedback from Molly Fisk, Renee Gregorio, Willow Hein, Shawna Hein, and Tom Slater.

The Somatic Education community, Lomi School, and Strozzi Institute offered crucial developmental practice spaces for the embodiment principles that inform every aspect of Skills for Change. We thank Robert and Alyssa Hall, Richard Strozzi-Heckler, Catherine Flaxman, George Leonard, and Wendy Palmer for their founding and formative influence on our body/mind approach to change, including bodywork and standing, moving practices.

We are especially grateful to those who created Radical Psychiatry and who wrote the original "Red Book," *Radical Psychiatry: The Second Decade*, including Beth Roy, Claude Steiner, Becky Jenkins, Shelby Morgan, JoAnn Costello, Sandy Spiker, Marian Oliker, Mark Weston, Diana Rabenold, and Eleanor Smith.[2] They are a large part of our roots.

This work is like a folk song. Folk songs belong to the people—we're all welcome to write new verses and add our own embellishments. If enough folks resonate with the change, it gets passed on.

We hope that somewhere down the road there will be another group of empowerment advocates who see how time has changed this book's relevancy and feel inspired to write a book of their own.

Contents

Preface

One pivotal event in the summer of 1991 ignited the first glimmer of this book. I was thirty-three years old, a single mother of three, and the owner of a retail business in Northern California. With an environmental-activist friend, I attended a weekend camp-out celebrating the return of water to Mono Lake after years of thorny legal negotiations. As we carried victory signs and a symbolic fish along Highway 395 to the lake, I happened to meet Glenn Smith, a trumpet player from San Francisco. He and I talked, walked, and shared meals, and by the end of the weekend, we'd developed a life-changing alliance: between two people, certainly, but also between two perspectives and lineages of powerful teachers and teachings. It was as if I had been working all my life on an almost-complete puzzle. Glenn (and his teacher, Beth Roy) offered me the final pieces!

Glenn came to live with me about six months later. Within a year, I began to see a few clients and synthesize the work I now call Skills for Change coaching. In 1995, I sold my retail coffee and clothing business and have now been in my own coaching practice for over twenty years. This book is the culmination of four decades of interest, curiosity, and study. The theories incorporated into Skills for Change coaching represent my attempt to explain my own experience and the experiences of my clients.

I was the fifth child of a large Catholic family from Massachusetts. My parents believed in hard work and social change. Working part-time jobs as a nurse while raising six children, my mother taught natural childbirth classes in our living room. My father was a clerk for the Boston & Maine Railroad and served as the secretary/treasurer for his labor union. Most evening meals in our household were accompanied by a kind of formal dialogue. My father would introduce discussions about current social concerns, including labor issues, the Cold War, Vietnam, and the merits of various politicians. His Irish American heritage and experience in World War II added weight and value to his political perspective. My older siblings were encouraged to share what they were learning in school, and since my two brothers were most interested in science, and my mom had two master of science degrees, I was exposed to scientific method at a very early age. I understood innately the idea of detached observation as I looked around at my large family. And the concept of change, how to measure, predict, and affect it, got pretty well stuck in my head.

I was born at the tail end of the baby boom, which also gave me a very young "outsider" perspective. In 1968, our family, and the middle-class culture I lived in, was experiencing huge social unrest and transition. My mother entered the work force again after a break of almost twenty years. My oldest brothers married young, had children, and narrowly avoided being drafted into the Vietnam War. My two older sisters, both teenagers, hung out with their friends a lot, and I was too young to go along. My younger brother was six years old and adapting to the complexity of grammar school and after-school care.

That left me, at ten, young enough to be interested in being with my parents and old enough to be very curious and anxious about the state of the world and our family. My parents included me in long conversations at the kitchen table at the end of the day, where my preoccupations were discussed. *Why is there war? What is religion all about? Is there really a God? Why are people so often cruel to each other? Why are we here at all? Why is extramarital sex wrong? What about love and happiness—does anyone actually feel them?* My mother—at heart a cultural anthropologist—would do her best to answer my questions, while my dad, obviously uncomfortable, added a word here and there, mostly responding with facial expressions. Years later he told me he had not a clue really about life, love, or God but believed in the importance of human ethics and people behaving in ways that took care of society as a whole. He loved my mother and admired her willingness to take on the larger questions.

My mother died at ninety-three at the end of last year. In her day, she cofounded the Boston Association for Childbirth Education and provided key thinking and assistance in the writing of the childbirth chapter of the Boston Women's Health Book Collective's *Our Bodies, Ourselves.* She was considered a pioneer in the feminist health movement and gave her research and writings to Harvard University's Schlesinger Library on the History of Women. But she never published a book. Although my mother was a good writer, she didn't enjoy writing. She liked to read and talk, think, teach, and discuss. As a writer, I've walked in the echo of my mother's silence.

I too prefer the art of storytelling to writing. I love to listen to stories, consider points of view, engage in conversation, and provide doors to new thoughts and actions. I am similar to my mother in this way. In my client sessions, I rely on both verbal and nonverbal connection and conversation. If I have an innate talent, it is for listening, digesting, and reflecting. Most of my life I have written for myself, in journals, as a form of self-care. I write to understand what I've noticed, sort things out, and catch up with my mind. For me, the process of writing takes great effort—I began the *Access to Power* book project partly to inspire, partly as a personal journey out of the shadows of my social class and gender. Without considerable help, this book would never have been completed.

When I came to Northern California in 1975, I was introduced to the wild rivers and mountains and to the philosophic discourse of the Deep Ecology movement.[1] From those reference points, I learned to delve into my own beliefs and feel how they kept me identified with my mind and separated me from my body and the rest of the natural world. Soon thereafter, I attended a ten-day Buddhist silent meditation retreat, learning to listen to my breath and moment-to-moment experience within the silence. Through the 1980s, I engaged in my own healing journey, discovering feminist spirituality, bodywork, psychotherapy, and women's groups. In 1992, Glenn introduced me to his teacher, Beth Roy, an early member of the Bay Area Radical Psychiatry Collective. During mediation sessions with Beth, Glenn and I learned communication skills that helped us to listen to each other compassionately, cooperate as equals, and resolve conflict in our relationship. I enrolled in Lomi Somatic Education and spent several years training and practicing, learning to notice the cultural conditioning and holding in the body. For six years, I trained with Beth Roy, and from her I learned to identify the underlying contradictions and oppressive structures of beliefs within people's stories.

I studied with educated thinkers and theoreticians, Buddhist teachers, and strong leaders. I also learned from angry victims, sobbing children, addicts of every kind, and heartbroken people still hoping for answers. I internalized powerful teaching tools and theories, but it was watching my clients and students put my suggestions to the test—with courage and sincerity, and who generously shared their stories—that grounded these tools in me. Many of these people have asked for this book, and it is for them that it was written.

Six such clients/students and now friends/colleagues have been the midwives of this book. Estrella Acosta gave us the book's name, along with love and moral support. The remaining five helped me collect these ideas in words on pages, writing in their own voices about my synthesis of this coaching work we call Skills for Change. Glenn Smith, Paula Elliott, Marybeth Paul, Julia Carol, and Nancy Shanteau (listed in order of their appearance in my life: 1991–2004), all carry the work and are wonderful coaches and teachers, each in their own way.

My husband, life partner, and colleague, Glenn Smith, as I've said, introduced me to Beth Roy, who became my primary teacher and mentor. He's been continually generous and supportive of me during the development of Skills for Change. Paula Elliott, a nurse and social worker, was one of my very first clients, and Marybeth Paul, a massage therapist, came a few years later. Both Paula and Marybeth applied every single one of these tools and theories to their personal lives in all contexts, with their husbands, ex-husbands, children, friends, and extended communities. They are both inspiring teachers and mentors in our community. Julia Carol, already versed in social justice through her participation in grassroots anti-smoking campaigns, was a powerful instigator for the writing of this book. She is a visionary, optimist, and life coach who pushed for the potential of Skills for Change coaching to help a wider audience. Nancy Shanteau, the youngest of us, radicalized young and already a somatic coach when I met her, quickly became a bold innovator and practitioner of this work. She is a natural teacher, a writing coach, the founder of a coach-training program, and bridge to the next generation.

At the onset, we planned to write *Access to Power* mostly collaboratively, with me as both peer and leader. We met as a group for several years until the effort, complexity, and slow progress became too strained for a number of us. At that point, the group graciously turned the book over to me to do as I wished. It had been challenging for me to have others write about concepts I had spent so much time updating and synthesizing, and I was relieved to have final editorial rights over the book. In the end, we each wrote sections, and with Nancy Shanteau's help, I edited the manuscript to make sure the theory matches what I teach. Nancy and I wrestled with many, many revisions, each bringing our strengths and depth of experience to the difficult work of depicting Skills for Change coaching on the written page. We changed the names of clients, family, and friends to allow greater privacy to those whose stories we are telling from our own viewpoints.

We've been through a lot together to get this book from concept to form, implementing all the tools we teach: We've cleared difficult feelings that came up, negotiated and renegotiated, supported and appreciated, taken on internalized oppression and normalized conflict, created plenitude in the face of scarcity, and taken as long as we needed to complete the book with the least injury to all. Most importantly, we remain friends and colleagues, despite much stress and many complex interpersonal dynamics. It has been honest and real.

We hope this book helps you make deeper sense of your life, inspires you to take power and make change, and strengthens your compassion for yourself and the rest of us on this swirling planet.

Julia Kelliher
Nevada City, California
June 2014

"There must exist a paradigm, a practical model for social change that includes an understanding of ways to transform consciousness that are linked to efforts to transform structures."

—bell hooks

PART I
THE COMPLEXITY OF OUR LIVES

One • Of Course

Julia Carol

Why don't I know what I really want? Why can't I make myself do what's good for me? Why do I often feel so overwhelmed? Is there something wrong with me?

These are some of the questions I have asked myself, and I find my work with clients often addresses the same questions. Here are some other questions: If life is such a great gift, why is it often so difficult just being alive? If relationships are so fulfilling, why do I feel insecure about or frustrated with my relationships? Why can't I just be happy?

Sometimes the thoughts are in the voice of a screaming inner critic, and sometimes they're just a nagging buzz in the back of our mind, draining our energy like an unpleasant radio station.

The first good news is that we're not alone. While it's true that we are all individuals and unique unto ourselves, we share more than we may realize with one another in our culture. Given the cultural messages we've internalized, it's perfectly understandable for us to feel overwhelmed, trapped, or to think something is wrong with us and that we need to be fixed.

So we're not crazy; we just respond naturally to the messages we've received from our culture and families. Our families also internalized restrictive messages, and of course they passed them along to us. Some messages float through the mainstream and some through many subcultures, depending on our race, religion, gender identity, sexual preference, socioeconomic class, region, ability, mental/physical wellness, and age. Those messages that come in the form of "absolutes," or right-and-wrong rules, often serve to produce feelings of disconnection and create in us a lack of love and compassion for ourselves and others.

I am passionate about my belief that despite cultural pressures we all face, we still can create powerful, positive change in our lives. I have firsthand experience using the tools shared in this book to ease various forms of struggle imposed on me, and my clients, by our own inner critical voice and external circumstances.

In my mind, it all begins with our DNA. While some animal species birth babies with instincts allowing maturation and independence in a matter of days or months, the human species is born quite dependent on adults of the species to nurture and raise us and to teach us how and who to be. We are designed to learn by watching and mimicking. We also listen to the stories we're told by our immediate families, neighbors, teachers, and community, and in modern times, through the ubiquitous media messages we're exposed to. As children, of course we soak up these cultural stories like dry sponges.

We're also pack animals. Not only do we learn how to take care of ourselves by imitating others, we also replicate the behaviors and postures of others so that we may "fit in" socially. As we learn to internalize cultural expectations and follow the cultural rules, we are rewarded socially (and it turns out this is nature's way to help us remain safe and aid our very survival).

SO WHAT'S THE PROBLEM?

Let me be blunt. Many of the messages that we have received from our culture are not conducive to a healthy and loving relationship with our minds, hearts, and spirits, nor with our family, friends, and communities. Also, the intent of the message givers wasn't totally pure. I recently read a bumper sticker that asked, "Who is profiting from your self-loathing?" In other words, what money-making business (a cosmetics company, cigarette company, food and beverage company, pharmaceutical drug company) is profiting from us not feeling good about ourselves?

We in the United States have a multitude of cultural perspectives based on economic class, race, gender, geography, education, and so on. And in addition to these diverse slices of cultural pie, there are "mainstream" cultural messages that all of us as U.S. citizens have been spoon-fed and dutifully consumed. For now, let's call these mainstream cultural messages our "shoulds" and "should-nots." They're the rules we've digested from a culture that has also taught us right from wrong, good from bad, and how to live in order to be accepted by our community.

DUALITY

Most of our parents thought they were doing a good job parenting if they taught us right from wrong. We were instilled with the message that we should be "good." We got punished when we were "bad." As an alternative, this book offers the concept discussed in many nondualistic religions and by many wise teachers: we cause ourselves suffering when our worldview is overly simple, when we hold our values in terms of "all or nothing/right or wrong" absolute thinking. The problem with absolutes is that they limit our ability to see the whole complicated, colorful picture and keep life in context. The either/or model limits our choices. In the moments we're able to leave the dualistic paradigm and instead bring curiosity to the complexity, and search for a deeper understanding of ourselves and others, we are more empowered to create change. The thirteenth-century poet Jalāl ad-Dīn Rūmī is often quoted as saying, "Out beyond ideas of wrongdoing and rightdoing, there is a field. I will meet you there. When the soul lies down in that grass, the world is too full to talk about. Ideas, language, even the phrase 'each other' doesn't make any sense."[1] When we leave duality as a worldview behind, the resultant spaciousness offers us many new options and ways of seeing our lives.

So when we combine our natural tendency to internalize cultural messages that aren't all healthy and life affirming, along with our culture's propensity to reduce life to dualistic thinking, we begin to understand why so many of us find our internal broadcast tuned to a disturbing station filled with unpleasant propaganda and painful static.

INDIVIDUALISM

Among the most oppressive of our unhealthy internalized cultural messages in the United States are those within a philosophy of individualism. The message goes something like this: The United States is a place where every child who works hard enough can grow up to be anything they want to be (including president of the United States) and have anything they want (big house, car, latest "stuff"). Furthermore, part of our freedom is the pursuit of happiness, and nothing stands in our way of achieving our goals and being happy.

While this message sounds lovely, and it may work well for some, the inherent message is that if we have not achieved whatever goals we might have for ourselves, and if we're not entirely happy with our lives, there is something wrong with us. However, this internalized individualism doesn't actually translate into individual rights or equal power for all people. It just ends up meaning that we're on our own, alone, and it's our fault if we're not thriving.

Most of us have soaked into our bones the story that we're completely responsible for the quality of our own lives, so we focus on ourselves and those individuals closest to us when we want to make a change. We've been taught that we have the power to create the lives we want. And so we try. And if our lives don't turn out the way we thought they would, we have ourselves to blame, and we resolve to work harder on ourselves. We try to stifle our complaints because no one likes a whiner. The truth is that it often takes us the better half of our lives just to know what it is that we really want—if ever we do know—because we've accepted so many messages about what we would want if we were good enough, smart enough, if we were to please our families or peers, feel successful, and get societal respect and approval.

How many of our choices are really our choices to begin with? Sometimes it's difficult to tell. Career choices, family/relationship choices, religion, politics—how much of our lives have we chosen ourselves, and how much have we chosen in order to please our culture or our community? And an even more frightening question: would we really be able to do what we wanted if we knew what it was?

We might be able to do what we want to, if it happens to fit into the constraints of our economic structure and isn't too out of step with mainstream values. For example, our culture occasionally pays lip service to supporting the arts, but in reality, there are very few artists (of any medium) who are able to survive on the merits of their craft. The truth is, if we choose to be a painter, singer, musician, or an art historian,—we are going to face economic challenges that are not of our creation and are not our fault. We still can choose to follow our passions, but we'll spend less time and energy wondering, "What's wrong with me?" if we know from the outset what we're up against. And we're all taught that to get ahead, we need a college degree, but I know a lot of people who worked very hard to get a degree, and all they have to show for it is student debt.

Also, for many people, myself included, college was just too far out of reach. I supported myself through three years and dropped out during the first semester of my final year because I was too exhausted working and going to school full time. I wasn't able to live in a dorm and focus only on getting a well-rounded education—and nowadays, it's even tougher. At the time, I held myself 100% responsible for my failure. Obviously, I was just a quitter. I assumed that the system worked, and so it must be all my fault that I couldn't hack it.

So if a child grows up wanting to be a doctor or an astronaut or a professional baseball player, it's not just their own hard work that will ensure their success. The part of the problem that makes me angry is this: We judge ourselves by how well we meet societal expectations, and yet society isn't always concerned with making sure those expectations are viable. Rugged individualism doesn't translate as "choose your own values"; it ends up meaning we're on our own in terms of responsibility for meeting society's expectations.

This message of individualism does not come just from mainstream capitalists who perpetuate the story that if we work hard and follow the rules, anything is possible in America. It also comes from religious leaders who preach that being "good" will bring us the life we deserve. We can find this same flavor of individualism in best-selling New Age books that profess to use quantum physics to prove to us that we create 100% of our own reality and can manifest anything if only we understand the "laws of attraction."

I'm a big believer in claiming individual power and creating positive change, but it's not an all-or-nothing situation. Some of what happens in our lives is pure luck, some fortunate and some unfortunate. Hard work can be helpful to our lives—and I applaud individual goals and dreams of a better life. But there are some harmful untruths to the philosophy of individualism that make it more difficult to change our lives.

We're not all born with the same opportunities. And our society does not equally support all of us in the choices we make. We face various inequities that impact our power over creating our lives, including but not limited to access to money, health care, higher education, child care for our families, clean air and water, and others. There are also different cultural expectations based on race, gender, geography, and so on that are imbedded in each of us and quite difficult to overcome.

When we assign blame, we enact the good/bad, right/wrong model. Blaming ourselves for our perceived failures keeps us stuck. When we get caught in the blame paradigm, we work to change only ourselves as individuals. Alternately, we might see injustice and inequality in our society and work collectively to effect cultural change. We might use the personal power we do have to change policies that will produce a country with full opportunity for all individuals.

When we break the collective spell of individualism, we are able to take a long, honest look at who we are and how we naturally evolved to be the way we are. We can say, "Of course we're having difficulties." We are better able to hold both ourselves and our society with compassion. Then, given the realistic options we have, we can work to change ourselves and our culture from an empowered place, with as much community support as possible.

SOCIETY SHAPES OUR STORY

"All things are subject to interpretation; whichever interpretation prevails at a given time is a function of power and not truth."
—*Friedrich Nietzsche*[2]

When we begin to discern between cultural values and personal values, we start to ask ourselves questions: What's my experience? How did where and when I was born affect the cultural messages I soaked up? What are the "shoulds" and "should-nots" that guide me through my day? Which cultural norms nurture and support me, and which are disempowering? It's a great exercise to check out our own life circumstances in the context of the social and political environment in which we grew up.

I don't even want to know how many hours my young, sponge-like mind soaked up 1950s and '60s commercials designed to make me think I needed to see my reflection in the kitchen floor, avoid ring around the collar at all costs, and eat a breath mint with a drop of Retsyn before I spoke to my friends. The first naked woman I ever saw was Barbie; I thought vitamins were pills that looked like Fred Flintstone, and I knew the men in the white hats were supposed to be the heroes. That was just what I soaked up from television. The little girl next door taught me that if I lied I wouldn't get any jewels in my crown, even if I made it to heaven, and if I touched myself "down there," I'd burn in hell.

My teachers taught me that Christopher Columbus discovered America, and I had to take a "time out" in the corner when I dared inquire as to whether the "Indians" had not discovered it first. My parents dutifully told me I could grow up to be anything I wanted to be— an astronaut (I was born in 1957, the year of Sputnik), a doctor, or a lawyer. I wasn't sure they were right, as it seemed to me that most of the powerful jobs were held by men, so I privately set my sights on being a secretary, mommy, or waitress (really, I did).

I also got the message that all of my hopes and dreams depended on me. If I worked hard and applied myself, the world was my oyster. That's what I heard with my ears. What I saw with my eyes were news stories where white mothers in Boston yelled at young black children in buses as they were integrating formerly whites-only schools. I was told in school about the First Amendment and saw on television the footage of college students at Kent State University being gunned down by the government for protesting the Vietnam War.

Somewhere in the back of my mind, I knew my teachers expected more of me than they expected of the Mexican American children, and we all expected the Asian kids to be the smartest and the quietest. In junior high school, I was denied the choice of wood or metal shop and forced to take home economics, like all the other girls. While my parents were very liberal and progressive for their time— and consciously tried to convince me that girls and boys should have equal rights and opportunities—even they could not escape the traditional gender roles they'd internalized. Though my mother went to graduate school while my father worked (almost unheard of in the '60s), my father was still the one whose moods we all tip-toed around. He had the final say about almost everything from the setting on the thermostat to whether or not the television was on—he was in control, and my mother did whatever she needed to do to avoid upsetting him, most of the time.[3]

The messages I internalized about sex and romantic relationships caused problems I'm still cleaning up today. I was caught between the cultural norms of the '50s (where a housewife's work was under-valued) and the new emerging norms of the '60s (where women still did all the housework, only now they "got" to enter the work force and earn wages, as well). Don't telephone a boy first, but split the check in a restaurant. Be a virgin, but know how to have multiple orgasms.

As we unearth the stories that we grew up with, we might feel overburdened by the pain of our history. Or conversely, our story may have so much privilege that it's hard to see any roadblocks or "shoulds" that got conveyed. Whatever the story, when we exam-ine our personal history and identify the systemic "of courses" that shaped us, we normalize our experience and are able to take our-selves "off the hook" of self-blame.

In his book *Outliers*, Malcolm Gladwell references scientific research and analysis of observable facts to come to this conclusion: "Why do some people succeed, living remarkably productive and impactful lives, while so many more never reach their potential? . . . [The successful] are invariably the beneficiaries of hidden advantages and extraordi-nary opportunities and cultural legacies that allow them to learn and work hard and make sense of the world in ways others cannot." Our "success" is both a product of our hard work and a benefit of our social context. We do not exist apart from our environment, and our success is created in context with the social world in which we work and live.

Our internal negative messages to the contrary, we are not bad, crazy, lazy, stupid, or any of the other labels we sometimes use on ourselves or others. We're normal people who make choices and exhibit behaviors and feelings, fears, hopes, and needs that are all perfectly natural once we view ourselves compassionately and understand the ways that we internalize cultural oppression. Some of our behaviors serve us well and are qualities to appreciate and cherish—and some may hinder us. As we lift the veil and see that there's nothing wrong with us, and of course we're the way we are, we begin to recognize which internalized oppressive messages are obstacles. As we see where we came from, and understand how it makes sense that we did what we did to survive, we begin to have more choice, to change our internal beliefs and then our bodies, feelings, words, and actions.

Two • Power

Julia Kelliher

When I was twenty-three years old, I lived in California and gave birth to my first baby. Far from my hometown and parents in Massachusetts, with my husband at work, I was alone with my newborn. At first, my new baby slept a lot. While I was peacefully occupied washing the dishes or paying bills, she would start crying, and I would pick her up and offer her breast milk or loving attention. I wanted to comfort her.

My daughter's power to obtain food, shelter, comfort, affection, and soothing was solely based on the power of her loving attachment to me, her mother, and other caregivers. My own limited access to food, money, and other outside support caused me a great deal of anxiety. And both my limited access to resources and my survival anxieties affected her directly.

I saw firsthand that the world is unfair and arbitrary right from the start. As infants, we have no control over what happens to us. We're born into a cultural and social setting where our caregivers have harder or easier lives, and things start happening to us, without any input from us other than our ability to express our needs through crying, smiling, and body language. Our first lessons about power are that we don't have much, and we need to get as much as we can from the people around us.

As a mother, I felt more love for my innocent newborn baby than I had ever felt for anyone before in my life. I thought I would probably sacrifice anything for her sake. Ironically, I also felt incredible resentment toward my baby for wanting so much from me when I wasn't getting many of the things I wanted and needed. I was often scared, tired, and hungry, and I felt angry about the personal neglect I experienced as an isolated mother at home. On top of that, I felt ashamed. I thought I was personally defective as a mom for feeling anger or resentment. I had so far in my life not found a way to earn enough money to live, grow much food, or build an adequate support system. And here I was having horrible feelings in the one powerful job I had as a mother. I thought of myself as weak and pathetic.

I now understand that what I was experiencing was a huge degree of powerlessness, which resulted in a sense of personal shame. It wasn't innate power that I lacked; it was power related to the social world, power to access what I needed as a young woman and mother. And my family's powerlessness wasn't a result of laziness or stupidity in my husband or me. I was plagued by depleting and dispiriting thoughts of shame and blame, and they greatly decreased my ability to make changes in my situation.

My first conscious awareness about power came after I entered the world of business. Our local co-op needed a new bookkeeper, and someone suggested I might be able to start a home business doing bookkeeping. I read some books on business, got lessons from a bookkeeper, and started a small bookkeeping service with just a few clients. A few years later, after my second pregnancy and the birth of twins, one of the retail businesses I worked for came up for sale, and through acts of luck, determination, privilege, and courage, I managed to procure it. I was twenty-six years old at the time. I had three young children all under the age of three, and I was in a near panic as I tried to run my life and the business. In the midst of a difficult negotiation with one of my employees, she exclaimed in exasperation, "You can do whatever you want. You're the boss!" I was stunned into silence. It was time; I had to look at how I was using power.

My employee's statement, though vastly oversimplified, was also true. I was a boss and had more power than my employee did. This truth was in stark contrast to my inner sense of shame and powerlessness. The resultant confusion and inner dissonance launched me into a personal inquiry into the concept of power and what it actually looked like in my own life and the lives of those around me.

In this chapter, I will share my exploration into what power means and the kinds of power we encounter in daily life. We will compassionately consider the limits and opportunities that power offers us. With more awareness, our hope is that perhaps we will begin to see more realistically what's possible and envision an attainable, balanced, and satisfying future for ourselves.

WHAT IS POWER?

Power is part of our day-to-day life. We use it, enjoy it, struggle with it, and are blind to it and to the effect of it. Power is complex, yet we intuitively understand power is at work in our experiences. We sense power at play and respond to it, often without consciously understanding what "it" is.

Power is defined loosely as "a measure of a person's ability to control the environment around them, including the behavior of other people."[1] But I, like many people, had related to the concept of power as either "bad," something that was used against other people, or conversely, something "mysterious" and beyond my reach. The word *control* was even worse. I knew some people had a lust for power (Dr. Frankenstein, for instance) and heard that some people were just "control freaks," but they were not people a good Catholic girl wanted to emulate. Wikipedia validates these confusing messages about power, stating, "The term *authority* is often used for power, perceived as legitimate by the social structure. Power can be seen as evil or unjust, but the exercise of power is accepted as endemic to humans as social beings."[2]

We all live in a complex world of social rules, relationships, and numerous kinds of power maneuvering. Everyone has personal needs. As *instinctual* animals, we naturally assert our physical and instinctual powers to meet these needs, sometimes at the expense

Oh Good, Conflict!

GLENN SMITH

So, is conflict good? Yes, conflict can be good! It can be informative and productive and spur positive change, even when it is surprising, upsetting, frustrating, or infuriating. Of course, if too much pain and damage have occurred already, it may be difficult to arrive at a positive end. We've all had experiences of emotionally, if not also physically, damaging conflict. This naturally causes us to want to avoid conflict and think of it as bad.

Yet, if parties in conflict communicate in relative calm, greater understanding will eventually result. After differences are aired, creative and fair give-and-take solutions may be negotiated. Along the way, we identify common goals, desires, and points, and our relationships flourish with shared action. Or at least we negotiate the terms for respectful distance. Unaddressed conflict tends to fester, perhaps leading to worse discomfort later. Skills for Change practitioners emphasize the role of power in conflict, work to uncover hidden conflict, and understand the roots of overt conflict. And when we become skilled at conflict, while it might not be easy, we open a doorway to change.

of others. As *social* animals, however, we also need to be in relationship with our family and tribe in order to survive. Our need for social approval can compete with needs that are more personal and selfish. We *fear* being shunned, but we also have strong *desire* for well-being and pleasure. This contradiction, when left unexamined, creates much strife and suffering for us.

In the 1950s middle-class suburban neighborhood outside Boston where I was raised, conflict and power struggle were seen as unpleasant, unkind, dangerous, and/or wrong. Nowhere was I taught that conflict was just a normal part of life, in which people have different needs and different degrees of power, and that negotiation of these needs is important. Once I started looking at power, it made total sense that I wanted control over my life, as did my children and employees. When I accepted that power exists, not good, not bad, I began to learn and engage in the joy, pain, and responsibility of power as I managed both my family and my new business.

Most middle-class U.S. citizens have some limited amount of power to create happy lives. First, we develop the power to know what we really need and want, as opposed to what we have been taught to believe we want. Then, we use our power both individually and collectively to free ourselves from cultural indoctrination and the resultant fear and addictions. Last but not least, we take action to gain access to the things that truly support our satisfaction and well-being.

When we come out of confusion and into clarity about what power is and how it functions, we may then access our existing strengths and resources. Our conscious understanding helps support empowerment, and our empowerment supports positive change.

TYPES OF POWER

Our personal power may help us get what we want through our use of inborn intelligence and talents, but power also exists outside of ourselves in the social environment. I used all kinds of power to attain and build my business. My innate intelligence combined with the benefit of good education helped me learn about business and make a business plan. I used my white, middle-class cultural background to confidently network with friends and family and broker loans. My youth and female warmth allowed me to charm great employees, and my "mother of little kids" identity helped me garner sympathy and support from customers. I used the power of U.S. citizenship and capitalism to fuel my economic growth.

One way to learn how our personal power intersects with the social world is to segment power into five categories. Beth Roy defines these types of power as *personal, transactional, contractual, cultural*, and *structural*. Roy stresses the fact that these categories are not distinct from one another, and in almost every instance of power, they overlap.

Roy also states, "I think of power as something we *do*. It is a means by which we accomplish, or are denied well-being. Power is a process going on between and among people, a multi-layered and ever-shifting set of relationships. *Shaped* profoundly by the social structures within which we live, power is *internalized*, manifesting as feelings of entitlement and insecurity. It is *enacted* in transactions between and among people, *embodied* in cultural practices, and *played out* in organizational roles."[3]

Think of power as *the ability to get what we want or need*. The following is a way I have come to understand the differences between the types of power:

- **Personal Power:** Our sense of confidence, how we express ourselves, our use of language, our confidence in our bodies, our talents and natural gifts—these all translate into expressions of personal power.

- **Transactional Power:** The way we behave in relation to others, and use our words, body postures, eye contact, and so on, communicates and negotiates power. Radical Therapists, borrowing heavily from Eric Berne's Transactional Analysis, identified three broad categories of transactions with power. For example, we can try to overpower another person ("power play"), try to find a way to meet needs mutually ("cooperate"), or we can give up our needs and take care of others first ("rescue").[4]

- **Contractual Power:** We generate sets of agreements, tacit or explicit, between or among people to distribute power in particular ways. These contracts shape individual transactions and organizational practice and fall under the governance of laws and regulations, thus reflecting the influence of structural power.

- **Cultural Power:** Our language, traditions, spoken and unspoken rules, and beliefs of religion, ethnicity, and geography are all examples of how cultural power pervades our lives. While our family's values significantly impact our beliefs, cultural values are as often transmitted via the media and our peers in our socialization as young people. Mysterious elements such as the shape of our bodies can impact our experience as we soak up the complex, interlocking preferences of our culture.

- **Structural Power:** Power relations within large social structures (such as capitalism or racism) are conducted within systemic power frameworks based on laws, policies, and local practices. Our face-to-face interactions as well as group dynamics occur in the context of these larger systems of power.

POWER IN ACTION

We were all children once, with parents or caregivers, even if we have never been parents. Being a child is one shared human experience in which we have all felt our powerlessness and the need to cultivate more control and power over our world. For that reason, as I review my own experience with my firstborn baby, we will look at how types of power are experienced and then enacted between a parent and a child during those first few years of their life together.

First, let's look at the context of structure, culture, and contracts. With enormous good fortune, both my husband and I were born with implicit *structural* and *cultural* power as white-skinned, middle-class United States citizens at a historical moment of growth and affluence in U.S. economics. In my nontraditional marriage, my husband and I had a traditional division of labor agreement that I would be the primary parent. From that agreement, I took the *contractual* power to have enormous impact over my child's day-to-day life. At the same time, I was still just a young woman with few career skills, very little money, and dependent on my male partner. His greater confidence and ability to get jobs was partly due to his *cultural* power. By virtue of being a woman in a patriarchal culture, I lacked both competency and access to resources. That in turn affected my *structural* power in terms of economics. I remember writing the words *trapped* and *powerless* in my journal.[5]

Out of desperation and necessity, I eventually connected with other mothers and tapped into a kind of tribal *cultural* power that occurs among women caring for children together. Mothers may be rich, middle-class, or poor, light-skinned or dark-skinned, but all over the world mothers usually share a kind of kinship in motherhood. We then have access to the collective *cultural* power of motherhood that men, as well as women without children, are denied. Even though women experience a rise in *cultural* power with motherhood, most mothers (regardless of social class) also experience a decrease in economic *structural* power.

Many middle-class men, my first husband, Michael, included, have a slightly different experience with power when they become fathers. When taking on the role of breadwinner, often fathers maintain whatever economic *structural/cultural* power they had before parenthood but often face a decrease in freedom and choice within the confines of their relationships with their partners and children. Fathers often feel trapped in a kind of *contractual* and *structural* "privilege" that involves working for money. Work, while providing economic power, frequently robs fathers of the energy to emotionally or physically nurture their relationships with themselves or others.[6]

These gender-based roles in families with children often create distance between men and women. Michael and I were a young couple with all those incipient struggles, and our marriage was troubled during those years. Nonetheless, as a young mother, I had far more *structural* power in my life as a result of being in a marriage with a strong, able-bodied, educated, middle-class young man, rather than having to raise my children on my own. This power was then part of my children's lives as well. Even later, when we were divorced, having Michael as a committed co-parent continued to give me a sense of support and security I would not have had without him.

Both Michael and I left our homes on the East Coast and came to California, so we had lost the sense of *structural/cultural* power that came from being part of our white-skinned, middle-class family's community. Michael and I had gotten married partly to access more family support, which increased our *contractual* and *cultural* power in the context of a culture with a religious and social bias toward heterosexual marriage. My parents had six children, my father came from poor Irish working class roots, and we grew up blue-collar working class, so I had internalized a certain sense of insecurity, with very little net to catch me if I fell. Michael, however, came from a middle-class family who could help us out financially, and he worried much less as a result. In this context, my daughter, Heather, was learning something about her own *cultural* and economic power.

Though she was not conscious of it, Heather had inherited *structural* power by virtue of being born a U.S. citizen, white-skinned, healthy, and nice looking. Luckily, she had been born in the context of huge cultural changes rising out of the feminist and civil rights movements. Being a girl child was not detrimental to that *structural* power while she was still a baby. She was born at home, with loving community around her. With trees, rivers, and good weather, Northern California was a beautiful home environment. She slept in our bed and had the *cultural* power of access to breast milk on demand, thanks to my involvement in the subculture of the natural childbirth movement. Being a cute and beloved only child in her first two years gave her a lot of power in our household.

Now let's look at *transactional* and *personal* power. Heather and I both had lots of innate and instinctual *personal* power. We were intelligent, creative, healthy, and attractive. We both had a connection to the natural world as a result of living in a beautiful place. We spent time singing, reading, playing, and eating healthy food. Heather and I both had physical strength and health that translated into humor, fun, and creativity. Heather had a kind of innate caution that kept her from having accidents.

In our *transactions*, I tried to teach cooperation by negotiating with her even when she was very young. When I spent too much time catering to her needs without my own being met and was burnt out, and I started to resent taking care of her needs, Michael often took a turn, so Heather and I avoided the worst kind of power struggles. As I disclosed earlier, like many parents and children, Heather and I had competitive tones in our *transactions* pretty early on. But when her twin siblings, Jared and Sarah, were born, our competitive struggles got much worse. She wanted attention. I wanted rest and sleep. I needed to take care of two new infants. The twins' birth had been difficult, and they were born two months premature. Modern medical advances had kept all of us alive, but Sarah needed lots of hospital and medical care that created more scarcity of time, energy, and attention for all of us.

In the context of scarcity and fatigue, I frequently noticed myself using *transactional* power in the form of power plays. I resorted to primitive use of control through statements laced with threat, like, "Stop it!" and "Do it because I said so!" I even combined threats with physical force, such as pushing or slapping her hand. Although I felt horrible about this behavior, I also felt desperate. I had been treated that way myself as a child, so it was familiar. In response, Heather became more aggressive in her attempt to get attention from me, unrolling toilet paper, drawing on the walls, poking the babies, and talking nonstop.

The *transactional* power struggles with children are very real. When adults speak judgmentally about children manipulating parents, saying, "You don't want them to control you," I find myself rather flabbergasted! Of course children try to manipulate parents! What power over their lives do they have other than trying to control what their caregiver does or doesn't do? As parents, we often try to get rest, food, or quiet, and children try to get attention, food, touch, or playtime. Our respective needs are often at odds. Children often pursue their own needs by interfering with their parents' comfort level through the use of their limited *transactional* power by screaming and/or crying. Children's *cultural* and *structural* power is severely limited, so it makes sense that parenthood is rife with *transactional* power struggles.

OUR PERSONAL/POLITICAL LIVES

Children try to maximize their power by accessing it from their parents. And of course, parents get burnt out by their struggles in the face of their family's real lack of resources—time, money, energy, and so on. Parents and caregivers of all kinds sacrifice many of their basic needs in order to provide for their children. Community, economic, and emotional support from others can provide *structural* power to beleaguered parents and reduce the stressful effects of *transactional* power struggles. Unfortunately, individual parents often do not seek this kind of support and instead turn to their own *personal* power. Turning inward rather than outward for the solution is supported by individualism and the "personal responsibility" cult of modern U.S. culture. But no matter how much we might try to change patterns of behavior in *transactions* using all of the *personal* power we have at hand, a certain amount of power to be happy exists in the world of externals.

In the United States, we often suffer from deeply mystified and depoliticized personal lives to such an extent that we might end up trapped and trying to change *personal,* internal relationship dynamics without looking at the *structural,* external component. Our culture encourages us to avoid the fact that "the personal is political," and we become more disempowered because the political is both hidden and interwoven in our personal lives. When we don't identify the sources of *structural* and *cultural* power in our lives, we often end up feeling powerless and blame ourselves and our closest relationships for our personal limits.

We thus begin to empower ourselves when we look clearly at the difference between types of power, identify the best sources of power for our circumstances, and thereby create the most realistic change. Without consciousness and awareness, no change is possible. If we still feel stuck and unable to change, it's not our fault, because knowledge by itself is not enough. With knowledge, we can begin to gather our resources, build our communities, and take the actions required to make the changes we want in our lives.

Three • Oppression, Alienation, and Empowerment: Loss and Recovery of Power

Julia Kelliher

Many times during my days and weeks, I hear myself or others around me complain that although they *think* they "should" be grateful for what they have, they *feel* funky, depressed, or lost. Some of these complaints are grounded in real material difficulties: lost jobs, house foreclosures, debt burden, money troubles, and fear of an uncertain future. Many of the younger folks in my life are having difficulty finding meaningful mates, work, or community. Relationships feel unstable and insecure. Jobs are hard to find. College is expensive and doesn't promise the same economic advantages as in the past. Affordable housing is limited. Our choices to commit to mortgages, children, or long-term marriage are very frightening. Life on this earth as we know it seems unsustainable. As if these material concerns are not hard enough, I also hear a tone of hopelessness and powerlessness that infiltrates most conversations. This mysterious malaise is at once palpable, yet challenging to address.

Compared to the majority of people in the world, those of us who are middle-class U.S. citizens experience enormous access to material and physical comforts of all kinds and have a relatively large degree of power over our lives. And yet among this same population, we experience chronic anxiety, disease, depression, unhappiness, and high rates of suicide, domestic violence, drug abuse, and other forms of emotional and social distress. In fact, statistically we suffer from those kinds of problems more than many of the so-called less-civilized cultures in the world.

As Skills for Change practitioners, we continually confront the fact that amid relative abundance of resources, we and many of the folks in our community of clients and students have a sense of "dis-ease" and dissatisfaction in our lives. We see a complex web of cultural and political influences that teach us to disconnect from a sense of belonging, from our bodies, from aliveness, and from a philosophical/spiritual center.

The philosophic concept of alienation is enormously useful as we attempt to unravel the murky complexity of this kind of human discontent and find a way through it to more empowerment and meaningful human activity. In the 1970s, the Radical Psychiatry Collective created a powerful sociological formula describing how three aspects of cultural influences tie together and form the trap of alienation.[1] As we reflect on the complexity of this formula, it's important to keep in mind that the forces impacting us via the culture are largely unexamined by individuals, and even then, habits of culture are hard to break. We internalize these forces without awareness or choice, and people are often horrified and confused by their own complicity with systems of oppression as they begin to awaken to the scale and impact such systems have on our individual lives. This is a good place to be self-compassionate and also seek support and kindness from others as we face the reality in which we live.

The alienation formula goes like this:

Alienation = Oppression + Mystification + Isolation

The assumptions implicit in this theoretical formula are the following:

- We are all either subtly or overtly *oppressed* in some way by the complex, competitive hierarchy of social class, gender, race, and other "accepted" social divides.

- We cannot recognize our *oppression* because the system we live in has been shrouded in *mystification*. We are fed injunctions and beliefs that reinforce the social divides. These beliefs are dualistic and false; they protect the system and blame the individual.

- We compete against each other as individuals to build our own happy lives, and therefore we are divided and *isolated* and do not come together to *demystify* the *oppression*; thus, it remains outside of our awareness.

- As *isolated* and unaware individuals, we do not join together to take our power in collective action against large systems of *oppression*; we are *alienated* from our power.

Taken together, our *oppression* plus *mystification* plus *isolation* forms a self-reinforcing loop that results in our *alienation* from our power. We cannot change as isolated individuals, and we cannot change what we cannot see or name.[2] Our attempts to change are constantly thwarted, and the shroud of mystification makes it incredibly difficult to even see the choices that will make our lives different, better, and more satisfying. Skills for Change tools and concepts have such a powerful impact on people's lives because we demystify these forces and reveal possibilities that are otherwise difficult or impossible to see.

Let's take an example from my personal life and examine how the forces of alienation played out during the incredibly complex stage of human puberty, when so many cultural conditions come together and put enormous pressure on a single person. Between the ages of ten and sixteen, I fell in love with folk dance. And under the influence of oppressive and mystifying cultural forces, I gradually experienced a sense of core alienation and ultimately suffered a tragic loss of personal joy and power. My parents began folk dancing in Cambridge and Boston around 1967, at the height of a renaissance in folk dance, about the same time folk music became a mainstay of the 1960s counterculture. My mom and dad found enormous joy and empowerment in the community and music and wanted to share it with their children. I took to the world of folk dance as if the music were already singing in my blood. It was what I lived for during my teens, traveling through Poland with a folk dance company when I was fourteen and performing in a Woody Guthrie tribute at the John Hancock Hall in Boston when I was fifteen. I actually received pay for the the Boston performance, which was pretty amazing! When I danced, I felt alive in my body, connected to fellow dancers, optimistic about the future, and very empowered.

As I blossomed into a full-bodied woman, my Catholic parents switched from being supportive to being cautious. They were concerned that I was young and beautiful and that older men were attracted to me. While their concern was understandable, the withdrawal of their support for the folk dance I loved was incredibly painful and confusing (*isolation* and *mystification*). Gradually, my flirtations with men became more sexually charged, and I became even more scared and confused. I was being sexualized constantly. Men would mention my breasts, blossoming figure, and mature physical appearance. The attention was both appealing and invasive (*oppression*). My parents' desire to shelter me combined with their Catholic morality and sexual repression complicated the situation by making me responsible for protecting my seductive body without any real guidance or education (*oppression*). The *oppressive* and *mystified* forces of power and hierarchy in the form of accepted cultural beliefs about sexuality and gender began poisoning my authentic experience.

Instead of going to the folk dance events to dance, I focused more on men: *Who was going to ask me to dance and what would happen between us?* I began to obsess about my relative sexual attractiveness, felt competitive with other women, and was further *isolated* from most of my community as I hid these confusing feelings. My love of dance had started out bringing me exquisite joy; now I was beginning to feel *alienated*. I was alone (*isolation*) and submerged in contradictory messages (*mystification*) in the landscape of sexism and adult relationships, long before I was ready (*oppression*). I would leave the dances early if a man I liked wasn't there, or I would leave with a guy and spend the rest of the evening kissing him in the hallway. I wouldn't be able to sleep at night, full of shame about what I had done. Instinctively, I kept most of my emotionally charged, confusing thoughts and behavior a secret from my friends, siblings, and parents (*isolation* and *mystification*).

At sixteen, I auditioned for the best professional folk dance group in Boston and was accepted. A few days later, I was unaccepted because they were afraid I was too young; the group had a history of sexual activity among the members, and they were worried they couldn't protect me on tour. When I spoke of my dream to study folk music and dance in college, my father discouraged me, saying, "You can't make a career out of folk dance." My optimism for the future was destroyed by a combination of my father's disapproval and my crushing disappointment at being rejected by the performance group. The overwhelming swamp of sexual confusion in my social relationships vastly diminished my genuine passionate relationship with dance, music, and my body. I was engulfed in the trap of *alienation* with no way to get out. In this state of excruciating loneliness, defeat, and powerlessness, I looked for any solace. I started a relationship with an older man, moved in with him, was disowned by my father, and stopped dancing altogether. It was years before I came back to dance, and it was never the same.

The web of complex, overwhelming, and alienating social forces made dance a minefield of sexism, disempowerment, and self-doubt. My joy, lightheartedness, and innocence could not survive the attention I attracted. Even in recent years, when I go dancing, sometimes my experience will become uncomfortable based on subtle competitive behavior or someone else's desire to be near me. While I can now dance and enjoy it, based on all the unlearning of alienation I've done, the outer world still contains external forces I can't control and often don't like. Dance itself, like music and singing and many other acts of art and community connection, is polluted in our society with "image-ism" and perfectionism as well as sexism. We cannot escape the competitive hierarchy of values that causes us to covertly (sometimes overtly) compare ourselves with others and rate each other according to competency, clothing, beauty, age, and attractiveness. It's heartrending to feel the love I hold in my body for dancing and to contrast it with the intense challenge of being in a social space and powerless over my experience. I feel it as a tremendous loss most of the time.

OPPRESSION, PRIVILEGE, AND HIERARCHY

Systematized oppression is one of the main influences that cause people to become alienated from their experience. When large groups of people hoard power and deny others access, this is *oppression,* and it is exercised, implemented, and codified into practice and law by the privileged elite. These structures allow access to benefits (such as voting or membership in powerful institutions) to a select group of people and limit or disallow access to others. Sometimes the limits are enforced by law, and other times by a complex set of unwritten but socially mandated rules.

Our situation is further complicated because even when we have a great deal of power in our lives, as I did as a young woman, we have internalized a very insidious and pervasive process whereby we become unaware of or alienated from that power. Most American citizens are at least mildly oppressed by the power structures of larger systems such as schools, businesses, religious institutions, and/or government regulations. That oppression becomes woven into the invisible fabric of culture. We then internalize a felt sense of powerlessness but are unaware of where it comes from or what it means.

Systematic indoctrination into a cultural belief system has far-reaching effects and continues to be mandated through control of information. Without help, it doesn't occur to us to question the beliefs that surround us. We become submerged in the culture's dominant assumptions. Then individualism and competition further separate us from access to knowledge by isolating us from each other. Alienation from our bodies, our minds, our instincts, and our communities prevents us from truly experiencing the power to change almost anything.

In the context of a dominant culture, we come to accept "the way things are" early in our lives, and unless we consider, analyze, and seriously challenge the social system, we remain blind and stuck. In the United States, within our competitive hierarchical class system, middle-class Americans embody both the oppressors and the oppressed, standing on some midpoint on the ladder of success, neither at the top nor bottom. We try hard to reach one more rung of success, seldom considering the cost to us or someone else.

We internalize cultural and structural hierarchy when we take on the beliefs that support and continue our place in that hierarchy. This internalized hierarchical system has two elements: oppression and privilege. We internalize oppression when we recognize our one-down position, and it becomes part of our self-definition. This reaction occurs to insure our survival in the face of potential punishment or social rejection. In sociological theory this primal survival mechanism is referred to as *internalized oppression*. Some people in very oppressive cultural or political circumstances cannot rebel against the internalization of oppression without continued threat of punishment.[3] Even as people of democratic developed countries who have gained more structural power in our lifetimes, we may never challenge our internalized oppression, as we still carry fear of social exclusion.

Conversely, internalized privilege occurs when we occupy a one-up position in society and protect it by unconsciously agreeing with its assumptions. We even more rarely challenge our internalized

Perceived Advantages and Disadvantages

MARYBETH PAUL AND GLENN SMITH

Some disadvantages carry a stronger cultural judgment and stigma than others. For example, it may be a greater disadvantage to be a person of color than it is to be short, depending on the neighborhood we're in and our aspirations for power, invisibility, attention, or safety. Disadvantages that appear to be under the control of the individual (overweight, shy, dirty) rather than inherent (old, female, of color) tend to invoke different kinds of cultural judgment and oppressive circumstances. Culturally and structurally, it is a greater disadvantage to be poor than it is to be highly sensitive. Being in ill physical health is equally disadvantageous to women as it is to men, but women's appearance tends to be subject to more attention and commentary from others. The following table lists common perceived advantages and disadvantages within our culture:

Perceived Advantages	Perceived Disadvantages
male • white	female • person of color
young • wealthy	older • poor
assertive • outgoing	shy • quiet
tall • analytical • funny	short • intuitive • serious
healthy • physically fit	weak • ill • chronic disease
slender • able-bodied	overweight • disabled
emotionally contained	emotionally expressive
well-groomed	casual personal appearance
decisive • business executive	slow/pensive • manual laborer
advanced education	high school dropout

Members of progressive-thinking movements, Skills for Change included, tend to believe that anyone or any group that feels "less-than," or one down, in a democratic or cooperative structure actually deserves *more* than equal time or an equal say. When we say *one down*, we refer to someone who is less powerful, either structurally or personally. Children are one down to adults, students to teachers, renters to landlords, and in a couple, while the power differences are very personal and unique, any big systemic structural differences often need to be taken into account. We take it seriously when anyone, or any group, with a history of oppression or who hails from a culturally disadvantaged group, voices frustration or other feelings of being one down competitively.

When someone is one down in a group, everyone else by default ends up being one up, even if they don't *feel* powerful. One-up and one-down statuses emerge from the complex interconnection of interior perception and exterior experience. If someone *feels* one down, she casts others in the role of being one up. When we can calculate the financial cost of structural differences, there will also necessarily be a systemic hierarchy of one up and one down, reinforced by laws, regulations, and practices. Within these structural differences, those who are one up, even while being dedicated to equality, may have a tendency to ignore and deny the effect of the uneven playing field created by different cultural power, roles, skills, and habits. The one-up person will tend to speak his or her mind easily, while those who are one down may initially express their dismay and, when ignored, fall silent. The one-down person or group eventually may either withdraw or rebel in some fashion. The conflict comes closer to the surface but often in a way that focuses attention on specific issues, people, or groups rather than the underlying power dynamic. The following table shows some differences in communication style between advantaged and disadvantaged individuals or groups:

privilege because the benefits in structural power are often too great to consider forfeiting, despite the personal costs of isolation and loneliness. Our privilege is an invisible helper, and while privilege is visible to the oppressed around us, those with privilege often find it difficult to become conscious of and acknowledge the benefits of their privilege. Those with privilege have also struggled and worked hard to achieve their success, and yet they have been traveling downriver with the current. Facing oppressive forces is like trying to swim upstream. No wonder privilege and oppression are such divisive forces in our culture and our lives.

If we reverse the alienation *formula*, we see a way to become empowered. *Knowledge* cuts through the confusion of *mystification*, *community* leads us out of *isolation*, and combined, *knowledge* plus *community* help us take *action against oppressive forces*. Here is the "empowerment formula":

Advantaged/One-Up Communication Styles	Disadvantaged/One-Down Communication Styles
direct • rational	indirect • emotional
declarative opinions	conditional until upset
strong voice	weak/silent voice
overt, oppressive	covert, disruptive

When we form cooperative groups, before conflict arises, we attempt to build group resilience by identifying people's protective safety reflexes, communication and competitive styles, and structural and personal power. With our collective awareness, we attempt to creatively negotiate agreements to share power more equitably and address differences. And we continually reiterate the process to reflect our current feelings and needs.

Empowerment = knowledge + community + action against oppression

After my daughter, Sarah, completed a bachelor's degree in computer science at a prestigious university, she was plagued by insecurities and self-doubt (*internalized oppression*). She applied for many jobs and in some cases wasn't even interviewed before she was turned down. She felt devoid of the sense of power and confidence one would imagine she would have after years of enjoying education and receiving good grades. She began to imagine that she lacked the skills and talent to work in the field of computer technology (*mystification*). As a young woman, she had been discouraged overtly and covertly by the cultural stereotype of what a "computer tech" was, namely, a very driven, obsessively focused, white-skinned man (*oppression*). Her self-definition did not match this internalized stereotype of success (*mystification*). She didn't know anyone else in her predicament; she didn't know other women in the industry, and her male counterparts were mostly far more confident (*isolation*). She was precariously close to giving up on her chosen career path.

In her pain, Sarah reached out to some trustworthy and powerful adults for guidance and help (*community*). She revealed her difficulties to them even though she felt ashamed and vulnerable to do so, and those adults helped her separate her internalized oppressive beliefs (*knowledge*) from her personal authentic beliefs. This process helped her to reclaim her considerable transactional powers, weigh through job possibilities, research more options, and determine what was best for her. She was then able to *take action against oppression*. She realized that her strengths and talents didn't actually fit in the traditional computer programmer environment, that the contracts associated with those jobs were actually oppressive to her, and she began looking for more satisfying solutions to continue her passionate interest in current technology. Instead of colluding with her internalized oppression and agreeing to a one-down position that matched the gender stereotype, or giving up entirely to hopelessness and despair, she became creative and empowered in solving the dilemma. She found a master's program at U.C. Berkeley that combined the study of technology, information, and sociology and felt her power and self-confidence return (empowerment). In the context of a supportive community, she blossomed. She reclaimed her authentic love of learning and became optimistic about finding a position in the work world as a more aware and empowered woman.

Sarah's experience not only brought her out of her own personal sense of alienation and powerlessness, but it also motivated her to help others (both men and women of various ethnicities) see the invisible barriers for marginalized groups in the primarily white, male world of technology. She continues to create contexts for compassionate conversation in her community to take further action against the oppressive and painful divides she and others encounter in the often cruel world of competitive hierarchical dynamics. Escape from alienation not only reconnects us to ourselves and others, but it motivates us to heal the social divisions that hurt all of our hearts. Ultimately, we are able to come back to an essential and richly connected relationship with this amazing world.

INEQUALITY AND THE POWER OF LOVE

I suppose if I believe in anything large in the way of concepts, it's got to be love. In 1967, Martin Luther King Jr. said, "Power at its best is love implementing the demands of justice. Justice at its best is power correcting everything that stands against love."[4]

One of the most tragic disappointments of social inequality is the way it blocks loving connection across social divides and exacerbates the *alienating* effects of *oppression* and *mystification*. Social inequality creates a loop of disconnection: *isolation* between groups of people leads to a lack of information about each other; *mystification* leads to resignation and hopelessness that impedes any action we might take to correct the very inequality and *oppression* we are experiencing. Equality, on the other hand, promotes more community and connection and supports love. Most of us know the pain of wanting to include people in our lives when financial, cultural, or material differences get in the way. If one of my friends has very little money, and I want to have dinner at a restaurant with her, this inequality creates immediate confusion and tension. If I pay for dinner, though it is an obvious answer, I might actually exacerbate the inequality and create more separation rather than inclusion. This same problem exists with all kinds of social activities. It takes privilege to maintain a car, bicycle, computer, phone, and home, and such material objects are crucial for mutual social connection.

Working with social inequality inside our loving relationships is confusing and arduous work. There are no easy answers or quick fixes. In order to willingly share power and privilege, our mutual commitment to love and caring within specific and significant relationships is a most powerful motivating factor. Connection to something larger, combined with an invitation into each other's lives, is what helps lead us to do the work. When we try to connect "human to human" within a cultural context riddled with structural power imbalances, it is imperative that we balance our power differences. But it's hard work and at times frustrating. If there's not a serious interest in loving relationships, the extra work of cooperation may not seem worth it.

Whether we are looking at differences between personal levels of power or policy levels of power, we may find the motivation to work for more social justice when we ask ourselves, "What's in it for me?!" "For the sake of what?" In other words, what is the risk-reward energy expenditure? The effort to love and connect across inequality can seem hopeless as we face confusing tensions and underlying conflict. Therefore, we can feel much more comfort and safety being in groups of people who share similar amounts of structural and cultural power. If we wish to engage in social justice in our personal

Blindness to Privilege

GLENN SMITH

I was educated early in the way wealthy and connected individuals and groups may abuse their power through racism, sexism and many other forms of dominance. I also have a highly developed—some might say overdeveloped—sense of fairness inculcated in me while I grew up with competitive sibling dynamics. And I am a white male, oldest sibling of four who did well in school through college. Though I had considered some of my internalized prejudices, realized my privilege, and thought I was very fair, I learned that I was blind to how my assumptions of privilege and my actions and manner affected people of less-advantaged groups.

Two incidents with the same ex-lover, whom I will call Wendy, were helpful in opening my eyes. The first occurred when I attempted to spontaneously show Wendy an easier, more efficient way to slice avocados. Much to my surprise and indignation—I meant well—she instantly and angrily rejected my attempt to "help." Through several subsequent conversations, I finally understood that not only did I jump to giving advice without asking or being asked, but my manner in this and previous events telegraphed my confidence and assumptions that I knew better than Wendy and that my help would be appreciated. As a woman, middle sibling of three, and less confident in some areas, she resented not only my unsolicited advice, but especially my confident assumption that my help would be appreciated.

A second incident with Wendy occurred later in a rather heated argument. We weren't yelling, but were definitely speaking intensely, and Wendy said something that made me very angry. In frustration, I walked to the other side of the living room and loudly kicked the bathroom door. I knew it wasn't hard enough to cause damage, relationships, though, it is important to hang in there with social inequality and do what we can to help solve the problem both politically and personally. Although the direct sharing of resources by those who have more with those who have less does not shift underlying systemic inequality, we *can* become active in our communities to expose injustice and learn from those who are oppressed.

and I did not understand the effect it had on Wendy until a later mediation session. She was understandably startled, but she also felt scared, threatened, and incensed at my action. I could not understand. I was across the room and facing away from her; I wasn't yelling, and thought I wasn't directing any threatening action toward Wendy. As Beth Roy was able to help me see, just the fact that I am a somewhat confident male, larger and stronger than Wendy, created a different implication than if she had done the same thing. We live in a society where men *do* violently attack and attempt to control women with threatening behavior. Even though Wendy rationally knew I made a commitment not to hurt her, the cultural implications of a noisy demonstration of anger felt emotionally threatening to a smaller, less physically confident woman. I, as a man, would not have been threatened if Wendy had done what I did. My blindness to my culturally one-up status, plus my desire to vent my emotion in what I thought was a nonthreatening way, left me unaware of the impact I had on Wendy during our fight.

Without help from Wendy and Beth, I don't know how I would have discovered the impact my privilege had on my transactions, much less been able to act differently in the future. I can listen with compassion when I am told how I affect others, and I can keep trying to understand the many forces at work in a single transaction. I can't get rid of my privilege, but I can try to understand it, acknowledge it, and advocate for others.

If we find ourselves in a privileged position, and want to face the oppression of others, first we must be willing to feel the pain. Once we accept the pain, we may allow the power of love to help us open up, lower our defenses, and really listen. Respect for ourselves and others, compassion for all beings, and a desire to learn and love lead us out of the insidious trap of alienation, grow our connections with others, and ultimately provide us with the potential for greater happiness.

Power exists in many forms, and we access it individually, uniquely, culturally, and collectively. May we find ways to increase our power and learn how to see when we are wielding power or experiencing external oppression. When we find ourselves feeling helpless and powerless, may we know we are not alone. There is tremendous power and joy in allowing ourselves to love what we love and move toward what we love with knowledge and community support.

PART II
INTERNALIZING COMPLEXITY

Four • Culture Inside and Out

Nancy Shanteau

As I was filling out a stack of college applications in 1988, I encountered a set of questions about my racial classification. Was I White (Caucasian) or an Asian-Pacific Islander? Black? American Indian? Hispanic? The questions stumped me. I was raised white, with a French-Canadian surname and all the rights and privileges of a white, middle-class, suburban education. Yet my mother's parents, for all their white skin, called milk *leche*, cooked posole for Christmas, and had an unlimited supply of dried peppers sent from relatives in New Mexico. When I looked at my father's family, they were clearly white, but they also embodied racism, sexism, classism, arrogance, and materialism. I didn't want to be like them. When I spent time with my mother's family, we laughed, danced, celebrated good food, and were kind to each other.

My maternal family was Spanish American, hailing from Albuquerque, New Mexico, with a genealogy traced back to exile from the Extremadura region of Spain. When they came to San Francisco after my mother was born, my grandparents blended in with the diverse immigrant Latino community populating the service sector in the tourist hotels. A conversion to Catholicism availed my mother the best private education my grandparents could afford and sealed their assimilation into San Francisco's immigrant working class. As a waitress and an upholsterer, my grandparents saved their money, supported their local unions, and voted Democrat. Neither of them graduated from high school during the Depression; both had worked to help their families survive. When my mother went to college to study science, she soon stumbled against the rigors and demands of self-initiated education. Her parents were uninformed as to what support she needed, and without assistance to work through the obstacles, she dropped out of school in favor of work, marriage, and mothering children.

That left me, at seventeen, the first grandchild in my maternal family lineage to go to college. I claimed them, their heritage, and the nurturing I received in my grandparents' home: I checked the Hispanic box on each, put stamps on the envelopes, and sent my applications to colleges across California. Little did I know that my seemingly small act of claiming cultural heritage would shape my university experience. U.C. Berkeley was my school of choice, and with that selection, I chose one of the most proactive affirmative action programs in the country. Over the next four years, I received invitations and opportunities designed to increase the success and graduation prospects of affirmative action students. I was often the only white person in the room—I know it sounds naïve, but it took me a couple of years to figure out what had happened.

It wasn't until years later that I realized I could've marched into the dean's office, taken myself off the affirmative action list, and reduced my confusing, overwhelming, and challenging face-to-face experiences with race and my own white privilege. Instead, due to that moment when I checked a box on my college application, I was on a fast track to learning about culture, its meaning, and how cultural values shape everything: our ideas, thoughts, bodies, and lives. For all the pain I experienced as a young person not belonging where I was invited, I would not change a moment; those years shaped me and made it possible for me to do the work I do today. My university experience led me to explore both the oppressed and oppressor sides of my ancestry, and I pledged myself to fight for everyone's rights, collectively cultivate a more compassionate culture, and advocate for a government that protects people rather than persecuting them.[1]

In this chapter, we explore culture to help us understand how we internalize cultural values and messages and where our internalized stories originated. Further, we discuss what we can do as adults to choose our relationship with our culture, its meaning in our lives, and how we can reorganize our bodies and actions in alignment with our beliefs and values.

CULTURE AND ITS MEANING

In Skills for Change coaching, we define culture as a collection of values and beliefs that are identifiable and reflected through the behaviors of individuals within a group. Culture in and of itself isn't material, nor is it dictated by a central governing body, though it is often reflected in and shaped by policies and laws. In the United States, the puritan work ethic is a familiar concept in conversational and pop cultural contexts, but it isn't written down in laws anywhere. Labor laws don't say, "People must work hard during their assigned work hours." With relatively high regulatory limits on labor practices, the laws governing the U.S. marketplace allow hiring entities to determine work standards and to oversee their implementation. However, there are injunctions, transmitted via transactions, that reinforce the message: Hard work is good. Laziness is bad. When I say these injunctions are transmitted through transactions, I'm talking about a lifetime of messages given in school, families, community groups, and workplaces. Each time the message is reinforced, an individual has his or her own reaction to it.

For me, raised in a middle-class, white-skinned, suburban household, I interpreted the messages I received about hard work to mean that if I worked hard, and I was successful, I would also be happy and loved.

Colonialism and Hegemony

NANCY SHANTEAU

Nestled in Nevada County, one of the whitest counties in California, Skills for Change Collective members and coaches are among the few who bring up the subjects of colonialism and hegemony in our community. Whether or not we are aware of it, the underlying basis of colonialism lives in our bodies, language, beliefs, internalized oppression, and access to power.

Colonialism is the centuries-long process by which mostly Western European countries have "discovered," immigrated into, dominated, subjugated, assimilated, genocided, and destroyed existing cultures and peoples and replaced them with a "mini-me" replica of the "mother" country's mores, ethics, language, beliefs, and power structures. Hegemony is an underlying threat of violence that keeps the status quo of patriarchy, white supremacy, and Christian-centric cultural dominance intact worldwide (look to the countries with the biggest militaries and find the elite of the hegemony).

When people who are privileged by the history of colonialism and hegemony interact with people who are oppressed by the history of colonialism and hegemony, very often there is a one-up, one-down power dynamic that goes unmentioned. One-down, or oppressed, people tend not to mention their feelings of oppression unless they feel safe, and one-up, or privileged, people tend not to notice and/or deny that underlying dynamics exist. As Skills for Change practitioners, we name power and make it visible to all. We identify power inequities, attempt to balance them whenever possible, and advocate for everyone's rights to safe transactions, spaces, and communities. Often folks in the middle class in the United States are both oppressed and oppressors, and how we identify tends to depend on the particular transaction we have just experienced.

While this basic act of naming power can seem awkward, often it is accompanied by a sense of relief by the parties who are one down. When I'm working with someone who has a vastly different cultural background, I might say something like this: "I want to acknowledge that we have really different backgrounds, histories, cultures, and upbringings and have been affected by those experiences in ways that privilege and oppress us. I can see some ways we are different and imagine there are others that are invisible to me. I am committed to naming them as they arise and dealing with any power imbalances as they come up between us. I hope you will trust me if you feel unsafe at any time by letting me know what you are feeling, and I promise to share what I feel and see also."

I might then give some examples of the power I hold: the privilege of being the coach, a woman who has verbal and emotional intelligence, the power of nurturing, the privilege of white skin color, English as a first language, education, an able body, heterosexuality, and so on. "I want you to know that I consider it my responsibility to educate myself about power differences, and if there's a book, movie, or other reference that you think would help me understand you better, I'd be happy to read, watch, listen, and so on." If clients then want to explore their own privilege and oppression and how the differences between us could impact our work together, I consider that conversation to be incredibly valuable to the work we will do as coach and client.

Fundamentally, it is not helpful, though it is incredibly normal, to feel ashamed of privilege and oppression, one-up and one-down status. A bury-our-heads-in-the-sand ostrich approach to privilege and oppression does not make them go away, and we miss the opportunity to align our strengths with our vision for the future. Ideally, each of us will understand and check our privilege to ensure we don't abuse it, honor the history and experiences of others, and work together to create a world where everyone's contributions are valued.

Consequently, even when my hard work inspired rejection or competition, which would seem to contradict my belief that I would get love from my hard work, I continued to pursue hard work and intelligence as a way to connect with others. While it's true that hard work is part of why I feel loved in my life, I also now attribute feeling loved and happy to other behaviors, like my willingness to listen and to be compassionate and my sense of humor and play. Do I work hard at these things? Sometimes. But mostly they are ingrained ways of being, and they feel natural. Culture is nebulous in this way, both unique to an individual and also systemic, influenced by economics, religion, public policy, our skin color, appearance, ethnicity, class, language, gender identification, sexual preference, physical or mental wellness/ability, age, and geography.

THE VALUE OF CULTURE: CULTURAL VALUES

Cultural values exist within a web of geography and history. Our current address, where our parents lived when we were born, and where we were raised all impact our cultural mix of experiences and values. Every day, we navigate a complex network of cultural values, norms, and assumptions, all contextually dependent on our position relative to those norms.

Take me as an example: I was born and raised in a suburb of the San Francisco Bay Area, surrounded by a mostly white-skinned, middle-class community (*skin color*, *geography*, *class*). My mother's family name was Garcia, and both my grandparents were bilingual, though they'd raised my mom as an English speaker to help her get ahead in school. I knew my surname was French Canadian due to the spelling, but I felt very little French-Canadian cultural influence (*ethnicity* and *language*).

My father was a college-educated, high school history teacher, and my mother didn't get a job until I was in grammar school (*class*). In her intuitive search for a better educational experience for my brother and me, my mother enrolled us in an alternative classroom called Open Education, with sixty kids, no grades, two teachers, and lots of family volunteers in the classroom (*education*). I staged a protest at the age of seven, and my mom, who had been taking my brother and me to the local Catholic church and to religious study programs, stopped insisting we go to church (*religion*).

My parents started their family squarely middle class, and my father's paycheck as a teacher often felt a little tight. Mom shopped at co-ops, buying cheese and meat in bulk, and we had a freezer in the garage for all the packages of food we froze. She made our clothes until it became cheaper to buy them in stores, and while I always had enough to eat, I remember being sensitive to expenditures of money, as if there might not be enough. Later, my mother got a job as a secretary, and her paycheck made the family finances a lot easier. First I and then my brother became "latch key" kids; we came home from school on our own, called Mom at work to let her know we were okay, and then did chores and homework and played games until our parents came home (*class*). When I was twelve, I read a book on my mom's shelf, *The Dinner Party* by Judy Chicago, and discovered an alternative women's history. My unusual grammar school education had already presented Native American history side by side with more traditional U.S. history, and by the time I finished reading Chicago's descriptions of women's oppression and persecution, I was fully ignited as a champion for equal rights for all people (*education*).

My middle school and high school experiences were much more challenging than grammar school, not because I wasn't smart enough but because I was fat. I was teased, bullied, and ostracized, and it took me a long time to make friends (*appearance*). I identified as a heterosexual woman—though I had a gay best friend in high school, I didn't have questions about my sexual identity (*sexual preference*). I was able-bodied, but my fatness led me to believe I wasn't good at sports or physical fitness, and my only glimmer of a different, more physically energized world came through my love of dancing (*physical ability*). While the community was wide-spectrum middle class, the popular kids in school all seemed to be upper-middle class, and I knew my family wasn't as affluent; we had less disposable spending money for cars and clothes (*class*). During this time, my father got his masters in psychology, finished his Marriage, Family, and Child Counseling license, and became a high school guidance counselor (*education*). My mom pursued an interest in New Age spirituality through her membership in a woman's group and by attending workshops on dreams, crystal therapy, and meditation (*spirituality*). By the time high school was over, the privileges of whiteness, a middle-class upbringing, and the tendency of folks in our neighborhood to normalize their cultural experience as if it were invisible, all shaped me into a restless young person who was itchy to get away from the suburbs and the safety they represented (*geography*, *class*).

As we are doing our own cultural inventory, we consider geography, class, skin color, ethnicity, sexual and gender identity, physical and mental ability, group memberships, immigration history, language of origin, education, oppression, and responses to oppression and how they shaped our family, community, and our own identity. The child of a doctor will have a very different life from the child of a farmer, laborer, or political activist. If a person identifies as a lesbian, she might contend with another set of cultural and social norms in the lesbian community, plus a complexity of responses to her sexual orientation in each of her cultural contexts. Our choices of career, education, and significant romantic relationships add additional layers as well. If we are chronically ill or have a missing limb, our bodies and world views may be further shaped by our experiences in the health care system as well as in our daily lives. Cultural norms and values magnify, contradict, and nullify each other, and they compete for relative importance in our lives and choices.[2]

"WHAT IS MY CULTURE?"

Our individual cultures are unique, and we are our own best detectives. As we discover our own cultural influences, we may notice how our family upbringing was different from our greater cultural experience, where we choose to align ourselves with our culture and where we choose to depart from our culture for the sake of our futures. I call this process unplugging and replugging our cultural and personal values—imagine an old-time switchboard operator who disconnects and reconnects telephone cables. Our culture may offer us tremendous strength through ritual, tradition, and a sense of belonging and also sources of pain from rejection, a sense of nonbelonging, and the constriction of rigid belief. Some cultures emphasize individualism and a bootstrap success model, and some cultures produce strong community values and a deep fabric of connection. How we orient ourselves to various cultural influences will depend on where we come from, what serves us and our communities best, and what we want for ourselves and our futures.

Through this process of self-reflection and cultural reflection, we end up with values that represent a composite mixture between the values we learned from our culture and those we learned from our families and communities. This complex approach to personal and cultural values offers a dynamic array of solutions. A fantasy gaming community offered me a feeling of belonging within an unwelcoming high school hierarchy that determined who was popular or unpopular. I have witnessed how, in the gay community, someone's "family members of choice" will offer support if they are struggling with cancer, financial troubles, or rejection from their families of origin. In an article entitled "Appellate Recourse to the Supernatural: Kithitu Among the Akamba," Jelvas Musau discusses the use of cultural rituals to help villagers mediate conflicts.[3] My friend, a Malaysian American peace worker, realized he could develop a hybrid leadership style, a combination of the gentle communalism of his village of origin and the visionary declarations of his new home in the United States. He discovered he was happiest when he sat with people, told and listened to stories, and helped each of them cultivate their own leadership to bring peace to their communities. The solutions we generate out of our cultural experiences are a beautiful meld of diverse strengths, and our unique expression of our culture is a gift to our community that only we can give.

Cultures are increasingly hybridized, assimilated, and colonized through contact with each other. And just as there is a hierarchy of cultural and systemic oppressive forces, there is a hierarchy of cultures. Like it or not, advertisements tell us who we are as a culture and reflect the current cultural standard for "normal," as well as top status in the cultural hierarchy. Thus for decades, since the beginning of television, most commercials featured white, middle-class, even midwestern U.S. citizens doing suburban activities like eating TV dinners and getting cats out of

The Language of Power

NANCY SHANTEAU

Subtle language codes are among the ways one-up people flex their power muscles. New York City isn't just another city, it's *the* city, as if it is the only city in the world. Such a claim on the general, normal, and commonplace is a coded act of power. The *majority* in the United States ought to be based on specific issues and values and composed of a collection of voters, but the word *minority* doesn't refer to a quantity of people; it refers to a racial classification defined by those with the greatest power. If people of color are minorities, then the majority is white people, or to be even more specific, white, conservative, Christian men. But in many, many geographic locations, white folks are a minority in population. They get to claim the term *majority* because white people in the United States still hold the majority of the power. The term American is another such claim on the general. The North and South American continents contain many nations, peoples, and cultures, yet in the media and around the world, American means a U.S. citizen, a person who lives in a single country on one of these continents. Likewise, in many map views of the world, the North American continent is depicted as proportionally larger than it is, and it is often centered in the visual field. These subtle trees. Gradually, the "normal" family has shifted to include people who live in cities, people of color, and gay people. Despite this minimal, gradual inclusion, in 2014 the majority of commercials and advertisements still feature white people, particularly white men, doing middle- and upper-middle class activities. Once we cultivate a heightened awareness of this pervasive cultural hierarchy, we start to notice how often white, middle class, and male equals "normal," while anyone else is "other." To move beyond our awareness of our current cultural context, we must question

cues suggest that the United States is at the center of the world, even though it is a relatively small land mass and takes up a small percentage of the total planetary surface.

As we discussed earlier in the book, the elite of the hegemony, the people with the biggest army and greatest brute strength, have the power to name and define their world. These types of coded signals of power might be invisible to the ones who benefit from the privilege of that power, but they tend to be aggressive and threatening to those who are oppressed. In the late twentieth century, there was much discussion of *political correctness*, a somewhat negative term for the social and even legal pressure on people to use inclusive language. As Skills for Change practitioners, we do our best to name the power at play in a given transaction, stand up for the folks at the bottom of the power hierarchy, and use language that shows our care for all beings. Thus, it might take a negotiation to discover how someone prefers to use language and then to memorize and learn the proper use of the new term. For example, my friend's daughter has selected a more gender-neutral name and has also asked people to use as few pronouns as possible, preferring they use a name instead of *she* and *her*. When we do this extra work, we show our respect for other people's dignity, personal power, and right to claim language to define their world. And such gestures of respect create radical change in how we think, speak, and behave.

the foundational theoretical models, values, and stories that shape our consciousness and ask ourselves what changes might serve our future. Ultimately, I hope we start asking how we might work together so that one person's future does not suppress the dreams and goals of another, or even better, how we might support everyone's dreams and goals.

THE PURPOSE OF CULTURE

In my experience as a white affirmative action student, I received an invaluable, invisible education in culture. When I was obviously ignorant and out of my depth, I learned to acknowledge my privilege, offer vulnerability instead of defensiveness, ask for help, do research, and educate myself. I received many blessings and learning opportunities, and it was hard and lonely—people didn't trust me to understand their experience, and they were right—I didn't. I made it through college one step at a time. Surrounded by many beautiful cultures and people, I strived for connection and belonging. I learned to speak out on behalf of those who had been hurt, disempowered, and oppressed, not to speak for them, but to speak for space so that they might tell their stories in their own time.

My story is a story of the United States, a human story. We each must figure out who we are, in our own culture and time. To achieve a life that satisfies our hunger for belonging and purpose, we must chart a course and make the necessary changes. It is important, challenging, necessary, heartbreaking, worthwhile work. Our culture may be obvious, or it may be elusive. Either way, it is a source of both power and oppression, and our work to understand our culture in all its complexity can help us go where we need to go, be who we need to be, and do what we need to do. This is my wish for all of us: may our culture help us learn who we are, find our purpose, discover an internally generated sense of belonging, and bring our best into the world.

Five • The Parent-Adult-Child Model: Understanding How Human Beings Work

Nancy Shanteau

Growing up, I lived in a sleepy suburban neighborhood where most of the fun took place in the cul-de-sacs rather than on the main street. We played dodge ball, basketball, and running games like hide-and-seek, where our objective to touch "home base" and be "safe" might be more important to us than looking both ways for cars. I didn't enjoy playing with the kids in the cul-de-sac directly across the street from us; all my friends lived two cul-de-sacs up from our house, and I could often be found there, running and laughing with a pack of other kids. Before I left the house, I was supposed to ask mom or dad for permission to go play and let them know where they could find me.

One day I didn't ask; I just went up the street. A couple of hours later, my mom came to get me, her face red and livid. She stomped up and hissed, "Home, *now!*" With the instincts of a child in trouble, I slunk home, calculating what I'd done wrong. Once we arrived in the kitchen, she informed me that she had spent most of an hour looking everywhere for me, and I was grounded for the rest of the afternoon. She told me I could play between the fire hydrant and the streetlight until 4:00 pm, which pretty much meant I couldn't leave our house.

I spent the whole time sulking under that streetlamp. I wished I was playing with my friends, and I felt very angry that I was grounded. I felt trapped. But at 4:00 pm, I ran into the house, asked for permission to go play, and when it was granted, ran back out and found my friends. I never ran off without permission again. I wanted to be good. I wanted my freedom, and I would do what my parents asked to achieve both goals. Now I look back and realize my mother must have been terrified that I was lost or kidnapped, and additionally inconvenienced by needing to look for me instead of making progress in whatever she was doing. The intensity in her voice was probably more fear than anger, yet I thought she was primarily upset because I had been "bad" and broken the rules. At the time, what I understood was that if I wanted to play with my friends, I had to do what my parents wanted.

This impulse on my part to do whatever it takes to be "good" still plays out in my life in many arenas and relationships. I tend to blame myself as the "bad" one when a relationship goes sour, and I will do an enormous amount of extra work on a project in order to avoid conflict with other participants. Even now, I find myself internally arguing over whether to raise a topic with someone: *Is it worth the risk? Am I better off handling it by myself and shouldering the burden of managing my feelings alone? Will I be punished if I do what I want?*

This chapter looks at how young people interpret the world and the rules in order to be safe and connected to primary caregivers, other adults, and each other and how those young interpretations often get solidified into adult orientations, worldview, and relationship habits. We will consider the origins of our patterned reactions and review a useful model for understanding how we cope with the challenges we face. We will see how this model helps us create more choices in our responses to events and other people and ultimately to chart our own course toward the future we want for ourselves.

YOUR SAFETY REFLEX: EMBODIED SURVIVAL MECHANISMS

We are naturally scared when someone almost runs us over in a cross-walk, when we trip and fall at the edge of a cliff, or when someone startles us by jumping out from behind a tree and shouting, "Boo!" Whatever the event, a cascade of instinctual biological responses kicks off, generating adrenaline and other chemical reactions that increase the speed of our response, decrease pain and mental processes, and help us take action, whether it might be to *fight, freeze, flee, move toward, tend and befriend,* or *dissociate.* This is our safety reflex.[1]

By the time we're adults, through a lifetime of experience, our safety system has identified and habituated the response or combination of responses most likely to keep us safe. Perhaps we are extremely fast runners—we are likely to have a *flee* response prioritized as a great strategy. Or perhaps we are slow moving; instinctually, we may have cultivated a *freeze* response to preserve our survival. If we had a physically abusive parent who was likely to hit us if we drew attention to ourselves, we might have overridden our tendency to run and *dissociated* so that we could interpret the parent's mood and choose the safest response: make a joke (*toward*), get him a beer out of the fridge (*tend and befriend*), hold still until she leaves the room (*freeze*), scamper upstairs to our room and cower in the closet (*flee*).

Our bodies and safety responses are extremely smart, fine-tuned by our environment to work exquisitely well. Yet they also tend to be unevaluated responses, so when a safety reflex becomes unnecessary, or even endangers us, we don't know how to stop it from happening. The danger we face tends to go down as we gain in age and power, yet the intensity of our safety response remains set at or above the level of greatest danger.

If we are accustomed to *dissociating* when a dangerous adult enters the room, we may continue this behavior when our boss enters our cubicle, even though she's never laid a hand on us or threatened us with danger. The sheer authority she holds in the relationship may be enough to set off our safety reflex. If our *dissociation* response involves constriction of breath and tension in the chest and shoulders, and if we now have high blood pressure and are under threat of heart failure when we get too stressed, we may be in greater danger from our historic safety response than from our fairly innocent boss, the external source of the stress.

OUR STORIES TAKE OVER

To add to the complexity as we grow up, we create stories to explain our safety responses. Let's walk through an example of how a safety instinct turns into a story. First, our bodies are stimulated—perhaps

My Armchair Theory of Human Development

JULIA KELLIHER

From the minute we are born, we interact with others in order to survive. In the book *Sex at Dawn*, authors Christopher Ryan and Cacilda Jetha propose that what defines us as most human and different from other mammals is our incredibly complex system of social interconnections. From family to tribe to culture to institutions, we have outdone all other mammals in the intricate and complex construction of our social systems. It makes sense then that our access to power as individuals is also dependent on an extremely complex social system.

The human baby starts putting together personal and social competence as quickly as it can. For example, we quickly use the ability to crawl not only to explore the environment around us, but also to crawl over to where our mom is sitting in hope she will scoop us into her lap and let us nurse. The ability to grimace, cry, or smile morphs into the ability to attract the attention of our adult caregiver so he will pick us up, rock us, or play with us.

by a loud noise, a car backfiring, some kind of physically startling experience that feels dangerous: the trigger event. Our bodies' instinctive response is incredibly fast, fast enough to allow us to put our hands out in front of us before we fall down. The sensory information about what has happened in the trigger event is passed to the limbic system[2], where our safety reflex kicks in, reacting with our particular variation of fight, freeze, flee, move toward, tend and befriend, and dissociate.

Our thinking mind (neocortex) is vastly slower, but when it is able to process the event, much of the mind's work is to figure out what happened (danger) and make a decision that will keep it from happening again (protection from danger). We evaluate the episode, call it dangerous or "bad," and then create a plan for how to be "good" so that bad things don't happen to us. In the case of a near collision with another vehicle, we might

As opposed to other mammals, human children do not learn how to use claws or fangs or camouflage or even muscular strength to survive. As children, we notice and respond to positive and negative signals in regard to the behavioral expectations of the adults around us. Some of our behavior is rewarded with hugs and smiles; other behaviors are met with anger or fear. Right move, wrong move. Our mammalian brains compile information about how to act within our culture with all its attendant stereotypes, expectations, and prejudices. Ultimately, we each find a way to fit into our specific culture of spoken and unspoken social rules.

As human children, we learn how to speak and act in our small family and extended community. This behavior is usually the best we can do at the time. We continue to learn as we come into adulthood, reacting to our environment and putting to use our best choices in each context. Our behavior takes on a sense of individuality and homeostasis. We are reaching for stability over and over again, and once we have reached full adulthood in our twenties, much of our behavior is set in place, becoming our "personality" or individual style.

curse at the other driver for thoughtlessness and incompetence (blame), or we might chastise ourselves for driving too fast or being distracted (shame). Perhaps none of these stories is true—perhaps a mechanical failure of the other driver's car caused him to veer into our lane. We'll never know unless we can ask him what happened. But we are likely to make up a story, and our bodies, words, and actions then reflect our belief in our story.

POWER AT PLAY

So how does power impact our complex set of triggers and responses, injunctions, and stories? Our bodies instinctually respond to power, status, authority, and hierarchy. We identify our role in the tribe or group and instinctually sense when to lead, defer to others, or get out of someone's way.

Internalized privilege and oppression further contribute to our expectations for position power in a given group—the more often we've experienced others deferring to our leadership, the more we expect to take power in a group. The more often we've deferred power to others, the more we expect to follow, or perhaps be rejected by, the group. All this analysis happens very quickly, before thought. We walk into a room, assess our position, and then act accordingly.

Evolutionary psychologists might say this type of safety assessment is "naturally selected" to preserve the greatest survival for our genes. If cooperation with others is more likely to produce survival, we'll be good at it. If dominance is more likely to produce survival, we'll be good at it. Our internal injunctions for safety and connection are good for survival, so we get very good at them. In the next sections, we'll look more closely at how these internalized injunctions arise.

THE PARENT-ADULT-CHILD THEORY

Eric Berne, founder of Transactional Analysis, noticed his clients seemed to have three distinct ego states that affected his work with them. He called these ego states the "parent," "adult," and "child."[3] In Skills for

Change, we expand on Berne's theory to connect how our safety reflex shapes our child ego-state development. We then describe the process by which we internalize cultural beliefs in the parent ego state. Finally, we identify how we can cultivate our internal adult ego state to increase power and choice in our lives.

The Parent-Adult-Child Model

JULIA KELLIHER

In Skills for Change, we modified Eric Berne's Parent-Adult-Child Model to mirror the neurological system more closely. We added a spine to remind ourselves that our automatic reactions, beyond thought, emerge from the body first, and then are explained by the mind. Finally, we may develop an internal adult consciousness to produce greater awareness, choice and compassion.

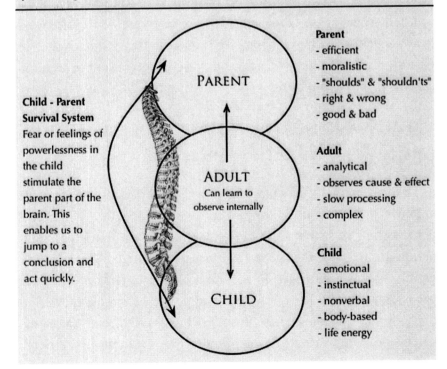

Child - Parent Survival System
Fear or feelings of powerlessness in the child stimulate the parent part of the brain. This enables us to jump to a conclusion and act quickly.

PARENT

ADULT
Can learn to observe internally

CHILD

Parent
- efficient
- moralistic
- "shoulds" & "shouldn'ts"
- right & wrong
- good & bad

Adult
- analytical
- observes cause & effect
- slow processing
- complex

Child
- emotional
- instinctual
- nonverbal
- body-based
- life energy

START AT THE BEGINNING: THE CHILD EGO STATE

The child ego state is the body: the original, playful, emotional, spontaneous, physical, passionate, fearful, creative, expressive self. We rarely experience a pure expression of the child ego state because the cultural beliefs and systemic power influences immediately begin to shape the construction of our egos. The original child state is unmediated by language or culture. Because we are immersed in the threat and reward of cultural messages, our expressions of a child ego state inevitably start to reveal cultural injunctions for our behavior.[4] However, we can recognize the child state in our feelings and sensations, be they joy, sadness, heat, coolness, fear, anxiety, streaming, tingling, dread, or aliveness. Our safety reflex emerges from the child ego state; we move *toward* connection for nurturing and sustenance; we move *away* from threat; we *fight* when we're cornered. These embodied responses are much faster than thought. We don't think, "I should brake," when an animal runs in front of our bike—we just seize the hand brakes and turn to avoid the collision. Then, as the adrenaline leaves our system, we look for ways to avoid another such experience. The child ego state is often not up to the task of avoiding future danger and powerlessness; we thus create an internal parent to protect us.

CRITICAL AND NURTURING VOICES OF PROTECTION AND CARE: THE PARENT EGO STATE

As children, in our acute vulnerability and powerlessness, we struggle to find ways to generate our own safety, power, connection, and feeling of belonging. This struggle, in our undeveloped, best-we-can-do manner, begins to shape the ego state known as the parent. This ego state rapidly assigns values such as good and bad, right and wrong to our behaviors so that we know how to behave to get the most approval and the least punishment. Because this part of us is tasked with safety, the parent ego state will start to sound more and more critical—after all, nurturing tends not to produce nearly as rapid and powerful results as intensity, cruelty, and fierce judgment.

The "critical parent," Berne's language for this ego state, is inherently an authoritative-sounding voice: it is a copy of the people in our lives we most admire, value, fear, and struggle to please. Thus, the parent ego state can end up sounding like our real mothers and fathers, teachers, and guardians. The critical parent ego state also reflects cultural values, mores, ethics, and rules: it is as Augusto Boal termed, our "cops in the head."[5] During the 1970s, the Radical Psychiatry Collective redubbed the critical parent ego state the "pig parent"; police were called pigs on the street, and the Radical Therapists wanted to highlight the political aspect of internalized oppression in their theory of the self.[6]

Because the pig parent ego state is trying to protect us, it will often escalate in its response to danger, treating each potential experience as *worse* than the greatest danger we've ever faced. When, as adults, we are trying to defang our inner critic, it can help to remind ourselves of the actual, perhaps deadly danger we faced and the tendency of the pig parent ego state to increase its vigilance tenfold, or a hundredfold, every time it failed to protect us from harm.

There is also a nurturing aspect of the parent ego state, still fueled by right and wrong dualistic thinking, yet more caring, loving, and soothing. Berne called this kinder voice the "nurturing parent." If our cultural practices encouraged self-nurturing internal commentary as well as self-critical internal commentary, perhaps we would hear our internal nurturing parent voice more often. However, in my experience as a practitioner, people's internal critical and nurturing voices rarely achieve equal balance. Sometimes I will invite clients to antidote every critical thought with a nurturing thought, just to see what happens. Most come back reporting that they had no idea how cruel they were being with themselves, how relentless the critical voice was, and how difficult it was to catch every instance and counter it with a nurturing statement. Either way, the parent ego state tends to enforce beliefs and stories that are externally generated; we are trying to be "good" to survive in a confusing world where the rules seem to change all the time.

MATURITY AND WISDOM: THE ADULT EGO STATE

The adult ego state is the final ego state to develop as we grow up. Reliant on the neocortical brain for its primary functions, the adult ego state processes sequential, analytical, cause-and-effect thoughts. The adult ego state helps us understand and hold complex and contradictory truths. When we are accessing the power of this ego state, we increase our ability to make choices based on personal values rather than external judgments. From our adult ego state, we organize, plan, problem solve, and make rational assessments of what is needed in a particular circumstance. The formation of the adult ego state enables our capacity for nondualism: Something can be good *and* bad, based on the context in which it is being expressed. We love *and* hate someone,

Dialectical Thinking

JULIA CAROL

"Do I contradict myself? Very well then, I contradict myself, I am large, I contain multitudes."

—Walt Whitman

Life is full of contradictions, or facts that appear to us as contradictory. Life is complex and ever changing. If we reject contradiction, we deny the reality of the nature of things, and we invite the critical pig parent to believe its own oversimplified story about the truth.

The dialectic process, as named by Plato in his writings on the Socratic method, offers a way to embrace the concept of beginning with one idea and then building on it, letting the contradictory nature of things add color and richness to the exploration. Rather than have two sides argue with one another, remaining steadfast in their conviction, teachers who use the Socratic method invite arguments feel happy *and* sad, hope *and* feel hopeless, all at the same time. In Western European philosophical thought, this capacity to hold multiple competing truths is called dialectical thinking. Holding paradox is a sign of sophisticated thinking and complex mental capacity and is a hallmark of the adult ego state. We also refer to the adult ego state as the fair witness, the compassionate internal observer, or the voice of reason. The development of this "inner adult" is essential to the successful implementation of Skills for Change in our lives.

In Skills for Change coaching, the development of the client's adult ego state is an underlying element of most client contracts. The adult ego state is a prerequisite for most clients to achieve their other goals, whether they are starting a business, working on their relationships, writing a book, trying to lose weight, and so on. In fact, the application to our lives of most tools in this book requires our use of the adult ego

that remain open to new information and examine fully and integrate all angles until parties in the dialogue arrive at the truth.

G.W.F. Hegel advanced the theory by supposing that contradiction is inherent in all things, and truth itself is a moving target.[7] Outside our own perceptions of truth, there exist constantly changing truths that take into account the evolution of truth, truth that contradicts truth, synthesis of those truths into a balanced truth, and then more contradictions.

All of these ideas can get very esoteric and academic. The aim for Skills for Change practitioners is to allow our minds and hearts to remain open and to handle contradiction by exploring its nature and being willing to hold opposing ideas until synthesis is found. I've found in my own life, and in my experiences with clients, that even once synthesis is found, it is temporary. After time passes, a reexamination from the perspective gained over time will embellish and add even more color, complexity, and a greater understanding of what I believed once to be "true." All this to say: Keep an open mind!

state: it is the source of our self-compassion, acceptance, discernment, and ability to tolerate complexity and contradiction.

We don't want to leave the child ego state behind, however. Instead, we aim to develop a life that is adult-guided and child-centric. After all, the child fuels our passionate interest in activities such as kite flying, obtaining an advanced education, playing basketball, cooking, having sex, plein air painting, practicing martial arts, playing video games, helping the homeless, crocheting, parenting, lake swimming, playing a musical instrument, developing friendships, learning another language, and so on. When we cultivate our adult consciousness, we are more able to create pragmatic changes in our lives that work for us. Without our child-based desires engaged, we can end up creating a robotic, mechanistic life, functional but without aliveness, excitement, ease, or joy. Our adult ego state also helps us work with our fears and be honest about what we can and can't do.

When we identify our safety reflex and ego states, we are more able to understand our internal complexity. Our reaction to conflict, such as tightness in our chest and a desire to leave the room, might be a safety reflex to move *away*. We may hear voices in our head saying, "Why did you do that? Who do you think you are?" After we identify these questions as coming from our pig parent ego state, we might ask: "What does that part of me need or want? What is it taking care of or protecting?" Our ego states may help us explain our internal splits and contradictions. We might say to ourselves, "So this is why I want both to stay in this relationship *and* break up. I want the nurturing, connection, and sex, and I don't want to feel trapped or stuck in a cycle of constant fighting. Of course, it makes sense—there are these different parts of me trying to figure me out and get me what I need!" Then our adult ego state may step forward and craft a solution that takes care of all our needs.

Six • Pig Parent:
How We Internalize Oppressive Beliefs

Nancy Shanteau

TRUE STORY
How the mind craves a good ruse,
any excuse to entangle you—sleek coyote
intent on mischief, monkey chattering nonsense
carefully chosen to wound, confuse. The mind
is rarely your friend. It aims for opposites,
argues that you're undesirable, lazy,
ugly, nuts, destined to always be lonely,
when in reality—take another deep breath—
like any dahlia bright under summer's sun,
zinnia, foxglove, leopard lily or china rose,
like the blue-bellied lizard warming herself
on a slant of granite beside this lake
or that cloud shaping itself into mares' tails,
you're incredibly easy to love.

—Molly Fisk[1]

I distinctly remember being five years old and feeling like every cell in my body was screaming at me. Screaming is probably a mild word to describe the experience. I felt like everything about me was wrong, and I was desperate to fix myself so that I would be loved, accepted, and chosen. I had entered kindergarten, a classroom by all accounts unusual, with sixty kids aged five to twelve, ranging from kindergarten through sixth grade, and two exceptional teachers. Being chosen seemed paramount, and it was everywhere. We were chosen for teams at recess, to play imaginary games, as partners in learning exercises. Everywhere, everyone seemed to be choosing each other, and even though I was often chosen, I was also often not chosen. The moments when I wasn't chosen were excruciating, and I was determined to fix it.

What did fixing it mean, though? "It" was the ineffable experience of inclusion, and none of the times I was included, picked, chosen, selected, or hugged made up for the times when I wasn't. Then I would be left out, lonely, lost. I was a brash, loud, exuberant, somewhat portly girl child, and I wasn't one of the "popular" kids. My response to these experiences was to try harder, be better, smarter. Of course, being smarter was a double-edged sword, but I was good at it, so I just kept getting better at it. The world of tact, relationships, empathy, and the dynamics of cliques and clubs eluded me, and I didn't know how to ask for help or do anything differently. I was lucky. By contrast, I believe my elementary school experience was incredibly gentle. I'm amazed that children survive the often violent, shaming, daily gauntlet of school. Still, I left school with a distinct impression that there was something wrong with me, something I didn't know how to change. I told myself if I just tried harder, I would figure it out, and things would get better. I began to internalize oppressive beliefs about myself that I was ugly, lazy, and would never be good enough, beliefs to help me survive in a frightening world that I didn't understand.

POWERLESSNESS AND THE INTERNALIZATION OF OPPRESSION

We start life so entirely helpless. As babies, we have minimum power to affect the world around us, and as we grow, we gain limited power and influence over our circumstances. Our powerlessness is over-whelming, and we protect ourselves from feeling the depth and extent of our lack of power by blaming ourselves for things that go wrong. If we don't have friends, it's because we're weird or ugly; if our parents don't give us as much attention as we want, it's because we're unworthy and bad; when we struggle in school, we must be stupid and lazy. This self-blaming instinct offers us sanctuary from the feelings of powerlessness—if we did something to deserve our difficult experiences, we can "fix" them. If we focus our attention on ourselves and what we did wrong, there's a chance we can improve ourselves and thus change our circumstances.

Unfortunately, this judgmental mindset focuses our attention too narrowly on an analysis of our own behavior (individualism) instead of on the bigger systems and forces that shape our everyday experiences. And we often pick our most successful strategies as the source and rea-son for our failure. I must not be smart enough or fast enough or work hard enough. We tell ourselves, "If I only work harder, I will be suc-cessful." Yet, who defines *weird* or *ugly*—how do we know when our preferences are ours and when they are shaped by cultural messages we receive from adults, our peers, and the media? We spend our time try-ing to fix what's wrong with us instead of evaluating the standards and values by which we are assessing ourselves. It's a hopeful but dead-end cul-de-sac that takes us ineffectively in circles, wastes our time, and disappoints our youthful dreams for a good life.

We can spend a lifetime focused on what's wrong with us and not look at the systems that keep us running in place because there's just enough of a kernel of truth to the story that our problems are our fault. And the great irony is that as we gain in power and become independent adults, we continue with these ingrained, habitual, self-blaming assessments. Even when we have the power to alter our stories, values, and standards, as well as the thoughts and actions that emerge from our belief systems, we continue to focus on ourselves as if we're the only source of our problems. All this focus on ourselves and what's wrong with us keeps us from taking collective action to change the larger systems of dominance that shape our world. We internalize oppressive beliefs that reinforce the systemic status quo, and we spend our lives working hard to change things that ultimately leave us dissatisfied and disappointed.[2] The cops are in our heads, and unwittingly we internally reproduce a belief system that controls what we want and who we think we "should" be. We internalize the rules, laws, and judgments of our family, community, and culture in such a way that we feel weighed down, even depressed. We feel the pressure of our internalized oppression. No wonder we feel so exhausted and overwhelmed sometimes.

"SHAME IS PIG IN THE BODY"

In the psychological world, this weighed-down feeling is commonly called shame. Shame is defined as "a painful emotion caused by consciousness of guilt, shortcoming, or impropriety," and "the susceptibility to such emotion."[3] The word *susceptible* jumps out at me as particularly interesting when we discuss shame in our cultural model. Shame is so interwoven into our construction of the self that many of our feelings, thoughts, and stories about ourselves and the world are shame-filled. We are susceptible to suggestions that we should feel bad about our behavior, our choices, our sense of belonging, and even our very existence.

The way human beings internalize oppression is extraordinarily creative: we shape our bodies to be as danger-free as possible; we tailor our thoughts to strategize safe connections and maximize the love we receive; we take on external values and rules, and they can sound like voices in our heads or appear as constricting impulses in our bodies. We may have vague but intense feelings of being exhausted, depressed, or lethargic. The ongoing voices and bodily constrictions become background noise, constant feedback on our daily activities. The voices—varying from cruel, judgmental attacks to subtle overplanning to an evaluation of every nuance of a meeting—become hardwired as thoughts, emotions, and physical tension. In Skills for Change, we call these voices and embodied tension the "pig parent." "Shame is pig in the body," says Julia Kelliher.

The pig parent acts as an internal police force, judge, and jury enforcing the external social rules for appropriate behavior. We learn a rulebook for greater success in the intimate settings of the family, classroom, schoolyard, and possibly church or community organizations—these are the locations for the thousands of daily transactions we engage in as young people. Our internalized oppression will be *much* harsher than the worst danger we faced in the world during our young life—it is the purpose of our safety reflex to keep us safe, after all. How could the pig parent keep us safe with timid, weak voices: "Maybe you should move out of the way, dear?" No, what we hear in our heads is "Get out of the way!"

The pig messages have a range of meanings. They might say we are weak, sick or ill, stupid, crazy, lazy, ugly, bad, or deserve to die.[4] We construct a set of strategies to help us succeed, and the internalized message is usually worse than anything anyone actually says to us, because the pig is trying to keep us safe by heading off dangerous behavior before it starts. These strategies contain a code to our unique and individual contexts. They are both universal and incredibly specific. They are wholly ours, and as such, can be reinvented. It's important to remember that the cops in our heads are not actually authority figures. They are manifestations of a terrified inner child who tries to figure out the adult world and uses intensity, harshness, criticism, contempt, and even cruelty to enforce behavior.

WHY "PIG"?

When we initially hear the term *pig*, or *pig parent*, many of us express a varied set of reactions, from revulsion to curiosity. Some of us complain that it makes the already difficult job of parenting even harder by demonizing aspects of parental behavior. Others say that labeling the pig with this negative term is no better than the pig itself and is inherently contradictory. Some have objected to the anthropomorphism of animals, saying that until we have more constructive and healthy relationships with both wild and domestic animals, we shouldn't drag them into linguistic distinctions about human behavior, or in other words, pigs are nice, and we shouldn't give them a bad name. Still others say that *pig* is an old 1960s Berkeley radical term, and we shouldn't use it because it sounds outdated and disrespects the police. Whatever the complaint, people who want to avoid the term *pig* have worked hard to come up with an alternative, and have usually failed.[5]

One of the reasons the term pig has stuck around in Skills for Change coaching is that it is a versatile word that lends itself to many uses. We might say, "I'm pigging myself," "I'm having a pig attack," "I pigged him yesterday when he came home with a bad report card," "Don't pig me about being late," or "My pig went crazy when my boss told me I was on probation." When it's tempting to judge ourselves because we see our pig but can't yet stop it, we remind ourselves, "Don't pig the pig!" Because *pig* is '60s slang for the police, this versatility brings with it the added benefit of indicating the inherent link between internalized oppressive messages. When we label the pig in these internal voices and external transactions, we remind ourselves of the social norms and injunctions transmitted to us throughout our lives and gain power over our internal state through the distance the label provides.

HOW THE PIG WORKS: DECODING PIG MESSAGES

We find the seven categories of pig messages hidden in our behavior and thoughts.[6] They support invisible norms that keep us stuck and prevent change. Thus, the people with the power keep the power, and the people on the bottom stay on the bottom.

Deserve to Die: This is the most destructive and pervasively potent of the pig messages. It is an "umbrella" pig message, and often each of the other messages contain deserve-to-die elements and refer back to this pig message. Variations on deserve-to-die messages include these: you're not good enough, you're not lovable, you don't belong, you suck, and it doesn't matter what you do. Deserve-to-die messages prevent us from pursuing our dreams, taking leadership positions, and asking for what we want in relationships and our lives. This pig message also encourages us to look for a silver bullet solution to make us feel good enough or that we belong. The deserve-to-die pig message goes hand in hand with expressions of resignation, a feeling of heaviness or apathy in the body, and a lack of will to take actions that will change the situation. When we have the worst expression of deserve-to-die pig, we suffer suicidal thoughts, or even attempt to kill ourselves. Even if we never actually want to die, the deserve-to-die pig message subtly or overtly suggests that we have failed to earn our place on the planet and are wasting precious space and resources. Taunted by our deserve-to-die pig, we seek approval from others, and yet no amount of external praise ever seems to fill the empty void of belonging.

Weak/Sick/Ill: This pig message tends to strike people who have physical ailments or disabilities or feel physically different, faulty, or inadequate. If we're weak, we'll be culled from the herd, rejected, isolated, and left alone to fend for ourselves or die. We'll be dependent on others for support and sustenance and require attention that we don't deserve—we believe we're physically broken. This message is deeply linked to a sense of low personal value (deserve to die) and also the productivity injunction associated with "lazy pig" (see below), for often when we are weak, sick, or ill, we are also unable to work or provide for ourselves and may even be dependent on someone else for our well-being. In cases of chronic disease or bodily difference, our weak/sick/ill pig might encourage us to believe we are basically flawed. Often when weak/sick/ill pig strikes, a flood of other pig messages follow, since many of us keep pig at bay with great effort and hard work.

Stupid: Poor school performance in our cultural model reinforces "stupid pig." Students receive grades that inform them whether their

---

Stereotype Threat: Intelligence, Test Taking, and the Election of an African American President

NANCY SHANTEAU

In 1995, researchers Claude Steele and Joshua Aronson published results of a study at Stanford that measured the impact of stereotypes on individuals' behaviors.[7] The study found that white students would perform better on tests when they were told the tests measured intelligence, while African American students performed worse. Steele and Aronson termed this vulnerability "stereotype threat." The students' fear of confirming a stereotype increased their physiological stress and affected their performance by up to 40%. Further studies found that students could fight the stereotype threat by cultivating resilient practices, such as when students remind themselves of their values and strengths before taking a test. The study was repeated when President Barack Obama was elected, and the stereotype threat against African American students' intelligence had diminished. Our beliefs shape us, our actions and reactions, and what we are capable of accomplishing. Change the belief, change what's possible.

intellectual, test, and project performance is above, meeting, or below standards. Even though schools don't automatically detect and reward genius levels of intelligence, we tend to label ourselves as intelligent or not based on our school performance. The intelligent are "successful and powerful." The stupid are "failing, slow, behind everyone else." As a result of this narrow definition of intelligence, we ignore other types of intelligence, including musical, emotional, street, spatial, aesthetic, and physical. Stupid pig is often accompanied with a cloud of confusion, which is also linked to "crazy pig" (see below). Stupid pig narrowly defines intelligence and keeps people from seeing their unique mental, perceptive, and creative gifts.

Crazy: Explicitly about people's mental stability, we struggle with crazy pig if we identify or have been diagnosed as cognitively different. Differences can include mental processing like dyslexia and attention deficit disorder as well as diagnoses such as paranoid schizophrenia and bipolar disorder. The codes of the *Diagnostic and Statistical Manual of Mental Disorders* (DSM) are used to categorize and label people's ability to function normally in social settings. While the clinical definitions of mental illness may assist practitioners in designing appropriate treatment for patients, the labels also shape social opinion as well as people's self-conceptions. One of the missions of the Radical Psychiatry Collective was to address the power inequity between therapists and clients and to debunk the idea that diagnoses were the primary reason people exhibit antisocial behavior. In fact, members of the Collective observed that when people's real scarcity (money, work, food, housing) was addressed, often their diagnosable behaviors minimized or disappeared altogether.[8] In addition to its relationship with sanity, crazy pig is also about other types of mental difference, whether in someone's thoughts, actions, or decision-making style. Logical decision making is valued in our culture, while emotional or intuitive decision making may provoke other people's judgment. People in one-down positions will often be labeled crazy because their experience is so vastly different from the experience of people who are one up and thus have the power to define *normal*.[9]

Lazy: Primarily associated with the protestant work ethic and the pursuit of the American dream in U.S. culture, lazy pig tends to come up when we are not as motivated as we think we should be in our desire for money or ambition to climb the success and promotion ladder. Lazy pig can be so strong that in the American middle class, we may internally attack ourselves even when we are outwardly busy and productive. Lazy pig may also encourage our intolerance and judgment for our exhaustion—thus, when we take naps or spend time in bed to recover lost sleep and energy, we might trigger a lazy pig attack.

Ugly: The narrow beauty standard in our culture results in people having eating disorders and taking on extreme diets, use of

How Ugly Pig Kills

NANCY SHANTEAU

Spain 2006: The Madrid Fashion Week organizers decided to limit underweight models' participation due to Uruguayan Luisel Ramos's death from malnutrition.[10] Subsequently, Spanish clothing manufacturers were required to use at least a size-10 mannequin in the windows of shops. A handful of countries followed suit, while other major fashion centers such as Paris, London, and New York refused to use a body mass index to limit models' participation—many famous models would not qualify for runways if such standards were adopted. Deaths from malnutrition due to eating disorders such as anorexia and bulimia continue to rise, and many young women still think they must starve to be beautiful. Ugly pig remains a deadly force, ultimately fulfilling deserve-to-die pig's message by killing its victims.

expensive beauty products, plastic surgery, and obsessive exercise. While the pressure to be beautiful is commonly discussed and suffered among women in our culture, short, fat, or slender men often also experience oppressive judgments, painful jokes, and reduced access to opportunities, relationships, and social success. Beautiful people are more likely to have job opportunities, friends, and access to resources available through relationships.[11] Because "ugly pig" results in competitive behavior among people struggling for limited resources, even people who are considered beautiful by many may still consider themselves ugly, focus on their flaws rather than their beauty, and feel bad about themselves and their bodies.

Bad: *Good* and *bad* are moral judgments based on cultural injunctions of acceptable and unacceptable behavior, and in Christianity, *bad* is akin to *sinful*. Most people relate to "bad pig" not as a direct label, but through its relatives. "Be a good girl." "Don't be a naughty boy, or you'll get coal in your stocking." "She's so selfish." "He's irresponsible." This pig message can additionally include behaviors that are criminal, addictive, or antisocial. The injunction to be good, obey, and play by the rules stifles creativity and free expression. Many cultural messages encourage us to take care of everyone else first, and we may be so far down our own lists that we rarely attend to our own needs. When we self-sacrifice, we often experience greater distance from and mystification around what we really want. Some people may have a counterphobic response to the good/bad messages that induces a rebellious acting out. Either way, bad pig cultural messages are a strong reinforcement method for the social norms and values that protect the hierarchy and status quo. Bad pig keeps people from generating alternatives to standard cultural practices.

Yikes! All this pig talk is heavy. Stand up, shake it off, dance around a little, and we'll move into the discussion of how we can begin to fight these messages internally, externally in relationship, and collectively in the larger social and cultural frameworks in which we live.

Seven • Getting Unstuck: From Pig Fight to Plan

Nancy Shanteau

We've talked elsewhere in this book about how real, systemic oppression in the world is perpetuated collectively and must be fought collectively. Just as collective action is the antidote to systemic oppression, individual internal action is the antidote to internalized oppression. We must fight the internal forces that weigh us down, much as we fight injustice in our communities, our nation, and the world. This is not to say we must fight internal injustice alone—collective action is just as important in fighting internalized oppression as it is in fighting systemic external oppression. After all, many of our internalized injunctions come from group experiences, and often a group's support can be the best defense against internal injustice.

In Skills for Change coaching, we call the process of clearing pig a "pig fight." Some people react strongly to the term *fight*, since it sounds as if we are inciting internal violence. In reality, a good pig fight will most often involve deep compassion and care for ourselves and others. We use the word *fight* because we consider internalized oppression an assault by large systemic forces on our well-being. We must do the work of choosing language for the process that inspires and supports us. We also speak of soothing the pig, sending the pig on vacation, releasing the pig from the body, finding an antidote for the pig, disarming the pig, and so on.

The good news is that it's possible to live mostly pig-free. I say *mostly* because we are swimming in a sea of cultural and social injunctions to be good, productive, sane, beautiful, healthy, smart, and to belong. These injunctions impact our bodies daily through verbal and nonverbal communication with others. Also the media, as well as our own stored patterns of thought, bombard us with messages of perfection. Our pig might get triggered when we see someone who has what we want for ourselves or when someone speaks or implies an assessment of us or our behavior.[1] For some people, the idea they could live pig-free might be oppressive because they think they "should" be able to achieve this goal. For others, the very notion of living without pig may produce a vibrant challenge that inspires them to achieve greater peace. We fight our pig when we notice what goals and aspirations inspire us and what thoughts produce heaviness and internal judgment.

In this chapter, I will introduce a systemic step-by-step process for fighting pig. As we experiment with the steps, we might find one step more successful or necessary than another. I encourage my clients to organize the steps in a way that makes sense to them and add or take steps away when they aren't helpful. I promise that these tools will begin to clear the mental and physical pig messages, and the emerging sense of freedom builds trust that we can dispel our internal pig, as well as the pig in the world around us. The pig fight is a progressive process. Remember, as we fight our pig, we cultivate our spacious adult consciousness, soothe the wounded parts of ourselves, and design a life that works for us.

NORMALIZE, OR "OF COURSE"

In fighting the pig, the first step is to normalize and reframe our behavior, thoughts, and choices and how the pig became a part of our daily existence in a cultural and social context, so we can understand why our actions make sense given our setting, training, and history. Of course we internalized the oppressive forces of systemic, structural, and cultural domination when we were growing up. All of the trusted adults in our lives—parents, teachers, guardians, babysitters, clergy—had also internalized oppressive values and were transmitting these values to us along with positive values that we may choose to keep. And of course we internalized these messages as rules for living, because we were much less powerful as a toddler, kid, adolescent, teenager, and young adult than we are now, and we had far fewer choices. Pleasing adults and adhering to the social rules meant that we had a chance to feel safe and loved.

When we normalize, we want to get as close as possible to the exact circumstances of our lives and to reflect back to ourselves why our struggle makes sense, given the situation we were in and the difficulty of our journey. Normalizing gives us an opportunity to tell a bigger truth about the past, and our experience, one that helps us understand why we suffered then and still suffer now. We try to tell the truth from our adult ego state, so we include elements of cultural and social context and remind ourselves of the contradictions inherent in our struggle to make a change that might be better for us.

NURTURE

The next step in pig fighting is to nurture. Nurturing can come from the parent ego state, where the nurturing is more right/wrong and dualistic, or it can be nurturing from the adult ego state, more likely to include the inherent contradictions of our situation. Examples of parent-based nurturing statements include these: "I love you just the way you are, no matter what you do." "You are the most beautiful person in the world to me." "You are perfect, wonderful and fabulous, and I love spending time with you." A parent-based nurturing statement might make us feel relaxed and happy, or it might sound like fingernails on a chalkboard, irritating and condescending.

Let's look at a nurturing statement constructed from our rational adult consciousness and see the differences: "You're not perfect for everyone at all times—some people find you beautiful, and other people don't notice your beauty at all. Part of why I think you're so beautiful is how much I love you; I enjoy your laughter and smile, because it means you're happy, and that makes me happy." Adult-based nurturing statements usually include a sense of context and personal preferences and may reflect differences across time and geography.

We start our adult nurturing statements with what's true, and then we say what's not true and what's also true. Often there's a kernel of truth in the pig message, and when we acknowledge what's true, we are more able to let go of our fear that the kernel of truth is the whole truth. Again, it's important to notice what statements help our bodies relax, and what statements increase our agitation. The best nurturing will bring us a sense of calm and a feeling of being understood, and perhaps some clarity on why we behave the way we do and the difficulty of making new choices for ourselves and our futures.

LABEL THE PIG

Once we've normalized and nurtured our experience, it can be really useful to label or categorize the pig messages, as they are often encoded and buried within relatively innocuous thoughts. Heavy and distressing sensations in our bodies are one way to identify pig-filled thoughts. The act of labeling offers us distance from our experience and sensations and thus increases our power and choice over our thoughts and feelings. Because each person's pig messages are constructed from a unique combination of family and cultural upbringing, one person may categorize a pig message differently from another person.

Labeling the pig messages can be surprising both internally and externally. During my first significant pig fight, I was shocked to discover that most of my thoughts and sensations were loaded with deserve-to-die pig. I thought deserve-to-die pig messages were impossible for me because I never had suicidal thoughts, even at my darkest moments. But as I described my pig messages, Julia Kelliher pointed out that they had the underlying theme of "you suck," and that was deserve-to-die pig.

Once I realized that I was dealing with a big pig attack almost all the time, I set about fighting. Within a few months, I'd reduced my thoughts by 70%. It sounds impossible, but it's true. Seventy percent of my thoughts, throughout the day, were either examining past occurrences to determine what I'd done wrong, and then chastising myself for my misdeeds, or planning the future to avoid screw ups. When I identified all these thoughts as pig, noticed which thoughts felt heavy and which felt light, and stopped the heavy thoughts, gradually the voices and painful sensations dissipated, until one day I realized I was thinking a lot less. My mind was quieter, and decisions were easier. "This," I said to myself, "must be what inner peace feels like."

Let's take the example of wanting to quit smoking and see if we can label the pig in our thoughts. We might think we are too weak to quit—this thought might be a combination of crazy pig and weak pig because the weakness is about willpower as well as bodily strength. There is almost certainly deserve-to-die pig because we probably think we aren't good enough, strong enough, or smart enough to quit. There's probably bad pig as well, since smoking is bad for our lungs and environment, and we might have stupid and crazy pig for smoking when we know it's not good for us. There could be ugly pig, for the impact to beauty, such as stained teeth, the smell of cigarette smoke, and dry skin. And we could have lazy pig for not working hard enough at quitting. Wow—that's every single pig message, all rolled up in the simple act of lighting a cigarette!

As we label our pig, we discover the power that comes from knowledge and insight. Throughout the process, we might continue normalizing and nurturing to help us get through the work—it can feel awful in the middle. We stick with the process and discover hope and progress in repetition. After a few pig fights, we start to see patterns and trends, and fundamentally it comes down to whether a thought is life affirming or life draining. When we stop our life-draining thoughts, we find ourselves living a pig-free life.

SENSATIONS/FEELINGS

It can be useful to unpack a label, for example, *sadness*, into its component sensations. When I feel sad, I feel a constriction in my chest and a squeezing, burning feeling in my throat, my face feels tight, and tears gather in the corners of my eyes. I breathe very shallowly and lose a sense of connection to my back and the lower half of my body. My stomach also tightens, and sometimes I feel nauseous. There's a lot going on in pig messages in the body, and it's often helpful to break things down to understand the complexity of the situation. Sometimes pig will show up only as a bodily phenomenon, without any corresponding thoughts.

Most of the time, pig messages are connected with a constellation of physical sensations. These sensations are contractions, reductions in the flow, movement, heat, and vitality in the body. They generally slow the vertical flow of fluids and energy by squeezing horizontally, along bands that Wilhelm Reich identified as "body armoring."[2] Armoring tends to compress in toward the bones and up or down toward the center of the body. Armoring is habitual bodily contraction, so ingrained that we no longer have conscious control over the holding pattern.

As we are fighting pig messages, our associated armoring may simply relax at the same time. Or we may find that we've done all the mental and linguistic work of fighting the pig, but the bad feelings and sensations still linger. Either way, another approach to fighting the pig is to fight it through the body. There are several ways to approach pig and armoring through the body: in conversation (we also experience conversations bodily), through individual movement practices, through paired or group practices, and through lying-down bodywork. Body scan processes can help build our knowledge of sensation, and our skill at keeping our attention on the movement, temperature, pressure, and emotions in our bodies.[3] Body-centered movement practices can also assist, though it's important to keep our attention on sensations rather than using movement to dissociate or flee sensations or emotions that are uncomfortable.

We keep going through the steps of normalizing, nurturing, labeling, and feeling as we discover more about our pig. The pig fight often reveals layers upon layers of history and self-belief. Sometimes, we've done all the cognitive work needed for self-love and acceptance, but we haven't done the work of releasing the pig from the body. Then the cognitive work could seem unfinished, or unsuccessful, but what's true is that the mental work is complete and just needs to be combined with physical release.

DISCERNMENT AND VALIDATION

Once we've labeled the pig messages, it's time to wrestle with the pig message's kernel of truth: we identify what's true, what's not true, and what's also true about the pig message. First we acknowledge there is some truth to the statement the pig is making, but it's not the whole truth. By doing so, we bring the kernel of truth down to size (what's true), then we tell the other truths, positive truths, or confusing truths (what's not true and what's also true) that don't fit rules or easy assignments of meaning. These other truths counter the pig messages. This stage of the pig fight requires our logical, mature inner adult consciousness to take charge and assert the reality around which we will organize our ideas, thoughts, values, and actions.

I often work with American middle-class white folks, especially men, who have trouble fighting their "successful-provider" pig. Those of us who struggle with this pig message receive cultural approval for being an economic provider for our families, and we often measure our worth by our income. Even when we don't buy in to these values in other aspects of our lives, we might have difficulty when we feel we can't earn enough money or when we have trouble doing the steps needed to answer phone calls, follow up on tasks, and complete projects.

One of the problems we face in fighting this pig is that it is strongly reinforced in the constant daily transactions we have with family, friends, peers, colleagues, and acquaintances. "What are you up to?" "How have you been doing?" "How are you?" These questions sound innocuous, as if they could have hundreds of meanings. In our lives, though, with a reduced emphasis on emotional relatedness and a one-up/one-down competitive conversational style, these questions are designed to determine status on the pecking order. Is he doing better than I am? Am I doing better than she is?

A client of mine, Joel, suffered from overwhelming negative thoughts about his ability to successfully provide for his family. We started fighting his pig by identifying what his pig says: "It doesn't matter what you do—you'll never get ahead. You're worthless, and you don't have any value to contribute. You don't have what it takes to succeed. Your girlfriend and your family will leave you, and you'll be alone when you're old." I imagine in Joel's case the kernel of truth is that it's harder to have connected, vibrant relationships in the midst of scarcity. When people are struggling financially, money becomes the focus of attention, and it's a challenge to make intimate and loving connections. While someone in the United States is often supported by her community during a financial crisis, there is often some degree of oppressive conversation, shunning, or even violent behavior directed toward the person who is asking for help.

Perhaps this admission of truth helps Joel relax a little. Yes, the difficulty is real, and it is harder to connect with others when money is scarce. So let's say we've successfully validated Joel's pig about his worth and value. What's not true? It's unlikely he'll ever be totally alone in his life. It's not true that he never contributed or made a difference. During this stage of the pig fight, it's important to be extremely specific. Last year, Joel made a big sale internationally, in a tough market. And over the past year, he worked during the summer on one job, with another team in the fall, and supported his family in many ways. Know that more pig might come out during this process—add it to the pile and keep fighting.

Once we've gotten through the "not true" part of the pig fight, we can go on to ask, "What's also true?" Is it true that all people will shun Joel if he isn't as successful as he's trying to be? Some people might gather to support him and his family, perhaps even the people and relationships he values most. Does Joel believe the only people who are valuable are those making a financial contribution to the world? What about poets, dancers, monks, disabled people, people who work in nonprofits and for social justice? What about au pairs, mothers, hospice workers, and the elderly? What about children? The work of nurturing has been systemically devalued in our culture. We generally do not get paid for love, compassion, caregiving, or laughter. Mostly, the human interactions of greatest value are unpaid.

As we proceed through the discernment process, looking for the most impactful "what's true" and "what's not true" statements, our bodily holding pattern will begin to loosen and relax. Often, clients will start to add to the pig fight, saying, "Yeah, and what about this or that?" Or they'll say, "Wow, I hadn't thought about it that way."

We continue asking, "What's true, what's not true, and what's also true," until we feel rebalanced, lighter, and hopeful, though perhaps still facing the sadness and discomfort of our imperfect and limited reality. The pig fight builds internalized empowerment: we increase our adult ego state's power and decrease the internal pig static that drains our positive momentum.

MAKE A PLAN

At this point in the pig fight, it might be a good time to ask these questions: "How do I want my life to look?" "At the end of my life, what do I want people to say about me, and how would I like to get there?" "Whose opinions matter to me, and can I satisfy them, or are they unable to be satisfied?" "Can I build an image of success that includes both work *and* relationships, play *and* effort?"

Making a plan has two steps. One is retroactive—if we could do that whole sequence again, how would we do it differently? There's lots of good information in analysis of a past situation, and it can be calming to know how we'd handle it if it happened again.

The second step is to design the future. Regardless of the past, how do we want our future to look? How will we get there? Does it seem realistic, or do we need to ask for help as we are implementing our plan so that we can do something collectively rather than individually? How do we want to feel as we move through the steps of our plan? When we generate plans with high chances of success, we're much more likely to build confidence in our compassionate adult ability to fight pig and design our lives.

This is a great time to practice something we can do right now—a way of being, expressing ourselves, asking for help—so when we go back into the world, we're prepared for the hard work of making real requests. For example, with Joel's financial difficulties, we might have him practice a way of speaking about his life that involves telling part of the truth and also telling part of what's hard: "Things haven't been easy lately. I'm really organizing myself around appreciating all the love in my life and the value of my friendships. Thank you for asking. I'm looking for help with international contracts, connections with suppliers, and someone who can help me organize social media outreach. Do you know anyone or anything that would be useful?"

PIG EXCAVATION

At some point in our process, we may choose to sit down and list every pig message present in our consciousness. Once we identify and categorize our personal array of pig messages, it's time to begin the process of shifting and clearing our pig stories and the habits that support or emerge from those stories. Such a pig excavation process can be extremely powerful, and we may want to ask other successful pig fighters to help us, since it can also be overwhelming. The more we understand about how pig works, the better we fight.

HAPPINESS, SATISFACTION, AND LOVE

Pig is generally a terrible basis for a life—playing by other people's rules doesn't generate happiness. The rules might not even create safety. They're just a construct, a formula that may or may not produce success, happiness, and love. And they are a formula designed to keep most people out of power because hierarchy and systems of domination require that many suffer for the success of a few. Pig fighting is worth every ounce of effort we put toward it, because when we are free from internalized oppression, we start to see external oppression very clearly. Change comes from our awareness of what we want, the choices that are available to us, and clarity about the collective forces opposing us. Our access to power arises from this knowledge, from our thoughtful plans put into action, and from the support of our communities. This combination of awareness, action, and support provides our greatest hope for a life filled with happiness, satisfaction, and love.

Eight • Competition and Scarcity

Julia Kelliher with Marybeth Paul

It was a lovely summer afternoon. I arrived at the potluck party hungry and a bit harried. Earlier, I had spent several hours preparing a fresh, direct-from-the-farm Chinese chicken salad. I'd skipped lunch. I saw dishes of rice, beans, cheese, bread, fruit salads, potato salads, and a few deviled eggs. I was trying to limit sugar, carbohydrates, and dairy in my diet, and besides, I just wanted my own favorite salad. Silently, I made a plan. I would leave my salad in the cooler until it was time to eat. When I got in line, I would put my salad on the table. That way I could take as much salad as I wanted and leave the rest for everyone else.

I don't like to think of myself as a selfish or competitive person, but at my friend's party, in the midst of abundance, I made a plan to get more than my share of my potluck dish. Many times, I share food and other resources. But I can just as easily push to "win" at others' expense, like speeding to the last parking space at the grocery store before another person gets it, or walking quickly toward a crowded restaurant, passing other patrons arriving at the same time to get a table before them. I'm not proud of my behavior. Just the same, when I become attached to what I want, and other people might get it first, I often feel helpless to control my competitive drive, my urge to win.

All human beings are born with instincts for both *competitive* and *cooperative* behavior.[1] We're also born with bodies that have varied genetic tendencies. Some of us lean toward more aggressive action, others toward stillness and caution. We also might have more acute or less acute hearing or vision. Based on the natural gifts and instincts we each carry, we respond differently from one another in similar situations. Our specific culture teaches us to some degree to lean toward competition or cooperation. In his book *The Moral Animal*, Robert Wright calls it tuning our knobs, as with a radio when we tune into one station or another. "Human nature consists of knobs and the mechanisms for tuning the knobs," and our ongoing reaction to our environment "adjusts the maturing mind accordingly."

Here in the United States, as much as we might be encouraged to treat each other as equals and value cooperation in the context of family and community, we are simultaneously encouraged (and in fact required) to compete against one another to be successful economically. When we go to school, we are trained to compete and prepare for work environments. Along with learning the basics of math, reading, and writing, we learn to vie for attention and strive to outdo everyone else for the same essentials. We may also give up, see ourselves as mediocre, or even losers, when we don't succeed at achieving the cultural standards and preferences. Those who are faster, brighter, and more adept receive more praise and rewards, and we also discover that if we move more slowly, are less outgoing, or don't conform well, we're not as highly valued. The qualities held in high esteem by our culture are not negotiable. If we don't measure up, it seems as if we will not only be left out of the group, but we'll be unable to "win," and thereby be "good." We learn to rank our attributes one up or one down relative to others, selecting our strengths according to the cultural value system and disregarding the parts of ourselves that don't fit. Our very identity begins to reflect the culture, either through alignment, conformity, resignation, or rebellion against the norms.

We thus begin to internalize the false belief that we must compete for a limited quantity of affection, nurturing, encouragement, compassion, patience, respect, or love. Our differing degrees of power of all types contribute to the competition we experience. Consider how, in organizational hierarchies, those with power dole out favors in a limited fashion. We enter a world stratified and organized according to external factors: birth family, skin color, athletic ability, intelligence, wealth, and geography. We then compete within our limited group for the resources available to us. Our awareness of our privileged starting position decreases as we rise in the hierarchy. Yet competition can make us feel as if there is not enough and that we must strive ever harder to be worthy of what we have. Scarcity and competition weave and intertwine. Like strands of a braid, it's difficult to distinguish one strand from another.

It makes sense that we might be confused regarding our feelings of competition. We are often not aware when we are feeling competitive. We can also feel guilty about our competitive feelings and thoughts because we're afraid they are unkind or judgmental. Yet, we don't know when it is safe to cooperate or even if we should. We may have internalized the pig ideas that if we behave more collaboratively, it means we are too nice or lazy or simply unfit for the world of survival-of-the-fittest capitalism. Giving up competitive behavior might stimulate the pig thought, "I'm a quitter," and we might think we aren't trying hard enough. In addition, we are afraid that others won't treat us generously or fairly even when we make the effort to cooperate with them. We might worry that if we try to consider others' needs equally to our own (win-win), we will end up betrayed by those acting unilaterally and competitively (win-lose). We don't want to be duped and end up the loser.[2]

As children, we have very little awareness of the so-called choices we make in response to our environment. But as we mature and our capacity for complex thought increases, we are better able to analyze the costs versus benefits of our internalized beliefs and resulting behavior. Hierarchy and competition are efficient, effective, and goal oriented. Competitive behavior also creates divisions and limits our sense of connection and trust with others. Cooperation and equality take more time and energy and can slow down decision making and progress toward a goal. They also open us to more empathy and connection.

What we practice most as children and teenagers becomes an entrenched pattern in our minds and bodies. These patterns make it hard to consciously choose between competitive and cooperative behavior. When we grow up in a highly competitive culture, the radio can get stuck on a competitive station. As much as we try to change the channel, many of us will find it buzzing in our heads at the worst moments. I think of this inner competitive radio station as "comparing mind,"—we just can't stop evaluating and ranking ourselves and others. When our best friend tells us they are going to Hawaii for a much-needed vacation, we have the thought, "Why

Material and Emotional Essentials

MARYBETH PAUL AND GLENN SMITH

Material Essentials	Emotional Essentials
food • clothing • housing	love • affection
money • health care	patience • encouragement
clean water and air	touch • community
relative quiet • space • time	belonging

don't I get to vacation in Hawaii? I've worked so much harder in my life than she has, and I haven't had a vacation in years." A beleaguered young parent complains how exhausted he is, and his single, underemployed friend with no children thinks, "Who are you to complain, with a loving wife, three gorgeous children, and a great job?" Often, these thoughts put us simultaneously one up and one down in the relationship and take us right out of a sense of equality. As much as we want to be happy for our friends, we might find ourselves feeling angry and shut down, victimized by some sense of lack that we previously hadn't even noticed. It's easy then to feel both ashamed and disconnected.

GOING FROM COMPETITION TO NEGOTIATION

The first step to untangling the competition/scarcity snarl is to cultivate adult conscious awareness in our relationships. Then we can notice when our competitive mindset is getting in the way in our connection to our friends and loved ones and assess if we really want the object of our envious feelings. Once we know we want something (more time off, an art class, to have children, a vacation, a better relationship, time to exercise, and so on), we can research its availability and make a plan to obtain it. The competitive mind becomes a resource for figuring out what we really want. Every time I have an urge to compete, or even just competitive thoughts, I ask myself, "Is this situation revealing a genuine want or need, or is this just a competitive reaction?" If I discover genuine wants and needs, I then ask myself if cooperative requests might generate better results than competing against my peers. We can use both competitive and cooperative instincts as resources to get what we want.

We do not have to be competitive with others in order to fulfill our innate ambition to improve ourselves and our lives. As a retail merchant, if I could stop thinking about what other merchants were doing with their stores, I could concentrate on creating the liveliest, warmest environment possible. Of course, I wasn't denying the competitive marketplace, but rather I was taking away as much of its pressure as I could. Instead, my internal desire prompted me to treat my employees fairly, have fun with color and light, and sell merchandise that was as well priced and local as possible. Our choice-filled response to our competitive impulses thus empowers us to achieve what we want.

THE TANGLED WEB OF SCARCITY AND COMPETITION

Up to a certain point, scarcity of food, shelter, and money make a huge difference in our ability to be happy. It's hard for any of us to experience much life satisfaction if we are cold, hungry, exhausted, sick, or lonely. Commonly we regard scarcity as pertaining to material essentials, such as food, clothing, warmth, housing, and money. But it also applies to other human essentials such as love, attention, and community. The *New World Dictionary of American English* offers this definition: "not plentiful, not enough to meet the demand, inadequate supply."

Scarcity becomes more difficult to solve when we cannot separate *real scarcity* from *false scarcity*. Scarcity that is real is based on an actual lack of essential resources available in our environment, right here, right now. When a person has been up for forty-eight hours fighting fires and, confused and inarticulate, begins dozing while sitting up, we could all agree that she is experiencing an actual lack of sleep. When someone has asthma and starts to gasp for air, we agree that oxygen is now in scarcity for this person, and we rush to do something about it.

False scarcity, on the other hand, is scarcity that is entirely constructed by thoughts, often fearful, competitive thoughts. We suffer from this kind of scarcity when we have a "feeling" of scarcity in our bodies caused by false beliefs or worry about scarcity now or in the future. False scarcity causes all the same emotional and physical responses as real scarcity, but it can be deconstructed by examining our ideas about what actually constitutes "enough." A common example of false scarcity in a middle-class environment might be when someone says, "I'm broke," when they actually have money in their pocket or bank account. Questions such as, "Do you have enough money?" and "Can you afford that?" bring up all kinds of confusing thoughts, conversations, disagreements, and comparisons when false scarcity is at play.[3]

In addition, real scarcity and false scarcity are often blended in a way that is hard to see or agree on. For instance, right now in my community of peers in Nevada City, many of us are scared that we will not have food, shelter, or money around the corner. Yet, not one of us is hungry or homeless in this moment. Most of us also have the resources to get help if we need it. This is false scarcity. At the same time, most of my friends are burdened by debt, some are unemployed, most are underemployed, and they all have internalized both oppressive and privileged competitive beliefs that they "should" be doing better than they are and "should not," under any circumstances, apply for a minimum-wage job or social services. While these friends are plagued by false scarcity about food and money, they're also experiencing real scarcity of many other tangible and intangible resources, such as time, health, sleep, extended community, well-being, and peace of mind. Because false and real scarcity intertwine in most peoples' lives, it can be hard to distinguish between the two.

We're further confused because some real scarcity is caused by natural events, like weather or overpopulation of a species in a particular habitat (*ecological scarcity*), while other real scarcity is caused by cultural constructs, such as banking systems, political systems, and large corporations (*systemic scarcity*). External hierarchical systems get internalized individually as systems of belief, such as competition and individualism. Those beliefs left unexamined can drive us to act in ways that reinforce the external system and our own individual experience of scarcity (*belief-driven scarcity*).

Belief-driven scarcity and false scarcity are both caused by large cultural systems and are individually internalized. Our beliefs and perceptions about life can get in the way of making powerful changes in our situation, changes which might alleviate some scarcity. In these kinds of scarcity, our internalized, oppressive pig beliefs drive behavior, which alienate us from our own insight into possible solutions or even the plenitude that sits right in front of us. These kinds of real and false scarcity can be solved using the empowerment formula: we can *demystify* and fight against internalized pig beliefs, gather in *community*, and find ways to take *action against oppression*. We can reduce belief-driven scarcity by challenging our internalized oppressive beliefs and making changes in how we organize our lives.

All kinds of scarcity weave together in our lives. It's nearly impossible to make positive change when the things we are unable to control are tangled up with the things we can control. We can spend time and energy fighting and pushing to change in ways that make our situation worse rather than better. Ultimately, sorting through the causes of our experiences of scarcity will give us the power to change what we *can* change. Within the relatively privileged sphere of middle-class America, we have enormous power to sort through the causes of scarcity and make changes toward more abundance and true satisfaction.

EXAMINING BELIEFS: EXPECTATIONS AFFECT PERCEPTIONS

The actual material and emotional resources available to us as we develop and grow have some bearing on how we perceive our relative abundance or scarcity. In addition, our expectations about what resources we "should" have now or in the future may also diminish our level of satisfaction with what we have.[4] Our minds that have learned to rate, compare, and compete for the top are very affected by the culture of "more is better."

The connection between perception, expectation, and experience became a topic of conversation early in my life. My father grew up in the shadow of his Irish immigrant parents' experiences of famine and poverty back in Ireland. He counted himself lucky to be born in America in 1914. By the time he married in 1948, he had lived through a tuberculosis epidemic (that killed his mother and six of his siblings), the Great Depression, and World War II. He saw himself as a very lucky man! He also told his six children how lucky we were. To him, we had an extremely fortunate life—full of comforts and resources as well as the social and political freedoms of capitalism and democracy.

But we children grew up thinking we were poor. We frequently felt physically uncomfortable and resented it. We saw our neighbors living far more comfortably, with financial and material resources we didn't have. We felt one down. The physical environment of our lives—a thermostat set to 50 degrees at night, very few blankets on our beds, two or three children in each bedroom, oatmeal for breakfast, hand-me-down clothing, chores on Saturdays, church and family dinner on Sundays—felt like deprivation to us kids but appeared as great comfort and security to my dad. Throughout my childhood, my father continued to express amazement at our perceptions of scarcity and experience of emotional misery.

The beliefs we have about life affect how we experience the degree of real scarcity or abundance that exists. What is enough? "Not warm enough" is a partially subjective statement. My father's version was based on survival, not comfort, "You are warm enough to survive." For me, "warm enough" means that I feel comfortable and that my body can relax rather than stay tensed up against the cold.

Manufacturers and corporations, swimming in the unseen waters of our cultural context and comparing minds, reinforce false scarcity, influencing our perceptions of what is enough. Through advertising tactics designed to encourage us to buy things, corporations convince us we need more or better than we have and that there is a limited quantity or time in which to make our purchase. This false scarcity feeds our pig, hinting or directly saying there is something wrong with us, something we must fix, that we are "not enough." Through media and other cultural interactions, we are bombarded with the message that the things we most value are scarce. And when there is genuine scarcity, we are led to believe it is our fault for letting it happen to us, not being hardworking or smart enough to protect ourselves.

Reexamining long-held beliefs helps us become more satisfied and empowered in our lives. It takes great efforts of self-observation and lots of support and practice, while we develop the capacity to choose what we believe and think. If we reevaluate exactly what is necessary and what is enough, we may find that we are able to be more content, less driven, and more able to connect with the values that inspire us rather than the ones that distract and confuse us. We may claim back our right to the satisfaction of community, love, and simple pleasures that don't cost money and do give us energy.[5]

THE SCARCITY OF TIME AND MONEY

By exposing the complex web that includes the current cultural ideologies as well as our internalized beliefs (which produce both *belief-driven scarcity,* and *false scarcity),* we can begin to understand what is really happening. For example, let's consider middle-class parents with young children. When parents are busy competing in our socioeconomic system, working jobs in order to provide their children with all the money and material goods they think are needed, their attention is being funneled into that pursuit, and the child's need for attention and time is not met (*belief-driven scarcity*). Parents may have plenty of love for their children, but it is common for children to imagine that there is not enough love for them (*false scarcity*) when they receive less attention and time than they want. A child may also rightfully fear that there will be even less time and attention to go around when a new baby is integrated into the household (*real scarcity*).

A friend of mine, despite incredible efforts to the contrary, including repeated conversation and family education classes, discovered that his three-year-old daughter thought she would have to leave and find a new family when her baby brother came home from the hospital. She packed a bag, and he had to stop her from walking out the door! He could not convince her that there was enough love in their family for two children by talking to her—it wasn't until she met her brother and was reassured consistently of her safety and belonging that she agreed to unpack the bag and stay.

Reclaiming some of our time back for unpaid labor (love, attention, nurturance, and play) could relieve some of the real scarcity felt by children and their parents. When we choose between fewer material and financial resources and intangible essentials, we face a no-win situation (*belief-driven scarcity*). Many times, as a young parent, I went without money to have more time with my kids, but it was hard to make that choice. It's also hard to negotiate safely in the current U.S. work culture. Many of us who are privileged enough to have good jobs are required to work long hours, often more than forty-hours a week, and are afraid we might lose our job if we ask to reduce our hours or take the sick time or vacation time that we have earned (*real scarcity*).[6]

A prevalent form of belief-driven scarcity in the working-middle class of today is the "glorification of busy."[7] More, better, and faster have become predominant national values. The current perception that being busy and unable to rest is a sign of success has been manufactured and marketed by corporations along with consumerism. It is one of the primary tools by which we unwittingly succumb to competing for more material abundance rather than taking time for the things that feed us more profoundly. Our mostly unconscious agreement with the culture of busyness causes a real scarcity of time that affects all our other transactions and relationships.

If we claim back some of our time in the time/money equation, scaling back our need for material consumption or expensive travel, we can then experience the abundance of love, attention, and enjoyment intrinsic to family and community life. It takes a lot of analysis and strategy to cover our needs for both time and money, but it's well worth the effort. It will require collective effort to change the workplace culture as well.[8]

SOLVING SCARCITY WITHIN A CULTURE OF COMPETITION

Let's consider an example where several kinds of real scarcity weave together within a complicated morass of competitive feelings, isolation, and despair. One of my clients, let's call her Theresa, is a white, single mom raising five sons. When I met her, Theresa worked a low-paying job and received some intermittent child support, which kept a roof over their heads and minimal food on the table.

Many nights, everyone went to bed undernourished, not because there wasn't enough food, but because Theresa was so exhausted and depleted that she didn't have the energy or creativity to make a nourishing meal. The oldest two sons, ages thirteen and fifteen, worked after school and provided a little care for the younger boys. But the older boys, being adolescents, preferred being with their peers and often neglected their younger brothers. The teenagers had already been indoctrinated in a competitive, individualistic system where they were embarrassed by their relative poverty. The youngest three boys sought out older kids, young adults, to provide the attention and nurturing they didn't get from their mom or brothers (or their absent dad). The boys argued among themselves over petty issues: whose turn was it to take out the trash or wash the dishes, who broke the lamp.

The youngest boys were in severe competition with one another to grab whatever of Theresa's attention they could. Even though the oldest boys had figured out they got Theresa's appreciation when they helped out, and they competed for her approval (which she was often too drained to express), they still resorted to arguing over things like who got a bigger serving of spaghetti. Every member of the family was striving to cope with scarcity. The squeaky wheel got the attention from Theresa, even when it was negative attention. They were all competing for the most scarce commodities of all, love and care from each other and their community and their mother's time.

How do we solve such deep, unmet needs? The answer is not easy, nor something that can be done all at once. In Skills for Change coaching, we first begin by normalizing the situation and helping the client see how systemic forces created and reinforced the scarcity and how competition for unavailable resources naturally resulted. We fight the pig the family members have for themselves for not being able to solve their problems, and we help them offer themselves compassion and understanding for the difficulty of their situation. And finally, we problem solve, situation by situation, until the scarcity diminishes. The conflicts caused by scarcity and competition cause emotional pain and, even when circumstances change for the better, leave emotional scars. Still, the healing effort is worth it—after all, it is exhausting to suffer scarcity and competition, and even though cooperation can feel like more work, it is work that empowers all, and it feels better.

In this way, Theresa and I identified the very real scarcity that was outside of her control, like her husband leaving her and the kids, and the unfair distribution of resources in our culture (*systemic scarcity*). We also examined how her individualistic pig messages told her she must take care of herself and her kids all on her own (*belief-driven scarcity*). Theresa had also believed that she must keep her nose to the grindstone, working overtime whenever she could, in order to have enough money for bare essentials (*belief-driven scarcity*). But no matter what she did, she never had enough time and energy in her day to get everything done, and there was never enough money (*real scarcity*). Theresa needed massive doses of compassion for all those factors so that she could have self-compassion. Often the first and most important thing we can do is forgive ourselves for suffering from scarcity and individualism and not being able to single-handedly change our circumstances.

I gently encouraged Theresa to reach out for more support, connecting with the food bank, other mothers, and some friends who didn't have children who might enjoy getting to know her kids. Theresa and I evaluated the economic reality of her life. She needed a minimum of $2,000 per month to pay for rent, utilities, and food. Making $9 per hour for forty hours per week gave her only about $1,350 per month take-home pay. Together with her child support of $600 per month, that gave her $1,950. No wonder she felt overwhelmed and hopeless! Her job barely gave her enough money to live on, and yet it robbed her of the commodities that were equally essential to her family: her time, attention, and energy.

The essentials of love, time, food, and clothing were all in short supply. And this scarcity contributed to feelings of low self-esteem for all of them. They had all internalized cultural pig messages that if they would only work harder or be better or smarter or more organized, none of this scarcity would be there, that it was their fault. They thought they should be able to fix it, but they couldn't. With all these beliefs blocking a wider view, they were unable to see the power they had to organize within their community. And it wasn't their fault that they couldn't see clearly within this web of beliefs in order to find solutions to such deeply mystified scarcity.

Theresa and I tackled one problem at a time. She asked for some help from a friend who had more financial resources. That person agreed to pay her rent for two months. She quit her job, started her own business doing housecleaning for $20 per hour, which meant she could work twenty hours a week and have more time with her kids. She could also then get to the food bank during the hours they were open (which she couldn't do before). She started a community dinner at her house on Sundays where she and some other mothers made food for their families together and made sure there were leftovers for the week. They played games or watched movies afterward. She went to the county to get her intermittent child support court ordered, so she would receive it every month. Slowly, she introduced more adults into the kids' lives. She encouraged her two teenagers to get jobs at the local bicycle shop and get involved with other teens in mountain biking groups. The boys began to feel more like a family and connected to each other. They mostly stopped splintering off in competitive factions and started pulling together more often, seeing the power in working together to create a better life.

CHOICE AND EMPOWERMENT

When we acknowledge that a competitive dynamic exists, we begin to demystify the inequality we feel. Many people will then experience relief and a sense of spaciousness. This spaciousness helps us further analyze the situation, ask questions about what changes are possible, and explore solutions. When we take more power over inaccurate and false beliefs that cause us suffering, we see more clearly our real beliefs and values. We delve more deeply into what we are actually experiencing, what we really want, and we discover what is really enough. We then ask for what we want and negotiate rather than launching into blind competition. By sharing our needs with each other, we create more intimacy and acquire the power to generate more of what we want in our lives, relationships, and communities.

There is hope and relief in working for more cooperation and positive change in our circumstances. Gently and consistently, transaction by transaction, we can slowly create more satisfying lives. This kind of change takes external help, something false scarcity can lead us to believe isn't available. The first step is to find the courage to reach out of our isolation and alienation. We can then, with help, find our way home to community, love, power, and choice.

PART III
CHANGE IS POSSIBLE

Nine • Theory of Change: Change in Our Personal Lives

Julia Kelliher

No matter how much personal, cultural, or institutional power we embody or rely on, our ability to control the events and circumstances of our lives is enacted within a social environment and supported or thwarted by internalized cultural beliefs and social circumstances. The actions we practice every day become patterns of behavior in our social lives. Once we have developed a satisfactory set of social skills to determine our survival, we repeat those strategies over and over again. We practice what has worked in the past and rely on our competency to deal with our social environment in predetermined ways. It then becomes very difficult to learn new beliefs, strategies, or patterns. Why try something new when the old ways served us?

Our desire to keep things the same while also wanting things to change is an enormous contradiction. And this contradiction is an essential part of being human. At a physical level, we want our heart to keep beating, our lungs to keep breathing, and for our internal thermostat to keep us at about 98.6 degrees. We want to have a home and a continual flow of food and other resources, secure, steady, and unchanging. Disruptions such as death, divorce, natural catastrophes, lost jobs, packing up and moving our homes, and losing money all rock our sense of stability and cause us suffering. From a place of comfort and security, we fight against change with all our might.

But wait a minute. We also want to change some things. We want to change the channel on the radio when it's bugging us and change our clothes when they're dirty and improve our relationships. We want to finish school, work, and projects. We want time to pass more quickly, and yet, we don't want to get old or closer to death in the process. Welcome to our rocky, compelling, complicated relationship with change.

What is change? Some change happens inevitably, without our say-so. But there are other kinds of change that are subject to our human will and influence. When we want more or less of something, we attempt to exert control over quantities and circumstances. Desire and aversion are the carrot and stick of motivation. We are constantly trying to change our environment in order to create stability, but that stability is ever changing by nature. Hence, we rarely pause our efforts to control, even when things seem stable in our lives. We put more clothes on to get warm when we are cold, but then conditions change, and we take off clothes and turn on a fan to get cool.

Alcoholics Anonymous took the following lines from a prayer by Reinhold Niebuhr: "Grant me the serenity to accept the things I cannot change, the courage to change the things I can, and the wisdom to know the difference." Commonly referred to as the "Serenity Prayer," these words both inspire and calm me. They weave together three important tasks in regard to change: acceptance, discernment, and action. When we *accept* the larger circumstances of life and our human limitations, we then may *discern* or decide what to do in strategic ways, and then engage in powerful *actions* that influence our lives. Ultimately, we *can* create positive changes in our lives.

THE COURAGE TO CHANGE

From the very simplest behavioral habit to the largest life transition, the process by which we influence change is complex, and it is easier said than done. A client of mine, Harry, told me about two small changes he made recently. Seven months ago he moved into a new house with a much smaller bath and shower stall. He did not have enough space in it to use his scrub brush when he faced the shower nozzle. For months he struggled. Then one day he turned his body 90 degrees so that he was sideways in the bathtub and lo and behold, he had arm space to scrub his back. In this same time frame, he had knee surgery. Every time he got in his car, his knee would hurt. This went on for months. As he was helping his elderly mother get into her car, he noticed how she led herself in butt first, sitting down and then scooping her legs around. He tried it, and now his knee never hurts when he gets into his car. Harry asked me, "Why did it take me so long to make those simple changes?"

It's hard to even see our habitual patterns. A new way doesn't occur to us until our awareness of the problem builds enough to feel the motivation to solve the problem! In the shower stall, Harry discovered a solution when his frustration pushed him to try something different. Harry used pain as motivation to try new ways to get into his car, but he also needed to see someone model a new move before he found a way that worked.

Harry's stories made me think of my own journey with seemingly small individual changes. I live in a house that, as the owner/builder, I worked with subcontractors to construct, bit by bit, over the course of about ten years. It has large windows, with no curtains, and an eastern view. The sunrise through my bedroom window in the morning is gorgeous. But that lovely aspect of my house has become very challenging recently. I'm in menopause now, and I have problems with disrupted sleep. In the summer, the sun shines in my eyes and wakes me up around six in the morning. I get overheated, which triggers hot flashes, and the heat and fatigue makes my life harder. For many years, I have thought about putting up curtains, and it's the obvious solution to my current problem. I could report all the reasons I haven't done it: limited time and money, not a priority, I like the light, I just never think of it at the right times, it's only a problem five months out of the year, no one ever taught me how to put up curtains. But why is it that my daughter as a teenager asked for curtains in her room, and we managed to get them up for her within a few months? That was fifteen years ago now! And I, instead, struggle most mornings in the summer. I still haven't even put the project on my list of things to do.

So, the real story behind me putting up with the distress of curtainless windows all goes back to the habits I developed to cope with fear and scarcity throughout my life. As a child I didn't have enough blankets in the winter to be warm or enough food to feel satisfied. My mom was reluctant to get medical care when I broke my arm because the expense wasn't included in her tight budget. It was nearly two full days before she took me to the hospital. I was sad and scared a lot of the time. As I grew up in a family with a real lack of resources, my coping strategies were reinforced by cultural pig messages. I was told over and over again, by the Catholic Church, teachers, parents, extended family members, and siblings that it was good to be able to tough things out, and that the tougher we were, the better our chances of success and survival. Other messages included these: "You should get used to not getting what you want." "You're such a wimp." "Don't be a drama queen." "No one likes a whiner." I developed a high pain tolerance and an ability to do without conveniences that other people thought essential, like dental appointments, salad spinners, hot showers, air-conditioning, new socks and underwear, and certainly curtains. Not bad habits, really. Frugality, endurance, and a high pain tolerance are definitely good qualities by evolutionary standards.

I still live fairly frugally now, but I have more resources, and I have updated my beliefs and values. It's no longer necessary to "tough things out" for the sake of my or my kids' survival. I *have* learned to schedule dental appointments, especially when I have a toothache. I finally put a salad spinner on my Christmas list, and I take as many hot showers or baths as I want.

After this writing, I finally put up the curtains. Success! This experience reminded me how hard it is to make a change, even one as seemingly small as curtains. My pain and fatigue level had not reached the threshold point where it outweighed the great survival values and strategies of "putting up with things." Prior to writing this section, the effort to make a change seemed far more daunting than remaining stuck.

Personal change is only possible when we become aware of our beliefs and actions, choose to believe something new, and then do something differently. And the something we might change is most often connected to an action that takes place in the context of a social setting: how we speak or act, when we speak or act, with whom we speak or act.

In the following sections, I will outline a theoretical approach for change as individuals that includes ways to observe our behavior in the context of culture, steps to see more clearly our present cultural conditions, and practices to change our lives and habitual patterns of behavior. I will also give examples of the kinds of changes we might want to make in our lives: a basic behavioral change and a change of life circumstances.

Keep in mind that this approach borrows from many theoretical perspectives and in no way is definitive or the final word on the subject. Theories are extractions from experience, not meant to supplant what we learn from experience itself. The map is not the terrain, but rather guidance to head us in a new direction and to invite us to explore change in our lives creatively and compassionately.

BASIC BEHAVIORAL CHANGE

One of my most vivid memories occurred when I was about twenty-five years old and well into my second pregnancy. I stood washing dishes, alone with my two-year-old daughter, while she played somewhere in the house behind me. Suddenly I heard a crash. Startled and scared, I turned around and saw a favorite bowl smashed on the floor in shards. Then I saw the look on my child's tiny, sweet face. She was terrified and beginning to cry. My automatic reaction of angry blame was bubbling up inside, despite the fact that I was clamping my mouth shut and refraining from yelling in anger, "Why did you do that? I told you not to touch that!" The intensity of my anger was being transmitted to her open, vulnerable body.

In the past, I had understood that my family and friends did not appreciate being snapped at or talked to in the blaming tones I would use. But I had also absorbed the message that having a temper and irritability were just aspects of my "difficult" personality. Any previous attempts I had made to contain or moderate my automatic behavior had been laced with futility. But seeing my two-year-old child's emotional reaction to her mamma's anger changed me. I knew that I did not want to cause my child to be afraid of me. That certainty catalyzed a strong commitment to changing a disturbing automatic reaction.[1] Never before had the awareness, the will, and the motivation all come together so clearly. My commitment to respond without anger is an ongoing practice, replacing old behavior with new behavior, that continues to this day, with my children, my lover, and my community at large.

We learn how to behave in our lives based on how the culture's written and unwritten rules combine with our innate personality and instinctual traits. Sometimes the habitual and automatic behavioral patterns serve us well all our lives. But sometimes our conditioned habits get in the way of making some important next step. While it can seem extraordinarily important to change, actually making the change in a pattern can seem nearly impossible. So then we need both an unlearning process as well as a new learning process, and to practice them simultaneously.

CULTIVATING AWARENESS

The first step to changing behavior and ultimately our circumstances is to learn how to accurately observe ourselves and our social context. As pointed out elsewhere in this book, our rational, nondualistic adult consciousness witnesses our inner and outer landscape. That same fair witness can see the child ego state's needs and emotions and guide our lives toward serving those needs rather than reacting from the cultural judgments of our parent ego state. When we enter the observer part of our mind, it's as if time slows down, and we can see what is happening.

When we are cultivating our internal observational skills, it is helpful to develop what is sometimes called a centering practice. We center ourselves in our bodies when we pay attention to our breath and sensations; we are thus present to our experiences in the moment. There are many ways to practice this kind of quiet, nonreactive witnessing, whether it is prayer, meditation, martial arts, yoga, writing, solitude, or simply walking.

Paulo Freire writes in his book *Pedagogy of the Oppressed* that the cultivation of "critical consciousness" is essential to uncovering the anatomy of our personal suffering. He encourages the kind of learning he calls "praxis": a practice of observation and reflection that uncovers the aspect of our own experience that is submerged in the hegemony of our cultural systems and otherwise invisible to us. Here are some steps to cultivate awareness and reflection:

- **Observe ourselves:** We start our observational practice by taking time to build our awareness of what is happening to and around us. We detach from our emotions and beliefs and try to witness ourselves and our environment without reacting. We reflect pragmatically on how our behavior is affected by the environment and how we affect others. We become the fair witness to our sensations, emotions, thoughts, and behavior.

- **Recognize our behavior:** We first learn to see a problem with our behavior by receiving feedback from the environment, our bodies, or important people in our lives. We try to face the feedback head-on without defensiveness or self-recrimination, using the nonreactive observational skills we have been learning.

- **Find motivation:** We need to have a strong motivation to change. In other words, "for the sake of what" would we try to change? We cannot change our way of being or our practices until we have the will to change.

- **Think contextually:** We look carefully at the limited cultural conditions within which we originally applied our innate talents. In what historic context did our behavior arise? We investigate how we learned the social rules and pig messages of our culture, how those rules were modeled and taught in repetitious ways by those around us, and maybe how the rules and pig messages still surround us now.

- **Normalize with self-compassion:** Our automatic habits make sense when we examine them with an eye to seeing how they reflect our innate traits and how they were reinforced or promoted by our environment. While we are powerful now, consider how helpless we were against the beliefs we internalized at the time. We bring compassion for the way we are hardwired to survive the best we can. Though our behavior may serve our survival, we understand that many of our automatic survival patterns make us stuck and cause us suffering.

- **See the difference:** We look carefully at the current conditions in our lives and see the difference between what was once useful and what is no longer useful in the present context. We see how our habitual patterns served us in the past and may again in the future.

- **Look for more feedback:** Once we have identified the central contradiction between what we want versus what we are presently doing, we seek more clarification. We might ask others around us for feedback or ideas or watch others who model behavior that is desirable to us.

Let's see how this kind of observation and reflection worked to send me on a path to change when my child broke that bowl. I saw my angry reaction to the bowl crashing as it happened. I was not blinded by rage. I could *observe* myself through my child's eyes. I saw the impact my angry reaction was having on her. I *recognized* in that moment that I was causing her to be afraid and that she was shrinking away from me. I didn't want my child to grow up in fear of my anger. I wanted her to trust me and feel safe with me so that I could

Getting the Pig Out of Feedback

Julia Kelliher

It is helpful to get feedback from those who know us. It can be hard to see ourselves clearly, and the addition of more eyes on our situation and behavior helps us see our blind spots—unless, of course, the feedback we receive is full of another person's internalized pig messages or their misunderstandings about us! In any case, if we remind ourselves that assessments are only stories, other people's theories about us that may have some truth but are not altogether true, it is easier to take them and use them well. When we hear an assessment of our behavior, we remember to treat it like a story. We remind ourselves that the story may not be wholly true, and then we analyze what's true, what's not true, and what's also true. We may find a kernel of truth in the story that, now pig-free, helps us in our journey toward self-discovery and change.

benefit from the sweet intimacy between us when she wasn't afraid. I was extremely *motivated* to care for my relationship with my child. Venting my righteous anger, or even protecting a favorite bowl, were not nearly as important to me.

I knew the historical *context*, 1958–1974, in which I had learned and perfected a habitual, fear-based pattern full of angry, judgment-ridden, find-the-blame reactions to the loss of a possession. My parents had gone through the Great Depression and World War II where food was rationed and their few material possessions were cherished. I was surrounded by the emotional repression of the '50s family culture in America. We had very limited income in my large family of origin, and all of us were forced to compete for scarce resources. I witnessed my parents and siblings model the repression of their emotions and needs, followed by big, emotional blowups. I also noticed how important it was to assign blame during those blowups to avoid punishment—those who were unsuccessful blaming others were punished, while those who were successful, redirected the punishment to others. Such blaming resulted in my internalization of the pig message that anyone who ruined or lost a material possession was lazy, stupid, bad, or crazy.

In my childhood, I had been discouraged from asking or negotiating for any changes in my circumstances. I was encouraged to stifle complaints. It made sense then and *normalized* my internal pressure cooker of unmet needs. And when a bowl broke or someone spilled a glass of milk on me, my historic context permitted me to yell. Suddenly, I felt entitled to voice my unhappiness, and all my pent-up frustration would come out in an irritable or blaming tone. My parents and siblings behaved similarly. I also think my temperament led me to be quicker to anger than some members of my family. Seeing the sense of my behavior opened the way for more *compassion* toward myself.

I saw that the historical circumstances of my growing-up years were no longer relevant to the moment in which my two-year-old daughter broke my bowl. It was 1984. Times were *different*. Bowls in America were abundant and cheap. In the past, adults were trained to repress feelings and needs. Now I had friends and a husband who wanted me to express my needs, rather than blow up when something went wrong. One friend of mine said that I seemed to have already lost the battle when I acted angry. He thought that I gave up on myself before I even considered asking for something and that my anger seemed to be coming from defeat. His *feedback* felt true, and I started to practice seeing my anger or irritation as an indicator of an unmet need. Now when I feel the signs of anger coming on, I try to ask myself, "What is wrong?" and "What can I ask for?"

Investigating, reflecting, and getting feedback from my children and friends in our current context allowed me to consider new behavior better suited to building a happier and more empowered life. Fortunately for me, at the age of twenty-six, I had all the necessary ingredients to begin a sustainable long-term practice of change that continues to this day. At the age of fifty-five, I rarely act in anger or snap at anyone, but the habitual tendencies are still there. If I need to express anger to get a point across or to fight against an attacker, I know I can. The difference now is, most of the time, I have a choice.

CHANGING OUR LIFE CIRCUMSTANCES

Changing our life circumstances for the better is an extremely long and intense process, requiring much investigation, reflection, awareness, and courage to act on our own behalf with new insights and practices. I met one of my clients, Annie, when she was twenty-eight years old. She was married and had one child who was about five. She and her husband came to my office to learn conflict-resolution skills to help their troubled marriage. I met with both of them and discovered that although both of them felt trapped and unhappy, she alone had been motivated over the last few years to try to make some changes. Annie and her husband were at a standoff, and neither would give up their position.

Annie had already identified some changes she needed and wanted to make. She wanted to find well-paid work, so she could support herself. She was motivated to exercise more, get healthier, make more friends, and have more fun. But she had to find a way to make these changes without her husband's support. He had set himself up as her opponent. When she began to eat better and work out at the gym, he made sarcastic and minimizing comments. When she developed new friendships, he acted extremely possessive and unpleasant when her friends were around. Annie discovered she couldn't make the changes she wanted while living with him. He was increasingly cruel to her and wanted her to continue giving up things for him. As she rebelled against her caretaking pattern, he became angrier and angrier, called her mean names, threatened her, and undermined her confidence in herself.

The whole conflict cycle drained her of the energy she needed to move forward in her life. In a private and very potent moment with her husband, he tearfully admitted to me, "I don't think I can support Annie in becoming more independent of me. I liked it when she was my 'fat girl' with few life options and low self-esteem. She needed me, and she took care of me. I know she deserves better, but I don't want her to change." He was not a "bad" man, but he didn't have the optimism or motivation to engage in the changes his wife had initiated. His desire to keep things the same and his fear of losing her drove him toward very "bad" behavior.

Annie relied on her adult observer to courageously face the central contradiction in her life of the moment: she loved her husband, but he was not willing or capable to change with her. Annie needed to practice lots of awareness, compassion, and discernment before she ever came to my office to get help. Once she knew that her husband wasn't able to participate in the process of change with her, she engaged in it independently of him. She was ready to move forward in the hard process of making changes in her life. Following are the eight steps in the process of change we use in Skills for Change coaching:

Dropping Out of Change

Nancy Shanteau

I've witnessed many smart, capable people who seem heartbroken around the change process. What I've learned is that we tend to be enthusiastic when we begin a new practice or try to change something. Our enthusiasm grows when we have an epiphany about why we did what we did or discover a new way of doing something, and we get excited about making a change in our lives. However, at some point in the process, our enthusiasm dims or even disappears entirely. It seems like we'll never succeed, that change is out of reach, and there is some sort of personal failure that keeps us from changing. This type of resignation around the change process is normal. Fortunately, there's a good reason we lose heart and a way to make it through the process and complete the change we seek to make.

Think of change as a range between 0% and 100%. When we are at 0%, we can only do the old behavior and are unable to do the new behavior at all. At 100%, we can do the new behavior 100% of the time, and we rarely or never do the old behavior anymore. When we begin a new practice or learn a new skill, we start doing the change a greater percentage of the time, from 0% to 10%, from 10% to 25%, and so forth, gaining in frequency of success as we continue to practice the new skill.

Up until we reach about 35% success at the new practice, we're usually pretty enthusiastic. After all, previously we couldn't do the new skill at all. But here's what happens—suddenly, as we near the 50% mark, our satisfaction often actually goes down. "Why can't I get this?" Perhaps we assume we should have been able to accomplish our goal by this point. Not too long ago, we were totally thrilled to do our new practice a third of the time. But somehow, a 50/50 success rate seems disappointing. "I shouldn't still be doing that old practice anymore. There must be something wrong." We rejigger our design, recommit to our practice, but our heart isn't in it. Soon we find we aren't practicing at all, and we've lost ground, perhaps altogether. We look for a reason we failed, and either pig ourselves for being too stupid to figure out a good plan, not good enough to make it happen, or too lazy to implement it or we blame the practice we chose. "Maybe that gym class just wasn't right for me."

Different people have different responses to this stage of the change process, and their reasons for giving up on change can be very personal. Perhaps we are the type of people who get so enthusiastic that we get overstimulated, anxious, and hyperengaged. Giving up on a change might be almost a relief because we can settle down, recover our strength, and return to a more normal pattern of energy. Or we might tend to forget we are in the middle of a change and find ourselves numb, distracted, or dissociated and then hard on ourselves for not keeping track of our new practice. "I must not really want this," we might say to ourselves.

I'm in the group that tends to feel disappointed and gives up on change because it doesn't seem to be working. If we experience this type of hopelessness and collapse around the uselessness of our efforts and the resigned feeling that change will never take hold, we might feel relief at not having to face the possibility of failure and the emotions that come with such a prospect. These types of emotional experiences might look a lot like our conditioned response to stress—we might fight, freeze, flee, move toward, or dissociate. Remember, change is a major stimulus, involves an increase in our respective power, and may trigger all kinds of responses in our nervous system, from fear to excitement, terror to numbness.

Whatever our reasons, we go on this way, picking up a new practice and then dropping out when we don't learn it fast enough, over and over again. Richard Strozzi-Heckler says of this starting-over process, "It's like putting a well on your property, and you dig a

- **Explore options:** We see how we are stuck, what behaviors and beliefs are keeping us stuck, and then we explore new possibilities. We ask friends and teachers what we might do differently. We consider and plan some changes that seem doable. We try something and compassionately assess what works and what doesn't.

- **Commit to practice:** We practice refraining from the old behaviors and beliefs. We practice something new. We'll have good days and bad days, two steps forward, three steps back, five steps forward. Learning is not a quick or linear process, so we need to cultivate endurance for the long haul. We strengthen our compassion and

bunch of three-foot holes when you only need one five-foot hole."[2] Just think—by the time we've finished digging the second three-foot hole, we've put in more effort than if we had just dug one hole to five feet. It's exhausting and disheartening when our practices don't give us what we want.

It's important at this stage to figure out what helps us stay committed. Sometimes we fall so in love with a practice that we make it through the difficult 50/50 stage. Sometimes we find a great teacher or a fantastic helper who knows that we need lots of extra support and encouragement around the 50% mark, and they help us reengage until we get to 65% success or more. Perhaps we can do an analysis to see what little changes we can make to increase our success rate.

Once we arrive at 65% rate of success, it's much easier to stay on track. We're only doing that old practice a third of the time. And 65% is pretty satisfying. Before long, we embody the skill and can do it most of the time. When we're making a change, it's extremely important to stay the course, keep doing the practice, and gain confidence in our ability to change.[3] We are much more likely to succeed if we are kind to ourselves, surround ourselves with helpful community, and give ourselves the time we need to achieve the change we seek.

awareness and take on practices that support the change we seek, such as walking, getting a massage, or writing in a journal.

- **Make mistakes:** We see ourselves do the same old thing. We congratulate ourselves for our awareness, and we try again.

- **Invite community support:** We include other people around us who support the importance and understand the difficulty of the change we are trying to make. We need to keep taking in loving feedback and encouragement, so we don't go back to the shroud of unawareness that nurtures the old, more familiar, and therefore "comfortable" pattern.

- **Fight the pig:** Our internalized "cop in the head" beliefs will come up in the midst of our progress, and especially when we have setbacks. It helps to remember we learned the right/wrong beliefs from our culture and we can unlearn them. A successful pig fight takes repetition and community support.

- **Take breaks and replenish:** When we are depleted and tired, we take a rest-and-replenish break from the effort to change. When we are in a state of depletion, it helps us to notice what pig comes up to reinforce hopelessness and cause us to want to give up. When we are more rested and have fought the pig, we will likely feel reinspired to start again.

- **Track our progress:** We create some kind of tracking system so that we can *see* when change has been made and reinforce our ability to know *how* we succeeded in behaving in a new way. Otherwise, our internalized pig messages may tell us we are not making progress and to give up.

- **Accept and appreciate ourselves:** We appreciate our efforts and accept the way we are struggling. We practice loving ourselves and the rest of this beautiful, mysterious world just the way it is. We compassionately hold the contradictions implicit in our human lives. We want to change; in fact, we strive to change. But even if we don't change, we're still okay. We find choice, safety, and love wherever it is in the present moment. Then we begin our effort to change again.

Annie applied these steps in the process of changing her life. *Exploring options:* Annie had already hit a threshold point. She was ready to find some solutions to what had become an untenable situation. She started to see me once a week to help her plan what to do. The first step we identified, once we understood the situation, was for Annie to live separately from her husband. She knew it would be difficult to ask him to leave their home since he didn't want the change. She knew she couldn't afford their large mortgage without her husband's income, and that knowledge made it easier to for her to leave her beloved home and rent a house on her own. Her mother, who was living with them at the time, moved with her so that Annie would have help caring for her daughter and paying the rent. Annie's mom had left her own husband about five years before and was still sorting out her own way in the world. It was a mutually beneficial arrangement for both of them.

Committing to practice: It was hard for Annie to leave her husband. She had loved him, felt grateful to him, and had tried to help him with his alcohol and drug addictions and erratic work tendencies. She felt sorry for him. She had rescued him and put his needs ahead of her own for so long that it was very hard to put her own needs first. Her reactive pattern had been to verbally attack and persecute her husband when he would goad her with cruel comments. Annie is very smart and would outdo his verbal abuse. Then he would be able to tell others how verbally abusive she was to him. She put her commitment and practice toward refraining from rescuing and caretaking her husband. She stopped herself from persecuting and verbally engaging in their fighting, and she examined over and over again the pig messages that told her to give up on herself.

Making mistakes: Of course, Annie made lots of mistakes. She would feel sorry for her husband and cave in to his demands, or rage at him, and conflict would escalate. Sometimes she would collapse and blame herself for everything. But she saw the negative effects of these setbacks and would reaffirm her commitment to doing conflict differently each time.

Community support: Annie needed lots of support from her community to make her way through this difficult experience. She sought out reality checks, perspective, and new ideas to stay the course. Her actions built stronger connections and friendships. She found a house for herself and her mother and found a job working for a contractor. Her love of exercise helped her to connect more with a female friend who went to the same gym. Annie discovered that many people cared for her, enjoyed her company, and understood the difficulties she was having.

Fighting the pig: If she hadn't gone up against all her internalized oppressive messages, Annie could never have stayed the course. Just when she was feeling stronger and healthier in her body, her pig would sneer, "You're fat. You'll never find another lover." Every time Annie made progress, the pig messages, especially internalized sexist messages, would intensify and tell her she wasn't worth the effort and that she didn't have what it took to build a happy, satisfying life. She needed much courage and help to sniff out the lies and fight the pig.

Resting and replenishing: The intense effort Annie made left her exhausted and depleted on many occasions. She would ask herself at those times, "Why did I ever go down this path?" I would remind her of the benefits she had already gained and encourage her to rest for a while. After making the emotionally and physically exhausting move to her new home, Annie spent time just sitting on the floor with her daughter, coloring with crayons, to replenish her energy before getting ready for the next step.

Tracking progress: Annie needed outside observers to help her track her progress. I was her primary outside helper, along with her mother and best friend. We were able to see what she had done, how it had changed things for the better, and to keep encouraging her as she took the next step. Otherwise, the pig voice in her head would tell her the patently false message that nothing was getting any better, just harder, and that she was simply "going from the frying pan to the fire."

Accepting and appreciating herself: Annie sometimes needed to stop putting her attention on the future and come back to the present moment and appreciate her relative safety and power. She and I developed a mantra to help her accept herself and calm down in those moments. She would say silently to herself, "I am loved, I am safe, and I have options," which was true most of the time.

Annie's story continues to this day. She is not living "happily ever after," but she does have a job she loves, many good friends, and a new relationship with a man who supports her in making progress in her life and is her partner in that process. She feels good about her body much of the time and enjoys its strength and health. She empowers her daughter and stepdaughter by modeling what it is to be a strong and satisfied woman. And she's acting more and more from a place of authentic desire rather than from indoctrinated beliefs and low self-esteem. Annie, alive and curious, is both student and teacher of those around her, and she mostly feels optimistic about the possibility of positive change in her future.

THE POWER TO CHANGE

The steps toward change outlined in this chapter are, regretfully, mostly useful to those with power, privilege, and many options. I, and my colleagues, truly wish we could change the larger systems of oppression in the world and create a more just society. We do as much as we can to promote a larger awareness of social concerns, and we teach some ways to work toward collective change. We also recognize that many people are so submerged in external forces of oppression that their only hope for more satisfaction and power in their lives is to organize as communities to fight the external forces and to gain the support of those who are holding more power in the fight. We envision a world where we who have more privilege become more empowered, and we use our power to learn from and ally with those who are more oppressed.

Internalized prejudices and cultural pig messages are inner impediments that are always worth addressing in both our personal lives as well as through social activism. When we fight against internalized oppression in our personal lives, we witness firsthand how the political is personal. Collective change is only possible when we become aware of our part in a larger system and then do something different collectively. From a place of more personal power and transactional power, we can organize more easily and accomplish more collective systemic change, which in turn creates fewer oppressive contexts and increases our choices even more. The spiral of empowerment feeds on itself and grows with time.

It takes quite a bit of work to see how our patterns of interaction are based on survival and to change the way we behave with others in order to get more of what we want and need. The work we must do to change includes the development of discerning self-awareness; confronting our personal, possibly conflicting needs; fighting the good fight when pig comes up; facing fears and long-term patterns; getting support; and practicing new kinds of interactions. Guided by clear observation, we rely on our ability to sort through beliefs and choose the ones we want. As we open to the support of our peers, we can increase our individual choices and empower our loved ones to do the same.

In a revised version of the serenity prayer I wish us all well:

May we all have the good fortune to have loving community around us who support our awareness of what we can change and what we can't. May we access powerful support, both inner and outer, to create positive change, incrementally and over time, those things that are worth changing. And may we come to peace and acceptance over the larger forces of life, human limitations, and the things over which we truly have no control.

Ten • Embodied Change: Body over Matter

Nancy Shanteau

I watched my hand reach for the phone, saying to myself, "Don't do it. Don't pick it up." Then the phone was in my hand, and I was dialing. It was the last time I would pick up the phone and harangue a coworker about a late project, and it was painful to watch myself. I'd been working on reducing my anger and hostility in the workplace for what seemed like a lifetime but was probably about six months. Through a coaching process, I'd identified how I wanted to act and what conditions at work encouraged me to lose my temper. I'd reduced my overtime, increased my frequency of communication around project timelines and status updates, and made sure I walked into people's workspaces and had regular conversations instead of doing things entirely by email. I regularly centered myself by balancing myself head to toe, side to side, and front to back, paid attention to my breathing, and brought my energy back and down. Still, there I was, with my hand reaching for the phone and words on my lips that I would almost immediately want to take back.

We want the changes that we are making to happen with the snap of our fingers, and sometimes it's that easy. But the rest of the time, when the process of change is slow and agonizing, we often give up, considering ourselves failures before the change becomes a choice. When I watched my hand move toward the phone, I was excruciatingly close to the moment of choice, but I wasn't quite there. The next time I thought of calling a coworker to yell about some missed deadline or mistake, I shrugged my shoulders and went on to do something else. It might seem like magic, but I had put many repetitions of intention and practice into creating that moment of opportunity, and I finally embodied the change I had been practicing. The moment of coinciding intention, awareness, choice, and action arrived, and I changed.

Many of my clients come to my practice for just such an objective—they want to stop smoking, eat healthy, lose weight, be kind to themselves, accomplish a goal, write a book. And they watch themselves doing things that not only don't get them what they want, but their actions take them in the opposite direction, and they lose hope. People's loss of hope in themselves very quickly turns to self-judgment, pig, and shame. Once pig and shame have arrived, the whole process of change becomes mired in self-doubt, self-loathing, self-disgust, and lots of other horrible feelings.

In this chapter, we'll consider how the body enters the change process, how we become efficient, successful change makers, what obstacles we encounter as we move toward change, and how the mysterious, sometimes magical process of releasing and unpacking our heavy load of history can open new pathways with ease and grace. We'll examine the impact of power and trauma on the body, consider our instinctual, animal nature, and look at how complicated change has become in our current cultural environment. We'll rediscover hope, and perhaps in the process, we'll make a plan to change something in our lives, with skill, patience, compassion, and self-love on our side.

LOSING OUR ADULT

When our safety reflexes are stronger than our wise adult inner voice, we often give way to habitual responses. Take Mike and Sally as an example: They are a middle-class couple, both with good jobs and children from different relationships. They have their children one week on, one week off and align their parenting schedules so that they have a week alone together and a family week with all the kids in the house at the same time. When Mike and Sally scheduled a Skills for Change mediation, they initially reported that Mike seemed to get very angry with Sally for seemingly unimportant reasons. Something about their conversational style was setting off an extreme reaction in Mike, and we set about mapping it out, to help both of them understand what was happening.

Mike noticed that Sally tended to react strongly when he reported having a conversation with his ex-wife, Natalie. According to Mike, Sally would get upset and exhort him to fight back, defend himself, or otherwise oppose Natalie's "unjust and irresponsible" requests. Sally's tone of voice would rise, and her speech would become staccato and clipped. As she spoke, Mike reported feeling like he was beginning to boil. Perhaps Sally noticed Mike's rising irritation, and her speech would speed up, increasing Mike's agitation. Finally, Mike would boil over and start yelling. Sally would instantly freeze, terrified at his anger. He would "shout himself out," finally noticing that Sally was shaking. Or Sally would unfreeze herself enough to fight back, engaging in a "who can yell loudest" match.

Mike would then clam up, distance himself, and take a time out, trying to calm down. Sally would interpret his withdrawal as abandonment and withdraw herself, icing over in a cold freeze. When Mike would come back to repair with Sally, he would find her in a sulk, uncommunicative and unwilling to talk to him.

Pretty frustrating, eh? How were Sally and Mike ever going to get to a point where they could listen to each other's needs and negotiate new agreements? Their responses to each other were hard-to-change legacies of historic safety reflexes and deep habit patterns.

When clients come in asking about this type of pattern and how to shift, I encourage them to look at the beginning of their response, before they've gotten too deep into the tit-for-tat fight sequence. What bodily options are available when Mike is sharing information with Sally and when Sally's voice is rising? What can Mike do instead of boiling over? Can Sally slow down instead of speeding up when she's talking?

Most of the time, when clients engage in this type of cycle, they have lost their fair adult witness and are responding solely from child and parent ego state strategies. It can be helpful to write out a map of the various strategies, plan new responses, and then practice the strategies to see if they work. Very often, I find that our plans

Skills for Change and the Embodied Enneagram

NANCY SHANTEAU

Like any personality-typing system, the Enneagram can at first seem like a secret code for judging other people.[1] "That's so Three of her!" "Don't take it personally; he's an Eight." "Sigh ... I just don't understand Fives." How many numbers are there, anyway, and what does it mean to know my number or anyone else's? In Skills for Change coaching, we use the Enneagram to help us understand ourselves and others, our strong drives and impulses, and how to coordinate with the tendencies and preferences of other people. We bring self-love and self-compassion to this exploration of our identity and use the understanding to increase our sense of choice and possibility.

The Enneagram is an ancient Sufi personality-typing system first brought to Western European awareness by G. I. Gurdjieff.[2] It offers immediately useful categories that help us recognize patterns of self-organization: patterns in our actions, reactions, stories, and the way we shape our bodies in response to the world. The Enneagram helps are too ambitious and that we have to find micro-movements that begin to meet the child ego state's needs. Perhaps Mike could choose to give Sally news about Natalie's latest request when she's relaxed after dinner, inviting her to listen calmly and offer advice only when asked? Perhaps Sally could notice when she is panicking and ask Mike to pause, soothe herself a little by putting her hand on her heart or thigh, and then resume the conversation when she's calm again? When an intervention meets the child ego state's needs, it achieves the greatest effect.

What I've observed in my work is that clients who experienced great danger in their precognitive years have the most work to replace their embodied child safety reflexes with adult ego state responses. Bodywork, EMDR, biofeedback, and other physical,

us see our default style, the styles of others, and to recognize the strengths inherent in each style. We can identify our reflex strategies for securing safety and notice what capabilities and tendencies emerge when we achieve abundance in our repletion and energy levels.

Ultimately, studying the Enneagram allows us to create options for change. Because there are nine types, a deeper knowledge of the Enneagram reveals many different ways people view and take action in the world. Our understanding of these differences not only helps us be more compassionate, the Enneagram also provides a fantastic list of possibilities if we want to choose a new way to be or act. Such a wide range of options dispels the notion of a right way or a wrong way—there are many right ways for many situations. Doesn't that sound liberating?

The Enneagram can be easily misused as a way to pigeonhole or typecast others, excuse our own behavior, or exploit others' fears and insecurities. If we resist the impulse to tell negative stories about ourselves and others, however, the Enneagram can become a tool for increasing compassion, understanding, acceptance, and options.

direct interventions seem to best assist the change process in these cases, often because the safety reflex was preverbal in the first place. If we learned something under intense circumstances, such as cowering in a corner while an adult was yelling at us to clean our room, we will likely need greater bodily intensity to unwind this fear—thinking our way through the problem simply isn't intense enough. If we practice a bodily shift—wrapping ourselves in a blanket, stroking our arms, brushing our hair—anything that increases the physical intensity of our experience—we are more likely to shift the patterned response.[3]

MAKING A CHANGE

Physical posture, stories in the body, trauma memory—these habitual patterns are not things we can change through epiphany, insight, or other mental processes. The thinking process of understanding, creating a cognitive framework for change, and making plans for a different future are all necessary aspects of the change process. However, if we don't then shift our historic bodily reflexes, change is less likely to happen. We must let the body catch up with the mind, and the body is a slower learner. It takes three hundred repetitions of a behavior to move a change into muscle memory, and three thousand repetitions to unlearn one behavior and learn another.[4] As Richard Strozzi-Heckler says, "We are always practicing something."[5] It makes sense that we want to choose what we are practicing, and when habit patterns and armoring are at play, we actually experience fewer moments when we are aware enough to make a choice. Too often we default to accustomed behavior. We can, however, choose new practices and infuse them with intention, invoke a supportive quality of being in ourselves, and allow ourselves to move toward a new shape and a new choice, again and again, until we take our unfamiliar practice from muscle memory to embodiment.

SKILLS FOR CHANGE BODYWORK

Wilhelm Reich, a contemporary of Sigmund Freud's, noticed when the talking cure didn't work for someone that a bodily intervention often did work.[6] Reich observed that "armoring," a band or pattern of horizontal tension, was no longer under the conscious control of his subjects. The subjects were not aware that their muscles were tightly held, and they couldn't relax the contracted muscles through effort or attention. They needed help to get their armoring to release. Skills for Change practitioners touch pressure points in the muscular structure to help the body release tension. Through conversation, we evoke the story, unwind the pattern, and allow the body to relax into a new shape. Bodywork speeds the process of change by unwinding the old behaviors and patterns and greatly supports the acquisition of new learning, behaviors, and patterns to support a client's desired future. It creates greater bodily spaciousness and by relaxing historic patterns of tension and overwhelm, ultimately offers clients greater choice in their daily lives.

Gina came to my office complaining of fibromyalgia, a pattern of generalized pain that affected her entire body, restricted her ability to work at a desk with a computer, and on some days left her paralyzed in bed, unable to get up. She was on an array of pharmaceutical medications that helped her return to everyday life, but some of the medications were very expensive. She was hoping to reduce her medication, increase her ability to work effectively, and change her life so that she was happier and more at ease in her body. As with all such coaching contracts, I did not make any promises to affect the disease itself. What we can promise to accomplish in coaching is a shift in our *response* to illness—clients experience reduced stress, increased relaxation, and bodily awareness. To accomplish this, clients track their symptoms, identify potential causes, and connect with a sense of purpose that generates greater satisfaction. We may hope for greater results, but certainly when the pain strikes, we *can* stop constricting our bodies or thinking anxious thoughts.

We began a two-pronged coaching approach to Gina's situation. We would talk about her life, sources of stress, how she worked, and how she might replenish herself to create more ease around her work. We tried a new schedule where she worked for no more than forty-five minutes at a time and took fifteen-minute breaks to walk and stretch, preferably outside whenever possible. After three hours, she would take an hour break. This meant she worked a longer day overall, but she soon reported a vastly easier bodily experience at her desk. Her productivity went up, and she became less fearful that she would lose her job.

We also began weekly Skills for Change bodywork sessions. Gina was anxious about receiving touch—she'd had a bad experience with a pain attack after a massage. I asked her to communicate with me throughout the session to let me know if she experienced any increase in discomfort. I touched and held pressure points that relieved tension in her body, supported her joints, and encouraged relaxation. We talked about her stored emotions in areas that were particularly tight. Sometimes she would get a clear memory of a significant emotional event, sometimes an image of a solid, muddy mass clogging her throat, heart, or breathing. We talked through the emotions as they arose and made plans for how she might support herself to shift patterns. The armoring in her body gradually began to release. Occasionally, Gina would call me on a weekend or overnight while experiencing a fibromyalgia pain attack. We would make an appointment and do bodywork to help ease the pain. Each time, the pain reduced, and the attacks grew less frequent.

After about three months, Gina changed jobs so that she could spend most of her summer working outside. Her pain from the fibromyalgia had decreased by half. During her summer job, she reported hiking steep slopes while carrying heavy packs and awkward equipment. She also said she hadn't felt so good in years. After a year of coaching and bodywork, Gina saw her fibromyalgia doctor, and they started reducing her medication. She still takes a couple of prescriptions, but she is mostly pain- and symptom-free. If Gina starts spending all day at the computer, her symptoms return. The disease isn't gone, but she has created a life where fibromyalgia has a vastly reduced effect on her body and mind. She is deeply satisfied with her results and experiences her current state as a "cure," even though she still takes medications and experiences symptoms. Gina's course of recovery does not offer hope to everyone who struggles with disease—the toxins in our world and the diseases that attack our well-being are real threats. Yet we can intervene in our response to disease, shifting our bodies and our stories to be more relaxed, aware, and self-compassionate. And sometimes those shifts produce extraordinary results.

PATIENCE AND COMPASSION

If the parent ego state gets results through domination, collusion with authority, and terror, the adult ego state gets results through patience and self-compassion. These are vastly different bodily states, with different internal chemical reactions. It is our assertion that practicing patience, self-compassion, negotiation, and cooperation are more sustainable bodily states and will produce longer, healthier life spans.

Change takes time. If we have struggled to make a change, there's hope. As we are kind to ourselves, we unwind the history of negative expectations and the stories we have told ourselves about why we fail. We then choose supportive practices and communities that help us shift our daily experience. We give our bodies the time they need to catch up with our lightning-quick minds, and we find that we make changes far more effectively. We have developed the skills to make changes with internal peace, gentle encouragement, and self-kindness.

Eleven • How Skills for Change Changed My Life

Marybeth Paul

Years ago, I couldn't have imagined that I would have the skills or the confidence required to hold a position of authority and power. Yet today I have a steady stream of coaching clients and students to complement my twenty-plus years offering therapeutic massage. I also have many rich and satisfying friendships, two grown children who are making their way in the world, and a partner with whom I celebrate over fifteen very happy, loving years. I don't take these blessings for granted since my life has not always been so functional. It has taken focused attention, determination, and much support to achieve this.

In 1986, after the birth of my first child, I experienced postpartum psychosis. Over the next six years, I had three more psychotic episodes. Recovery from each of these episodes took close to a year. Skills for Change helped me find and maintain stable mental health and to access power with love and reason. I would not be who I am today without it! I've claimed ownership of and learned to fully inhabit my life.

I was raised in the Chicago suburbs in the 1950s and '60s by working-class, struggling alcoholic parents. I was the youngest of three siblings. Transparently patriarchal, the hierarchy in our household went from my dad, the dominant heavy-handed disciplinarian, to my mom, the subservient martyr, with each of my siblings and myself acting out anger and frustration on one another. In comparing notes with peers of my generation, it's unquestionable that what went on in my household was far more oppressive than the standard of the day. We were beaten, belittled, and coerced into obedience and at times were literally threatened with our lives.

Like all of us, I took in the messages given to me as a young child. "You stupid idiot!" was spoken by everyone in my house when anyone made a mistake. "Stop that crying, or I'll give you something to cry about!" was my parents' frequent response when any of us would cry, whether in response to a physical injury, hurt feelings, or being beaten. "Don't you dare look at me that way!" were my father's words when I was scared or confused by an impending punishment or for not understanding a rule. Although I lived in a great deal of fear, I was determined to appear to be normal, like any other child or teen; thus, I never shared with anyone the full story of what was going on in my house until many years later.

We did have "normal" exchanges as well. There was laughter; no one exuded more enthusiasm about the possibility of going to the fireworks on the fourth of July than my dad. We had holiday gatherings with aunts, uncles, and cousins, almost always with an excess of alcohol, first around the dinner table and then around a poker table. Often there was tremendous upheaval; arguments that didn't erupt in violence often ended with people vowing to never speak to one another again. What I saw modeled was not what I wanted for myself when I was grown.

It wasn't until I established a strong sense of belonging to a community that I was first able to question beliefs I'd held since early childhood. Much of my life I had been isolated, either by shame, fear, or simply by logistics. I first felt a sense of belonging within the school community where my kids attended grammar school. Then I joined a Skills for Change group where, under the facilitation of Julia Kelliher and Glenn Smith, people helped each other solve ordinary daily challenges. I was able to hear other people process their issues, and I learned how to distinguish between a "story" (what I impulsively *chose* to believe in a situation) and what was actually true. I learned how to reframe my internal critic saying something like, "You stupid idiot," into "Yeah, not the best choice, but considering the situation, it's understandable how anyone might have done the same." I was able to see how the culture we live in colors our perception in very subtle ways and how to expand my awareness of reacting on "autopilot." I applied what was useful in my own life based on the successes and mistakes of others in the group. This included working one-on-one with Julia twice a month, once a month, then skipping two or three months, and finally meeting on an as-needed basis. Thinking of these appointments as tune-ups or tutoring is a reminder that it's about learning new information and that repetition and support are essential in times of greater stress or around highly charged transactions and situations.

There are now many people in my life who have similar values and problem-solving skills with whom I regularly exchange ideas. It is by getting out of isolation, and working diligently, both alone and with others, to learn and implement new ways of understanding and communicating that I have been able to find a voice and the confidence to speak. I've overcome tremendous obstacles. My life today is a heartening example of the power of Skills for Change.

Part IV
Putting Skills for Change
to Work

Twelve • Empowered Transactions: Cooperative Negotiation

Julia Kelliher

Empowered change is possible when we use our awareness, community, and power to negotiate skillfully with others in the world. Whether we are looking for loving relationships, satisfying work, or a more meaningful lifestyle, we first need to discern and prioritize what is truly important. Then we can look at where, when, and with whom we need to negotiate, and finally, we can take practical and specific actions that are geared toward a desired result.

I can recall a small example of this in my practice. At the end of one of my client Laurie's sessions, she came back and told me she'd locked her keys in the car. She began to complain bitterly.

"Why do these things always happen to me? I'm such an idiot. I have no one to help. My daughter's at work, I am completely broke, and I don't have an auto club card."

Laurie had a very strong pattern of getting stuck in feelings and stories of victimization, rescuing others, and thinking she needed others to rescue her. I told her this was the perfect moment to practice a new habit in the midst of a small crisis. I asked Laurie to make a list of possible requests she could make and a list of people who would be willing to hear her requests. She is a very intelligent woman, and once she shifted into her adult and out of panic and pig-laden despair (inner voices that said, "It's not okay to ask anyone for anything because it proves how pathetic you are"), she was able to generate several viable options, the easiest being to ask me if I had an auto club card and if she could use it. I said "yes," easily.

Laurie's success gave her confidence to continue making clear requests over and over again, developing stamina to hear "no" as well as "yes" to her requests. It has taken time for Laurie to excavate and go up against the pig-filled judgmental messages that make it hard to ask for things. Slowly and consistently, she is becoming more empowered in her negotiations and building a safer and more satisfying life.

The power of the observer is essential to change. When we can see the difference between internalized indoctrination and our genuine needs and wants, we begin to determine what negotiations are really important. Eventually, we might see the natural tension intrinsic to being a complex social mammal and identify the needs of different aspects of ourselves: part of me wants this; part of me wants that. By putting out dignified requests to supportive people in our lives, we increase our options, a sense of safety, and hence power over our lives. The following are three different contexts in which to practice Skills for Change negotiation: when there are equal rights and relatively equal power, when there are equal rights yet unequal power, and when there are both unequal rights and unequal power.

EQUAL RIGHTS, (RELATIVELY) EQUAL POWER: THE COOPERATIVE CONTRACT

The cooperative contract was originally formulated by the Radical Psychiatry Collective as "No Rescues, No Lies, No Power Plays." The positive version of the contract is this: "Ask for 100% of what you want, 100% of the time, and then negotiate to mutual agreement." That one little line includes the contradictions in our human nature: our self-centered desires to have what we want, while at the same time taking care to promote goodwill, equality, and respect between people in our social group. This is an incredibly empowering model of negotiation but only works amid relative equals, with many resources of time, patience, and material options.

In a world of hierarchy and competition, social injustice and inequality, the impediments to successful negotiation and resolution are vast. Rather than negotiate openly in the face of huge obstacles, we:

- *rescue*, silence ourselves, or give in when there is scarcity and fear and we are hopeless to do anything else,

- *power play*, take power without giving in to someone else's needs, push or coerce to get our own way when we think it's the easiest or best way to get what we want, or

- *keep secrets or tell lies* because knowledge is power, and withholding or altering the facts keeps us out of trouble or gives us more power in some way.

Negotiations break down frequently, even when we bring our best skills and intentions to them and the social inequalities are minimal: among friends, lovers, coworkers. We still have to face up to differences in desires, resources, and needs. It can be difficult to know what we really want, we can feel hopeless or depleted in the midst of the negotiation, and we might get angry or frustrated. And most often, there is some urgency to solve the problem. When we reach an impasse in the negotiation, we often try to avoid conflict and solve the impasse when one person gives in, a *rescue*, and/or the other takes power unilaterally, a *power play*.

We define *power plays* as taking power without the other party's agreement. Power plays are generally seen as selfish acts. With authority figures, we tend to accept them as rightful and powerful decisions. In our society, leaders are expected to act decisively, and if they don't, they are seen as weak. We hope those with more power will be benevolent to those with less power, but we rarely trust that they will

Internal Rescue

NANCY SHANTEAU

One of the big challenges people face once they learn about the cooperative contract is understanding why they have so much trouble asking for 100% of what they want, 100% of the time. I often see people struggling to resolve internal competing needs as they ask for 100% of what they want. The culture encourages us to be clear in our requests, and there are plenty of crazy pig messages in the culture that make people wrong for not knowing or being able to articulate what they want.[1] Internally, we often end up overriding or compromising one or another part of ourselves in an attempt to generate clarity for other people. This striving for clarity is in itself a rescue—in this case, one part of us is rescuing the other part, doing more than its share of the work and sacrificing its needs in the spirit of easy resolution.

Consider Norah, a mother of two children ages six and nine. Part of Norah wants to be a fantastic mother, soaking up all the finite, precious, good, and bad parts of her children's everyday lives, knowing they will soon be teenagers and then adults and gone, moving forward into their own lives. Another part of Norah wants silence, freedom, peace and quiet, and time to stare at the wall, sleep, and recover from all the chaos. Sound familiar?

Wendy Palmer, in her book *The Intuitive Body*, calls this type of internal competing need a "split." These are irreconcilable needs, both completely valid, competing for Norah's time, energy, and attention. One part of her has probably won the battle, over and over again, while another part of her has suffered. That suffering part may continue to suffer, or it may start to rebel.

I suggest that clients come up with a compound 100% statement, where all their needs are valid. With such a compound statement, rather than producing an internal rescue to offer external clarity to someone else (a process rife with potential resentment for that other person), they create transparency about their competing needs and include the other person in their struggle. If Norah only meets one of her needs and ignores the other, she suffers, no matter which need is getting met at the time. A compound 100% statement allows her to acknowledge, and then potentially meet, her unmet needs, all of them, no matter the number and how complicated, gnarly, or embarrassing they might be.

Norah, in sharing her compound 100% statement with her partner, may find that her partner wants to spend more solo time with the kids. Suddenly, her need for silent staring-at-the-wall time and her unspoken need for her partner to get quality time with the kids may both get met in a single swoop. She'll have to sacrifice being present for the fun times her partner and kids will have together, but her quiet self-care time will likely generate greater mutual appreciation on everyone's part. Sometimes it's hard to take breaks, but they are almost always helpful and regenerative.

I encourage people to stop and reflect when they are asking for their 100%—is there an unspoken met or unmet competing need that they could include? The wonderful part of this experiment is that extraordinary results usually occur, and when new solutions do not magically appear, it's still possible to ask for empathy, understanding, and compassion from everyone involved. Sometimes irreconcilable needs are genuinely unsolvable. And if we name them as such, the energy we've been putting into solving them is released, available for alternative uses.

Sometimes the skill is to recognize when change isn't possible, to accept our powerlessness and wait for a solution that is not yet apparent, consoling ourselves with compassionate understanding along the way. Either way, we end up with vastly more cooperative, intimate, and connected relationships—not just with others, but with ourselves as well.

be. In personal relationships, power plays tend to decrease intimacy and increase anger and conflict, all in the name of getting our way.

Recently, my partner and I had a discussion in which we disagreed about how to arrange the furniture in the guest room and what things were important to keep. I was sorely tempted to take control while he was out of town and toss out everything that I saw as unnecessary clutter. But once in the past I had gone through the medicine cabinet in the bathroom that way, and the memory of his hurt and anger revisited me. He has attachments and needs about material things that I cannot possibly take into account. So the thought of his reaction and the harm it would cause to our loving connection stopped me from doing what I wanted to do.

The Power of Secrets and Lies

NANCY SHANTEAU

In many contexts, there is more support and cultural bias for us to keep our stories quiet and "just get over it" than there is for us to clear the air by sharing our version of events, emotional reactions, and personal stories. Our stories become secrets when we withhold them from someone. We don't tell our stories because of our fear that others will react in retaliation or punishment; or to protect others from hurt feelings, reduce the conflict in our relationship, avoid shame or other bad feelings in ourselves, or escape the judgments of others; or because we wish a nicer story were true. Secrets buy us time, but they also create distance and separation in our relationships, and they put off current conflict for future, possibly vastly more escalated conflict later. A secret is a power play; we are unilaterally deciding what someone knows and doesn't know.

Like a secret, a lie is also a power play, but in this case, we are not just withholding information, we are obscuring the truth with false and misleading information. People tell lies and secrets for

On the other hand, we can give in to someone else's demands or sacrifice our own needs for others. This is what we refer to as *rescue*. For example, if I give up on my desire to get rid of unneeded "stuff" in the guest room because my partner has a hard time letting go of things, I will be giving up on my needs and power to make myself happy. And most likely I will feel angry and frustrated as a result.

Sometimes rescuing and self-sacrifice are considered proper behavior, mature, loving, and kind. In the case of parents and children, it is sometimes seen as good parenting but other times seen as weak. But, ultimately, rescue creates an imbalance of power. The person making

similar reasons. The child that says, "I didn't take it," right before the stolen gum is found in his pocket, is clearly trying to protect himself from the consequences of his actions. Sometimes people believe their own stories so thoroughly that they don't know they are telling lies. In *The Moral Animal*, Robert Wright relays a story in which Charles Darwin documents with horror his own self-delusional tendencies in his journal. We often tell lies to protect our own self-image and to control the image others have of us.

The "No Secrets" and "No Lies" injunctions are critical to the cooperative contract. We exit cooperative relationship and take power over someone else when we ignore this suggestion.[2] Secrets and lies have long been tools of the oppressed and are units of power. In cases of totalitarian regimes, secret keeping and lying may be the only ways a revolutionary group can protect itself. Secrets and lies are life and death in such situations. People keep secrets and tell lies for good reasons. In everyday circumstances, however, most people would probably rather hear the truth, no matter how painful, and negotiate what happens next, rather than have someone decide for them how to handle unpleasant information. When we are deciding whether to cooperate, it can be helpful to consider whether the relationship is cooperative, and act accordingly.

a sacrifice often feels a sense of moral superiority temporarily but can also feel resentful and disdainful toward the "victim" needing "rescuing." The person being rescued usually feels one down to the rescuer, and both people tend to feel angry and blame each other.

Ironically, as much as we might try to avoid conflict through the use of power plays or rescues, neither guarantees an end to conflict. In fact, in most cases, we avoid conflict in the short term only to perpetuate conflict in the long term.

COOPERATIVE NEGOTIATION: (RELATIVELY) EQUAL POWER

Let's take an example of how the cooperative contract works in a seemingly insignificant transaction. Recently, I worked with a couple, Dennis and Karen, who had known each other for about six months and were very much in love. Dennis had first come to see me a few years previously when his wife at the time, Lara, had quite suddenly left and divorced him, all in a matter of two months. He came to my office understandably devastated, shocked, and confused. Lara, Dennis, and I met together so that Lara could explain to him what had happened. In the session, we came to understand that Lara's unhappiness had built up over power imbalances in the relationship. Lara had seen Dennis as the "boss." She did not see herself as having equal rights, and she felt very justified in keeping secrets from him. He had tried to be generous with her. She had internalized his rescues as disrespect and resented his authoritative air. He in some ways did *not* respect her. They both had built-up resentment. She had become hopeless about anything ever changing. She made a unilateral decision to end the relationship (*power play*) when he would have liked a chance to cooperatively negotiate for change.

Dennis wanted to do things differently with his new love, Karen. In this particular session, when I asked them each what they wanted to address, they answered that they wanted to learn a shared set of communication tools and to understand how to bring their spiritual practices into their day-to-day life. Then Karen tentatively started to say that there might be one other small thing, which was unimportant, and she didn't know whether to bring it up. I encouraged her to say it, knowing that the small details are actually much easier to address and practice with than the more general topics. Quietly, she got out the words *toilet lid*, and Dennis responded with emotion, laughing loudly, slapping his knees, and rolling his eyes. Bingo! I knew this would be a rich example for them to practice negotiation with equal rights and equal power.

I instructed Karen to ask for 100% of what she wanted around toilet etiquette, and she went on to explain that Dennis was in the habit of leaving both the seat and the lid up after he urinated, and it seemed like such a "right" and easy thing to just shut them both. She had asked. He had agreed, and now he wasn't doing it all the time, only sometimes. I asked if she was annoyed by this, and she responded, "No, I just don't understand why he can't just do it. It seems to make so much sense practically and aesthetically."

I then turned to Dennis and suggested that maybe this agreement was a rescue, doing something he didn't really want to do in order to please Karen. He said, "Absolutely!" She was very surprised. I asked him to ask for 100% of what he wanted instead. He said that since he used the toilet standing up a lot more frequently than he used it sitting down, it was far more efficient for him to leave the seat and lid up all the time unless he needed to sit. He added that he had been taught by the women in his life that it was respectful to put the seat down for them but admitted that he didn't really understand why it was important to Karen to put the lid down, as it didn't bother him to have it open. He was in conflict because he really wanted to make Karen happy, but he didn't want to put the toilet seat or lid down every time.

This was great. Now we had their true needs and desires on the table, and I asked Karen if she was willing to actually negotiate for what she wanted instead of the subtle power play of endowed "rightness." "Well, of course," she replied, with what seemed like confusion and trepidation. Dennis began by saying that he was actually willing to develop a practice of putting both the seat and the lid down. All he asked in return was for

Karen to be more patient and less judgmental about it when he forgot. Dennis wanted Karen to be more curious about why his way might be right for him, and her way right for her, instead of there being only one right way.

Karen was still pretty confused by this notion, but she was willing to try to let go of her judgments of rightness and wrongness in the context of her spiritual practice. So she closed her eyes, took a deep breath, and tried to open more fully to the possibility that it might be morally okay to leave a toilet lid up. She asked for another example in order to help her understand.

I shared a story from my relationship of really believing that it is "appropriate and considerate" behavior to close cupboards in the kitchen after you open them and how my partner leaves them open a lot. I had to make a tremendous effort to see why it might be okay for him to leave them open, even though it bothered me immensely to see them open. She asked me how we solved the problem, and I told her he had, out of consideration for my more intense desire, begun a practice of shutting cupboards. If I saw one open, I tried to remind myself that it wasn't "wrong," and I just closed it for my own sake. If he began to leave them open more often, I would ask him, as kindly as I could muster, if he was willing to put a little more effort again in shutting cupboard doors. Karen immediately seemed relieved and nodded and said, "Yes, I understand."

It's hard to see power plays and rescues as they are happening, but if we can notice resentment later, it becomes possible to negotiate the issue that is underneath the anger. Often when agreements aren't kept, we can see later that the agreements were not mutually satisfying, and renegotiation is necessary for more mutual satisfaction.

HYBRID NEGOTIATION: EQUAL RIGHTS BUT UNEQUAL POWER

It is rare that power is exactly equal in any intimate relationship in which we are striving to respect each other as equals. But there are some relationships where the power is more clearly unequal, and acting as if the power is equal would simply be unrealistic and problematic. As we navigate such power differences in relationships, we end up creating a hybrid style of negotiating that combines cooperation and hierarchy in order to take care of needs for both intimacy and real-world structural power differences. Some examples of this are relationships between parents and children or intimacy between a healthy able-bodied adult with a disabled, sick, or elderly adult. Also in this category are close relationships between employers and employees or landlords and renters.

Let's take the example of me as a mother with my children. Obviously, children cannot be on equal ground with their parents, but that does not mean that they can't negotiate as equals some of the time. The art of this type of negotiation is for the person with more power to treat people in the one-down position with respect, let them know where they can negotiate as equals and when the one-up person will take the power. I taught my children that they always had the right to ask for what they wanted but that many times I as the adult would make the final decision. I could also ask them for things, in order to nurture more equality.

When my son, Jared, at the age of twelve, did not want to do his homework anymore, we had many complicated and emotion-fraught negotiations. At first, we just fought about it. I didn't understand why he even thought it was an option to not do homework, as I had been taught to unquestioningly obey my teachers in school. I nagged; he resisted. I couldn't make him do it, and I was unwilling to use punishment as a way to coerce him to do it. I didn't like using threats or other kinds of power plays against my children. Generally, love was more important to me than control, but I was scared about the consequences of Jared's behavior.

Finally, I realized that both Jared and I needed to examine more fully what we were arguing about! I asked him if he would just have a conversation with me and trust that I loved him and had his best interests at heart. He agreed. I promised to listen openly and respectfully to his reasons for not doing homework, and I asked that he listen to my perspective as an older, more experienced adult.

Jared told me he could do well on the tests by just listening in class, that he was well behaved and understood the material. I gave him information about the laws pertaining to parents' responsibilities for children and as much of a sense of future consequences as I could, based on my own information and experience. I also let him know that my love for him and my desire for his future safety and happiness were my primary motivations and that, as his mother, I did not want to shirk my duty or misuse my power in a way that would adversely affect his future prospects.

Over many months, Jared and I continued to talk about the issue respectfully. We researched and examined the specific consequences that scared me: (1) him being held back a grade in school and therefore slowing down his progress toward independence and/or causing him to feel bad about himself; and (2) him not getting good grades and therefore not getting into a four-year college. Jared reassured me that his teachers knew he was smart and liked him. He was fairly certain he would not be held back a year for incomplete homework. He told me he did not want to go to college, and if he changed his mind, he could always go to community college, no matter what his grades, and then transfer to a four-year college. It was a very arduous negotiation, but we did reach resolution.

We agreed that as long as his teachers would give him passing grades without him doing his homework, and as long as he did not foresee any need to go to a prestigious college that required good grades, I would no longer nag him about his homework. What a relief for both of us! He agreed to continue pursuing computer skills and get jobs so that he was ready to support himself without the need for a college degree. If he ever flunked a class, we agreed that he would come up with the next solution to take care of my need to know he would be okay legally, socially, and economically.

In the eleventh grade, Jared finally had a math teacher who flunked him for lack of homework, despite his good grades on tests and steady attendance. True to his word, he solved the problem himself. He researched "testing out" of high school. He took the test, passed, and started his own freelance computer business. To this day, Jared and I are extremely grateful that we were able to stop the "homework war." Instead, we came to a more sophisticated understanding of each other, the educational system, and the power relationship between us. Our long process demonstrated the radical creativity of the hybrid model of negotiating, where Jared had maximum available power to determine his experience, while my real-world needs and concerns about his well-being were also addressed.

HIERARCHICAL NEGOTIATION: UNEQUAL RIGHTS AND UNEQUAL POWER

The world is full of circumstances where power is unequal, and there is no commitment by one or both parties to work toward equal rights. In the typical U.S. workplace, decision-making rights follow the level of power an individual possesses in the hierarchy, even in environments where leaders say they value collaboration. More power means more rights and responsibilities over others. Often there is a spoken or unspoken understanding that certain people do *not* have the right to ask for certain things. Secrets, power plays, and rescues are often necessary strategies to accrue more power in an unjust social system. The question here is how do we practice basic human kindness and advocate for self-interest at the same time.

My daughter, Sarah, has been perfecting these kinds of strategies to establish a satisfying career in the computer technology world. Sarah had an enviable job in San Francisco for two years during the smartphone application boom. While she appreciated her bosses and her coworkers, many of her own needs for creativity and power went unmet. Her two male bosses had their own style of management and priorities regarding the contracts they selected. Though she felt free to speak up about what kind of work she preferred to do, ultimately they assigned her to the projects they thought best.

Recently, in a conversation we had about her career, Sarah told me the following:

> As a woman in the male-dominated technology industry, I have had to learn, first, the cultural expectations for my gender and, second, what is valued by the industry and how successful people (primarily males) act in that industry. If I only pay attention to the cultural expectations of a woman, then I'll feel vulnerable and like an impostor when doing the things I need to do to become more successful, like ask for raises or for specific

Tools of the Oppressed

NANCY SHANTEAU

I spent about ten years working in corporations, and during that time, I noticed a tendency among the leaders to talk about honesty, direct communication, and taking responsibility, particularly when employees were afraid, and gossip and rumors were flying around. There was a sense that the people who spoke about a situation in hushed tones were "bad," and the people who walked into the leaders' offices and asked direct questions were "good." I also noticed that when these times of high rumor occurred, often big changes were afoot in the organization—in other words, the rumors were the smoke before a fire.

Sooner or later an announcement would be made by the same leaders, notifying the employees and the world at large of a merger, acquisition, downsizing initiative, or other meaningful action. The employees' lives were impacted, yet the leaders who had asked for honest communication from the employees had lied, directly or by omission.

Gossip, rumors, snarky comments, jokes, defensiveness, criticism, complaints, contemptuous remarks, stonewalling or withholding contracts. If I only behave like the successful (male) leaders, that won't work either. I'll be seen as selfish, arrogant, or off-putting, and I won't be as liked or likely to succeed. To be successful, I've had to take on the qualities of the male leaders, like over-the-top confidence, frankness, looking out for myself, and the ability to interrupt, but at the same time, do it in a way that won't freak people out (since these attributes are not expected from a woman) and conform to standards of female gender expectations, like being a listener, negotiating with kindness, and taking into account people's feelings. The result is that I have to be completely logical and confident with lots of compassion and empathy for others if I want to succeed.

information, theatrical demonstrations, and many other one-down communication styles are often the only way people who are "down hierarchy" can gain access to information, share critical news, change minds, and hopefully influence decisions made by people who are "up hierarchy." It is convenient of people with power to dismiss or undermine such expressions. Until the power dynamic changes, the people who are one down will take power in all the ways available to them: they will use the tools of the oppressed.

When we notice people using a tool of the oppressed, we ask ourselves if they feel powerless. In a cooperative setting, once a feeling of powerlessness has been named, often the person feeling the powerlessness can identify a held feeling. Sharing her held feeling and story/paranoia can help someone feel heard, understood, and perhaps powerful enough to make a request instead. Most of the time, if we can shift the power dynamics, people don't need the tools of the oppressed. People use the tools of the oppressed when they are desperate. When people feel mutually respectful, have access to power and cooperation, and can negotiate for what they want and need, they tend to be happier, more hopeful, and willing to invest in a collectively beneficial future.

Sarah has learned to put aside her emotional reactions to things, to observe the larger systemic assumptions, come from her objective adult, understand power, be strategic with power plays and rescues, and negotiate from a place of confidence and clarity. That work requires much more energy than her forty-hours per week job would suggest. In general, a minority person in a hierarchical setting needs to *rescue* by doing the extra work of studying the ways of the majority, while at the same time dealing with the cultural propaganda about inequality. Many people in majority groups are taught (and want to believe) that sexism and racism no longer exist because we now have laws that have "fixed" all that inequality. So as minorities in a hierarchy, we have to fight against that kind of crazy-making story, find others who validate our minority experience, and study the ways of the dominant (white male) culture without losing who we are and want to be. In the absence of coherent understanding on both sides of power differences, no hierarchical negotiation is truly honest and, hence, cannot be cooperative.

EMPOWERED NEGOTIATION

Empowered negotiation is contextual and complex. No matter what the power dynamics are at play, and even if someone isn't willing to participate in a negotiation with us, we need to continually ask ourselves what we need and want. We must examine our own desires in contrast with culturally defined expectations, sort through internal conflicts, and do our best to negotiate wisely and respectfully. And throughout this complicated process, we achieve our greatest success when we acknowledge our efforts and bring lots of compassion for ourselves and others. Our world is full of inequality and oppression, and with each conscious step we take, we create more equality, power, and skill in our communities.

Thirteen • The Rescue Dynamic

Julia Carol

I was forty-five, and my mother was dying of ovarian cancer. As if this wasn't enough, she was my father's caregiver, he being in the middle-late stages of Alzheimer's disease. They lived in Southern California, and I in the Sierra foothills in Northern California—about a seventy-five-minute drive to the nearest airport. My only sibling, Kate, lived in Seattle and had a demanding government job. Ever since my mother's cancer fight had gotten to the palliative care stage, where everyone but my mother and father had accepted that her condition was terminal, my sister had been taking personal leave to fly down and see them every third week. I was closer in distance, and self-employed, and had driven down often—but not as often as my sister.

Now Mom was gone, and we had checked my father into a "care" facility (and I use the word lightly). The nightmare journey with Mom had lasted over two years. We still weren't finished. Their house and two cars had to be sold, their things sorted through and given away, sold, or stored. And the paperwork was overwhelming. My sister was going down to Southern California yet again, and I had said I'd come too. However, I was worse than fried. I was a train wreck, depleted beyond self-recognition. I wasn't sure if I was handling it well or if I was even in my right mind. I felt a bit crazy. I decided to seek professional support.

That's how I came to see Julia Kelliher and learn about Skills for Change. Julia listened to my story, and after giving me a welcome dose of empathy and compassion, she asked if I had heard of the "rescue triangle".[1] No, I shook my head. So she briefly described the roles of the rescue triangle, complete with a whiteboard drawing. She explained that when we say "yes" to others' expectations, but deny our own needs and wants, it's called a *rescue*. Julia drew the rescuer position at the top point of an equilateral triangle. The longer we rescue, she explained, the more resentful we may become. She said we are in rescue when we're doing more than our share or something we don't want to do. We are rescuing because we want to be "good," and we might also be afraid of what people will think of us if we do not.

The burnout we experience giving our extra energy in rescue depletes us and leaves us feeling powerless. She showed me how we lose energy as we move to the next point on the triangle, called *victim*. Most of us want to avoid the horrible feelings of helplessness, powerlessness, and hopelessness in the victim role, so it's very natural for us to rebel, which is our attempt to get some of our power back. That takes us to the last point on the triangle; she called it *persecutor*. In this role on the triangle, we often feel self-righteous and indignant, and we justify our feelings of impatience, irritation, frustration, and anger based on our story that we were wronged. Sometimes, when we act out this persecutor energy, we feel guilty and often go back to the rescuer position in order to feel "good" again, and we complete the triangle. Julia pointed out that we can spend a lot of our lives going around and around the rescue triangle, becoming more and more depleted. She suggested that a more cooperative way out is to begin to ask for 100% of what we want 100% of the time, negotiate to agreement, act on our own behalf, and try to find ways to stop doing so much of what we don't want to do.

She told me very sweetly and firmly that she really hoped I would choose not to go on the upcoming trip to Southern California! It was one of those "lightbulb" moments. Of course I was depleted and angry! I had done too much for too long, and although I'd been trying so hard to be "good," I had spent my soul to the last drop. I recognized myself in the rescue triangle fairly quickly. And yet, I still gasped out loud at her last suggestion. "Not go?" My mouth dropped open. "But my poor sister has given even more than I have, and she still has the energy to go! It won't be fair to her—she didn't ask for this either, and she's rescued more than I have! I love her, and I don't want her to resent me!"

Julia smiled reassuringly and said, "Your sister is handling this really dreadful situation in the best way she can, and hopefully in a way that works best for her. You can do the same. Talk to her about it; negotiate with her. Tell her the truth about how you feel and see if she still wants you to come." She explained to me that if I honestly revealed my needs and wants, and I asked to hear all of my sister's needs and wants, then we could negotiate the best scenario for both of us, and I wouldn't be in the rescue triangle anymore.

I left Julia's office feeling, although still seriously depleted, very much lighter and incredibly relieved. I was giddy just considering not going on yet another trip to that ghastly house where my mother died. I also felt I had permission to talk to my sister about this option. Julia had given me that permission; this is an important point. The cop in my head needed to be balanced by another cultural authority figure telling me to take care of myself, that my own life was important, and I had the power to negotiate for what I want and need. Further, she gave me permission to assume my sister was powerful enough to take care of herself.

During the drive home from Julia's office, I felt much more spacious, and I began to entertain other possibilities. We didn't really have to rush anymore. Mom was dead already. Dad was in a facility. Who cared if the house sat vacant awhile? I called my sister and shared my feelings with her. She agreed with Julia, that she needed to go because

The Rescue Triangle

JULIA KELLIHER

We experience the rescue triangle roles dynamically. While it may look as if we statically move from one role to another, often the feeling states of rescue, victim and persecutor are intermingled. In relationships, once we engage in the rescue dynamic, we each embody many roles, moving from one role to the next or bypassing a role so unconsciously it is hard to track.

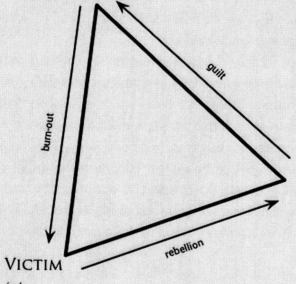

- does more than his/her share
- does something s/he doesn't want to do
- gives in or gives over in a disagreement
- feels guilty, resigned

RESCUER

guilt

burn-out

PERSECUTOR

feels
- angry
- self-righteous
- judgmental
- shut down
- punitive

rebellion

VICTIM

feels
- powerless
- helpless
- incapable
- hopeless
- low energy

she needed to be done as quickly as possible. She encouraged me to skip this trip and help her later, when I was ready.

I was still depleted, but I was finally out of rescue. I had more of my power back because I was making my own choices. When I went down the next time, it still wasn't my idea of a pleasure cruise, but because the decision to go was mine, it was much less onerous. And I can see in retrospect that I was actually helping my relationship with my sister instead of hurting it. I realize that if I'd had a different sister, she may well have had a different response. But I was no longer rescuing by doing what I thought was expected of me. Instead, I negotiated: I made my needs clear and listened to her needs and wants.

Let's look closer at the rescue triangle, how it relates to pig and power, the different scenarios that commonly lead us to enter into rescue, and most importantly, what it takes to get out!

THE ENERGY OF THE RESCUE DYNAMIC: RESCUER, VICTIM AND PERSECUTOR

Rescuer: We rescue when we do something we really don't want to do or when we do more than our share. We might rescue because we're too depleted to fight the pig parent voices telling us we can't say "no" to someone's request. Or we might find ourselves rescuing when we do something for someone unilaterally without negotiation, which may lead the person we're rescuing to feel powerless (or one down).

We deserve compassion for all the reasons we rescue. The rescuer role is shown at the top of the rescue triangle because it often appears to us, in the moment at least, as being the most powerful of all our options. When we burn out from rescuing too much, we go to the victim position.

Victim: We occupy the victim position on the rescue triangle when we feel one down or powerless in some way. This can happen because we've rescued too much, not gotten enough of our own needs met, or because we have scarcity of a resource (money, time, transactional power, skill, experience). Some people get stuck feeling like a powerless victim throughout much of their lives. Because people at this position on the triangle report feeling one down or powerless, we put victim at the bottom of the rescue triangle. Eventually we may rebel against the feelings of being stuck and powerless. The energy of rebellion helps us leave the role of victim and go to the persecutor position.

Persecutor: We enter the persecutor role when we attempt to get more power. While the term *persecutor* sounds mean and nasty, it can be a healthy impulse to take action in response to feeling powerless. We know persecutor energy is present when we notice emotions of impatience, irritation, frustration, and anger. Persecutor energy is usually accompanied by a massive dose of pig in our stories and our bodies. There are so many pervasive cultural stories and real experiences of anger being dangerous or "bad," we may feel guilty for being angry. Our culture denies us permission to be angry, and so most of us have not witnessed angry behavior handled in a constructive (not destructive) way. So if we express our anger, our guilt over behaving badly may carry us from the persecutor back to the rescuer position. Or if nothing changes even after we've expressed anger or displeasure, we might return to the victim role.

THE RESCUE DYNAMIC AND PROBLEM SOLVING: A TEMPTING TRIANGLE

Sadly, if we are unaware of the rescue triangle dynamic and don't have the tools to fight the good/bad messages from the culture, it's incredibly easy and common to get trapped and travel from rescuer to victim, victim to persecutor, and from persecutor back to rescuer. We can also take turns playing each role with another person.

As we learn how to apply the solutions to the rescue triangle dynamic in our lives, we learn to avoid many rescues. However, we may need reminders that it is incredibly human to rescue and that sometimes rescue is actually the best choice. A simple and important difference between "eyes wide open" rescue and "impulsive, reactive" rescue is the degree to which we persecute ourselves and others. Sometimes, we may not have any option that is not a rescue, and all we can do is offer ourselves gentleness as we choose the rescue option that is the least unpleasant.

Rescues are everywhere, embedded in the culture on a systemic level, and sometimes we simply do not have cooperative partners who are able or willing to negotiate with us. Even in an awful situation that we are powerless to change, our analysis of the dynamic can help us offer ourselves more compassion, explain why things are hard, and show us the ways we can take power in our response to the situation we face. Let's explore the roles in the rescue dynamic and learn how we get into the triangle and how we can get out.

HOW WE BEGIN TO RESCUE: THE CARROT AND THE STICK

Remember the pig parent? Our internal safety cop mindset monitors our activities and decisions to make sure that we stay in line and do what we should do, our internalized definition of what a "good" person would do. So our need for safety and inclusion prompts us to rescue. The pig story that hooks us usually has a carrot and a stick, a reward and a punishment. We agree to the rescue because we want to be helpful and fix the problem and to avoid what might happen or how others might see us if we don't. Often we have genuine fears of death, loss, injury, or dispossession. The carrot: We want to be a good person, and we want the outcomes we hope rescue will bring. The stick: We're afraid of conflict or a tragic result if we don't do something extra, such as drive our drug-addicted, homeless niece to her methadone appointment just before she's about to have a baby so that the baby has a chance to be born in a safer environment. We're also afraid of being seen as selfish and of the social punishment that might come with our actions. Sometimes, in order to stop rescuing people, we need to practice seeing them as more powerful than we've been seeing them, and give up some power. And, of course, we all want and need our communities to work and to be accepted by our friends, family, and peers, so we're quite normal for rescuing in this way.

Further, pig messages about what we should and shouldn't do aren't just internalized in our minds, but also exist in our culture, so sometimes our story about what will happen if we do or don't rescue might be accurate. For example, consider all the weddings, birthdays, retirement parties, and baby showers we get invited to: if we don't attend, unless there's a great reason ("great" meaning one that the cultural pig message of obligation finds acceptable), we may very well get punished in some way. The honorees may be insulted, find fault with our behavior, and respond to us in a way we won't like.

Sometimes when I explain how easily obligation turns into rescue, clients become confused and think I'm casting aspersions on our acts of duty and generosity toward one another. Certainly not! When we give of ourselves because we really want to, and we are giving from our natural generous impulse, it's a tremendously fulfilling gift to ourselves because we feel powerful, which raises our physical energy level. When we're doing things we don't really want to be doing because our internal "shoulds" put us under tremendous pressure, we may actually believe we are generous, but in fact, we're sacrificing ourselves. Our minds may not recognize our sacrifice right away, but our bodies do—gradually we feel depleted emotionally and energetically. It's in our nature as living beings to value our own needs and wants, despite internal and external pressures. As Audre Lorde says in *A Burst of Light*, "Caring for myself is not self-indulgence. It is self-preservation, and that is an act of political warfare."

The more depleted we are, the more likely we are to choose a rescue, since it takes energy to say "no" to the pig messages pushing us toward rescue. And the more we rescue, the more our energy is drained, and so we have even less energy to counter our internalized pig messages and stop rescuing. Competition, scarcity, and real or perceived danger increase the pressure to rescue and reduce our resilience and ability to cooperate, negotiate, and make different decisions. It's easy to see where the rescue dynamic generates a vicious and debilitating spiral downward into depletion.

POWERLESSNESS: THE MANY FACES OF VICTIM

Genuine victimhood exists—there really are wars, acts of genocide, and poisonings by pesticides. There really is structural and systemic oppression enacted by those who hold a great deal of power. There are acts of nature such as fires, earthquakes, lightning strikes, and torna-does and acts of fate such as freak accidents and genetic diseases passed down through generations. Our need to help and be helped in such circumstances is an exercise of instinctual compassion and a wonderful reflection of human nature. Thank goodness for first responders during disasters. They are doing all of us an enormous service.

A rescuer may be genuinely willing to help and a victim genuinely grateful to receive the help. Sometimes, over time, the meaning of the exchange can shift, as with parents and their growing children. When we give an eight-year-old lunch money and a forty-year-old adult child gas money, we enact vastly different acts of generosity, with layers and layers of relationship history and meaning piling on the back of the transaction. I witness senior citizens occasionally getting angry with their adult children once the power dynamic shifts; being elderly can mean we are no longer able to use our personal power in the same ways we have for decades, and it once again causes a shift in the parent-child dynamic that provides opportunity for hurt feelings and entry into the rescue dynamic.

The disability movement has extensively studied this easy slide out of appropriate caregiving and offers us much insight into why we go from generosity to resentment and how to shift the power and agreements in the relationship. People have accidents, they get taken care of, and at some point we treat them like victims far longer than may be necessary or desired. We can tell when the shift has happened because people start acting in a persecutory way toward each other. Whatever the cause, the one-down feeling of the victim state is oppressive. We might lose our ability to function, return phone calls, show up to work, and engage in normal daily activities. We might find ourselves incredibly emotional and have a difficult time recovering our ability to function. The victim state increases our vulnerability to illness and infection as our bodies' normal immunity may be compromised by our low energy. We may have trouble sleeping, eating, and performing daily personal hygiene tasks such as washing our hair, brushing our teeth, and doing the laundry. Or we may sleep too much and have difficulty getting out of bed. Some of us remain in victim state for a very long time, if we are very depleted and haven't the internal energy (or support or skills) to move out of the victim state. This victim state can go from depletion to a more dangerous depression if we remain stuck in a state of resignation about being powerless—this happens if we stop fighting our victim state, and our physical and emotional energy is suppressed.

Our internalized oppressive beliefs don't leave us alone in the victim role. As U.S. citizens, we're taught we could be powerful if we were good enough, smart enough, or worked hard enough. When we experience a lack of power or control over our destiny, it might be an invitation for any of the pig messages to rear their noisy heads. This internal dialogue tends to make the victim state worse, or it might trigger the energy of persecutor.

Some of us will turn our chronic victim state into a justification to demand rescues from others. We insist that we can't function without help, and we deserve whatever we need because our state is so much worse. However, our victimhood doesn't mean we deserve material assistance from the people closest to us. We might have a good chance to get help from others because they love us and care about our well-being. It's important for us to find the energy to negotiate and make an agreement for how the interaction can be more two-sided. Sometimes, all we can offer our helpers is our appreciation. If we can say, "I got myself in a deep hole, I'm really stuck, and I need your help. I wish I didn't have to ask, and please say no if you can't help me," we have gone a long way toward acknowledging our victim state, asking for what we want, and negotiating for an empowering outcome. We know we are moving out of the victim energy state when we offer ourselves compassion and accept our powerlessness. We gain in personal power as we develop the ability to take care of ourselves and ask for 100% of what we want in our relationships.[2]

TAKING BACK THE POWER: THE ENERGY OF REBELLION

The good news about the persecutor role is that persecution is our way of saying, "Enough! I am not going to take this anymore!" The feelings of persecution are signs that things aren't right in our lives, and we're not listening to the signals about our real needs and wants. Our seething persecution presents us with an opportunity to ask ourselves, "What's wrong?" For some of us, our awareness of our persecutory anger or resentment is how we recognize that we are rescuing by doing unsustainable work. Our patterns of rescue may create a cycle of depletion that could eventually result in illness, exhaustion, and loss of relationship. Persecutory energy is a healthy impulse away from the victim state.

There are warning signs that we're becoming persecutory, and if we recognize them early, we can handle our mood and actions responsibly. Our first sign is a feeling of irritation or crankiness. If we ignore that feeling, our mood in persecutor can grow angrier and angrier. When we're really angry, there's the risk of causing harm to ourselves or others if we react impulsively. In fact, acting persecutory usually exacerbates the problem, as our actions invite others to feel victimized, and then we're back in the roles again. Most of us wouldn't call ourselves persecutory when we're acting out the role; instead, we feel like a victim while we angrily complain and name the injustice of our circumstances. When we are expressing our persecutory distress, we're surprised to observe people distance and disconnect from us, citing our anger as overwhelming and too much. We may be turning our feelings of powerlessness into shaming and blaming (pig), expressed as criticism, complaints, and verbal and nonverbal contempt. Defensiveness and stonewalling can be more passive versions of persecutor, where we withhold our love, connection, validation, and care.[3]

The Pig in Persecutor: Adding Insult to Injury

Julia Carol

Our pig injunctions are largely responsible for our experience of persecutor energy, and yet we may say horrible things to ourselves for being persecutory! Often, our internalized cops in the head give us no way to win, creating a lose-lose situation by adding pig messages to the injury of the difficult situation.

Our circumstantial misfortune is an invitation for our internalized pig voices to lay blame and shame and dump a lot of all-inclusive piggy labels on other people who "obviously" caused our problems. In our persecutor energy, we might be the type of people who vocalize our frustration with name-calling or the quiet type who act passive aggressively or power play to get our power back. Or we might turn the energy inward on ourselves as shame and self-loathing. Usually our pig parent tells us we're "bad" (again!) and convinces us to move back to rescue—or to stop persecuting only to go back to a powerless victim state. When we fight the pig in persecutor, we are learning an important step on the path to asking for 100% of what we want. If we can articulate our feelings of frustration and powerlessness, we begin to understand what we don't want, and this clue can help us learn to identify what we do want. Step by step, we build the skills that help us change our lives.

When our culture of origin encourages us to give the greatest benefits of attention and nurturing (*rescue*) to the biggest victim, this persecution/victim dynamic can become pronounced and toxic. For example, one of my friends, Elizabeth, had a sister who noticed that if she was sick, she didn't have to go to school or do her chores. She learned that being a victim was a source of power in her family. As an adult, Elizabeth's sister complained (*persecution*) about her health and finances and how her siblings didn't appreciate or respect her. Elizabeth tried to make her sister happy by listening to her and appeasing her (*rescue*). Elizabeth was afraid of her sister's wrath and didn't want the conflict to escalate. But it didn't work; her sister didn't seem satisfied. Eventually her sister's "wolf in a sheep's clothing" complaints (*persecution*) no longer got her what she wanted—Elizabeth stopped responding to the complaints and distanced herself. Ultimately, Elizabeth decided her wedding would be better if her sister didn't attend, and that was the end of the relationship. Persecution as a strategy can backfire on the person using it.

When we've acted out our anger or frustration, taking out our feelings on someone else, we often feel guilty. This guilt can trigger a cascade of self-loathing and judgment and compel us to begin rescuing again. We end up back in the rescue role, further depleting ourselves, and beginning the process all over again. This can continue, over and over, until we find ourselves so depleted that we end up stuck in a chronic victim state, unable to take action at all. Or we may end up feeling like we're easily upset and frequently angry in particular relationships. Thankfully, there's hope.

With patience, time, and courage, we can use the energy amassed in persecutor to restore a healthy balance of power and get out of the rescue dynamic. When we recognize the dynamic and normalize the pattern, we are then more able to fight the pig messages that have us stuck, take responsibility for our part of the dynamic, and compassionately work to find our power in other ways. From the persecutor role, we gain energy to figure out 100% of what we want, and we consider if we have any contradictory needs or internal rescues that we need to address. We're no longer committed to our rescuer role, and we are fed up with the lack of power in victim. We're frustrated and ready to stop the rescue-victim-persecutor triangle and make a change. As we become more aware of how persecutor energy shows up in our feelings and behaviors, we look within, figure out what we want and need, and strategize about how to have more power in our lives (without oppressing others).

THE RESCUE DYNAMIC IN RELATIONSHIPS: THE ROLES AT PLAY

I grew up with a father who knew how to fix everything and seemed to enjoy being the one people called on for help—whether it was their cars, house plumbing, electrical problems, and so on. I assumed that all men had both the knowledge and got the same enjoyment out of fixing things. I do not know how to fix things, and when something around my home needed attention, I would ask my then-boyfriend, a mechanical engineer, to fix it for me. Not only did I need the rescue (I saw myself as a powerless victim), I had also internalized some privilege around being a woman and accepted the pig story that I deserved to have men help me with physical tasks because I was weak and they were strong. If he was too tired or for whatever reason did not feel like climbing on the roof to caulk the skylight or getting under the kitchen sink to see why there was a leak, he'd decline, and I'd get angry and persecute him. "It would only take about an hour! It would be so easy for you, and it's so difficult for me, and it's Sunday, so I can't hire someone, and it means so much to me! How can you say no?" I'd also use a line a lot of women use with men in relationships: "If you really loved me, you would help me." I might also recall any previous rescues I'd done for him as further evidence of the expectation I'd be rescued in return.

While I was feeling like a victim, my boyfriend probably felt perse-cuted. I have seen couples in my office whose pattern is to fight for the right to be the victim and demand a rescue. They each feel persecuted, so they each feel like a one-down victim, so they act as persecutor and go back and forth that way. In this way, when we feel like a victim but act like a persecutor, we justify taking power without negotiating the exchange in the relationship. We gain the added benefit of not feeling guilty if we feel righteous in our persecutory energy and actions.

The rescue triangle can also apply to organizations or groups. For example, in many U.S. nonprofit organizations, the organization is the victim of scarcity, and the volunteers and/or staff feel pressured to rescue too much, so they go to persecutor, feeling resentful of individuals who don't rescue as much as they do or resentful of the organization itself.

ESCAPE THE VICTIM/PERSECUTOR BIND: ASK FOR 100% OF WHAT YOU WANT

We begin to antidote the rescue dynamic when we:

- ask for all of what we want (we call this asking for our 100%),

- identify our internal conflicts and competing needs,

- negotiate and create agreements about how we'll handle the trans-action now and in the future, and then

- live by our agreements, or negotiate again if they aren't working.

This process is vastly more complicated than it sounds. Sometimes we know exactly what we want, and sometimes the situation seems so confusing that we'd rather avoid it altogether. Many of us do an internal calculation: we take our preferences and the other person's preferences into account, come up with the perfect solution, and ask for the com-promise we've arrived at in our heads. While sometimes our calculated request turns out well, often the other person takes our proposal as the negotiation starting point. If they had accepted our proposal, we might have gotten 70% of what we wanted; by the time we're done negotiating, however, we're furious because somehow we end up agreeing to 30% of what we want.

Consider this example: My husband and I are going out for a meal. I grew up in Los Angeles, and Mexican food is comfort food for me. However, I know that my husband doesn't care for Mexican food. So when he asks me where I want to eat, I decide to answer, "Let's get Thai food!" I think I'm being clever because I know he likes Thai food, and I'll at least get some chilies! My heart sinks as he replies, "Well, I'm more in the mood for soup and salad, so how about a salad bar?" What's happened here is that he thinks we're beginning the negotiation by asking for 100% of what we each want, whereas I rescued by taking his needs (or what I imagined they might be) into account before I answered the question.

My intentions were sweet and loving; I was trying to be a "good" and thoughtful wife—however, it's actually much more intimate to let him know what I really want. "Intimacy equals 'In To Me You See,'" is a quote I borrow from Stan Dale, cofounder of the Human Awareness Institute.[4] When I ask for 100% of what I want, I'm actually increasing intimacy. Using this same restaurant example, I now will begin by saying, "Well, I'd love Mexican food; however, I know you don't usually care for it, so my second choice would be Thai. What would you like?" This way, I'm being completely transparent in my request, including my desire to make sure he's happy with our choice.

VICTIM AND PERSECUTOR BYPASS

The energy of victim and/or persecutor can sometimes feel like a relief (we finally collapse or get angry and make a change). Others of us so dislike the feeling of either the victim or persecutor state that we put extra work into avoiding one or the other. When we skip moving into either victim or persecutor energy, we call this a victim or persecutor "bypass." Those of us who avoid the victim state will spend much more time trying to make rescue work, and experience the resultant extreme burn out of chronic rescue. It's also possible to whip right through the victim role of the rescue triangle and move into persecutor so rapidly that it feels as if we never felt the powerlessness of victim.

I've done this while driving—another car changes into my lane without signaling or leaving a safe distance in front of me: I yell out loud. I don't feel my fear, but it is there, because for a moment I am powerless, and my anger is my attempt to regain control of the situation. Others of us are afraid of feelings of persecution, whether in ourselves or others, and we avoid persecutor energy and go straight back to rescuing rather than face a potential conflict. When people don't recognize themselves in the rescue dynamic roles, often they have a pattern of bypassing one of the roles to avoid a particular energy state.

When we are bypassing an energy state in the rescue triangle, it is worth exploring how that energy could free us from old patterns and create new possibilities in our relationships. For example, I hate the feeling of the victim state, so I either find myself burnt out, exhausted and depleted, or I jump to persecutor and pick an unnecessary fight. When I allow myself to feel powerless and express how vulnerable I feel, often the entire relationship dynamic shifts. I feel heard and often receive nurturing and support that I wouldn't otherwise have gotten.

I've also learned that I can access the vulnerability and powerlessness of victim energy when I feel the impulse to rescue. Instead of thinking I know what's best and just getting it done (*rescue*) with the blind hope that it will make everything okay, I do much better when I pay attention to my resistance (usually it's coming from depletion or time scarcity) and accept my own one-down condition with compassion so that I give myself permission to negotiate with the others for an option that better suits my needs. When I avoid rescuing in this way, I am not just taking care of me, I'm taking care of the people I was tempted to rescue, as I won't resent and/or persecute them if we've avoided the rescue dynamic.

LIVING RESCUE-FREE

First the bad news: There is very little chance for perfection in our attempts to avoid the rescue dynamic. There's just too much genuine scarcity and power imbalance in the world influencing us to rescue, and not one of us is powerful enough to fight it all successfully all the time. So we begin by accepting that sometimes we will rescue. When we do, we rescue because the cultural oppression is too great to overcome (paying taxes, for example) or because it would break our hearts not to (our friend is crying on the phone at 2:00 am because her teenager isn't home yet and she's worried). One thing we can do in these situations, if we can't negotiate a better solution, is to recognize the rescue and choose it. Since much of the damage of rescue is caused by our feelings of powerlessness and our attempt to "fix it," at least by making the conscious choice to rescue, we are finding some degree of power. We're less likely to feel like a victim, and we're out of the rescue dynamic sooner.

I have greatly increased my energy and enthusiasm for life since learning to drastically reduce my unconscious rescues. In the beginning of 2006, I did an inventory of all the ongoing rescues in my life and began to strategize getting out of them. It was one of the most emotionally challenging things I've ever done, but with focus, courage, and lots of support from others in the Skills for Change community, I ended the year free of the larger, chronic rescues I was in when the year began.

I started with self-nurture. I dismissed ideas of perfection and went for good enough: sleep, nutrition (yes, I have some privilege here), time alone, affection, mindfulness practice, exercise, tying up loose ends, completion of projects. I paid attention during the day to what depleted me and stopped doing as many of those activities as possible. I began to focus my time on activities that helped me to feel replete. When we're replenished, we have the necessary energy to fight the culture's injunction to rescue.

The next tool I used in my campaign against rescue was community support. Remember: The pig is the voice of internalized cultural oppression. It was so much easier for me to stay out of rescue because I'd attracted friends, colleagues, and my husband who held the shared value of nonrescue. While others in my community (family, in particular) held to the values of duty and obligation, I had many alternative voices encouraging me to take care of myself and stay empowered by my choices.

Next, I had to know what I wanted. When this question was difficult, I gave myself lots of normalizing, nurturing, compassion, and encouragement: of course I was struggling; we've been encouraged by the culture to hide our wants and needs from ourselves. Systemic privilege and oppression affect our ability to know what we want. A wealthy, white male might find it easier to name his wants than a poor woman of color. That isn't to say that the wealthy male hasn't internalized messages that lead him astray, as I'm sure he has. I'm saying it is likely easier for him to learn to distinguish a "should" from a "want"; someone lower in the social hierarchy may have fewer resources and less community support to get her needs met. For many one down in structural power, it might not even be safe to ask for what we want, so developing a keen awareness of what we want might not be safe either. For me, I realized how often I was compromising between what I really wanted for myself and what other people wanted. I'd go to a family dinner, resentful of being there, and end up in an argument with my father-in-law that drained everyone's joy in the togetherness and shared food. I learned that if I declined most invitations and took care of myself, I was more likely to be curious and happy to see my in-laws, and the gathering was much more harmonious. My parents-in-law sometimes expressed their disappointment about my absences to me and my husband, but most of the time the guilt I felt was easier to deal with than the emotional repercussions of resentment, disagreement, and disconnection I felt when I rescued. I practiced new ways to say "no." Key phrases that worked for me include these: "I'd prefer not to." "Thanks so much for thinking of me, and I couldn't possibly do it that day." "I'd love to, and I can't make that work." Or I might make an alternate suggestion such as, "I can't go to a movie; how about a walk?" It's difficult to say "no" to people we love, and it was important for me to practice new phrases that felt authentic and loving and took care of my needs and priorities.

When I noticed myself feeling depleted or angry, I'd perform an internal rescue check to discover if I was in rescue. Then I would practice skipping the blaming and shaming, ask for what I wanted, and negotiate if possible. Or I'd just act on my own behalf if there were no way to negotiate.

When I realized I was rescuing with someone who uses the Skills for Change tools, I would first focus on getting myself replenished and out of strong persecution mode. Then I would apologize, follow the steps for clearing held feelings, and clear my resentment, and we would both ask for our 100% and negotiate for a win-win.[5] This would work most of the time, and when it didn't, we could agree to disagree until we discovered a solution that met both our needs.

In relationships where I didn't trust the other parties to cooperate, I did the work internally and offered myself compassion for anything I couldn't change outside myself. I first normalized the situation by assessing the cultural messages that lured me into the rescue (using the "of course" phrase), compassionately took responsibility for the rescue, and took steps to change the situation accordingly. I might attempt to negotiate, but if that failed, I would choose not to rescue and risk the other person's persecution, as well as the guilt inflicted by my internal pigs. I'd allow the guilty feelings to arise, feel their intensity, and see if they passed away with time. As I experimented, I learned what worked best for me in different contexts.

Finally, I realized that if I rescued, I'd feel resentment—and if I didn't rescue, I'd feel guilty. I decided that for me, guilt is often a better choice than resentment. I think this was because my resentment comes from a healthy and natural disappointment that I'm denying my own self-care. However, when I decline the rescue and feel guilty, the voice of guilt is from my pig voices, the voices of internalized oppression telling me I don't measure up.

Nowadays, I am much more aware of how and when the rescue dynamic is at play—and that awareness really helps! However, I sometimes find myself slipping back into the rescue dynamic. I've gained an even deeper awareness of how, as a woman in our culture, my unwillingness to rescue makes me appear like a "bitch" to myself and/or to others. Sometimes, I'm just not able to fight that pig, and I succumb. However, I've surrounded myself with supportive loved ones who remind me of my commitment to nonrescue living in my more intimate relationships. I renew my efforts to live by my principles most of the time, and when I find myself rescuing, I do so with as much self-care and compassion as possible.

SYSTEMIC OPPRESSION AND THE RESCUE DYNAMIC

Once aware of the effects of structural power imbalances and the harmful effects of the "-isms" in our culture (sexism, racism, classism, and so on), we can often feel angry and frustrated (*persecutor*) with the dominant cultural structure that is so hierarchical and the source of so much of our external and internalized oppression. With cultural messages, there is often no one to negotiate with, or negotiations happen very slowly, and we are genuinely stuck in an unjust situation. We can either go back to accepting the inequities wholeheartedly (*rescue*), seeing them but being resigned and hopeless (*victim*), or stay in what I call "compassionate persecutor." In compassionate persecution, we direct our persecution toward the system of oppression, while holding with compassion any individuals in it. None of us alive today created the systems of oppression, and even those who perpetuate them often do so because they have internalized privilege that may well be invisible to them. I still feel angry when I see cultural oppression—injustice weighs on my heart, and I want everyone to see the world how I see it. I have to be patient, join collective groups taking action on behalf of change, and then when change is within reach, hold myself with compassion for the ways I am limited and do my best to act on behalf of my perception of justice.

Being fully replenished greatly increases our ability to feel and act powerfully on our own behalf. It's important to analyze whether we have enough structural power to change something, or if we are an individual going up against a much more powerful system. Once we have identified the ways in which our lack of power is not structural, perhaps instead of a story of false scarcity the culture has sold to us, we can work to change our story. What we cannot change, we can work to accept, compassionately persecute, and organize to change collectively.

Internalized Privilege

JULIA CAROL

Privilege is often invisible to those who have it. However, it's often quite visible to those who do not have it. And it's natural to feel persecutory toward those who have privilege they're using unconsciously. To combat this tendency, we can learn to recognize our own privilege and find compassion for the nature of privilege.

We can strive to see our own privilege in a system of inequality as a two-edged sword and hold ourselves with compassion for having privileges others don't share. We can also try to hold compassion for those more privileged than we are. It's all more complicated than it at first appears.

When it's possible to recognize and willingly give up privilege, we may experience the increased intimacy that comes from sharing power equally in a relationship. Other times, even if we see our privilege, it is difficult to give it up. Unfortunately, there are times when giving up privilege feels more like going one down instead of becoming equal. For example, I imagine that most people reading this book have regular access to a hot shower. I know I do. Well, for the majority of human history,

The good news is that even a modest understanding of the rescue dynamic can lead to life-changing results. The day that Julia Kelliher introduced it to me, I glimpsed only a small aspect of the rescue dynamic's impact on my life. And yet, the limited insight I received gave me tremendous relief and subsequent energy and prevented what could have been an ongoing pattern of rescuer, victim, and persecutor with my sister. It was a while before our journey with our parents' decline was over, and what I learned about the rescue triangle saved me enormous difficulty and helped me get through the whole thing much more compassionately.

even the kings and queens had to wait while their servants fired up the wood or coal and heated water for a bath. Once a bath was cold, that was it. And most people weren't kings or queens. Even today, much of the world's population doesn't have clean, cold water on tap, not to mention hot water flowing from a shower. Now, I am all about balancing power and privilege, and I think of myself as a lover of justice and equality, but how far will I take my principles?

Suppose we could actually count the number of hot showers available and divide them by the number of people alive on the planet. Would I vote to make them available equally? It might mean I only get one hot shower a year, or one a decade. I'm not sure I can answer that question. I realize, of course, this idea of fair division of showers might seem a bit preposterous. Yet these types of environmental privileges, while seemingly insignificant in a single instance, amount to a significant difference in lifestyle when taken together. Household appliances and plumbing are just a few of the many privileges to which I am accustomed. And I might be willing to give up quite a few of my privileges, if circumstances allowed. I do find a great benefit in becoming aware of them, to the extent I am able to, and to working hard to reduce the harm my privilege causes others.

The more I've worked with the rescue dynamic as a tool, the more subtle the roles I've played in it when I do get caught up in the dynamic. In the past few years, I've used mindfulness practices to sniff out pig messages, and I keep working, compassionately when possible, to fight pig and remove myself from the rescue dynamic as quickly as possible. I'm more inclined to recognize my persecutor energy by sensing tension in my body and noticing feelings of anger (such as a clenched jaw and tightness in stomach) than with any story in my head about wrongdoing. I am more fully aware now that I really don't want to persecute myself or anyone else, and I imagine most of us would prefer to negotiate kindly whenever possible. The more I've explored the concept of the rescue triangle, the more pleasurable my life has become, as I've cleared most of the despair, resentment, guilt, and anger from my mind, body, and heart.

Fourteen • Stories: Filling in the Blanks to Create Meaning

Glenn Smith

I was sitting quietly in the kitchen when my wife, Julia, entered abruptly, noisily dropped bags on the floor, and began complaining about random things. I immediately assumed that she was upset and irritated. Since I was feeling sensitive, I quickly jumped to the conclusion that she was angry with me. I remembered that I hadn't done a promised chore. I then started to believe that she was angry about the undone chore, and I emotionally prepared my defense and counterattack before I knew what was really happening. In my confusion and alarm, I created a story that explained her actions.

Our stories about the world are ubiquitous and very creative. We use stories to fill in the gaps of our understanding. As in the previous example, we do this individually on a small-picture level to explain and add meaning to personal observations. In the big picture, there are cultural traditions that use narrative and storytelling to help us learn about ourselves, one another, and the world around us. We use cultural stories to make sense of mystery, to entertain, and to pass on current events, tradition, and history. Myths and parables are big-picture, collective stories that explain large forces and phenomena. Individually and collectively, we also create big-picture stories, such as philosophical, spiritual, and political theories to explain large existential questions. Just as big-picture stories give meaning to our larger world, small-picture stories help us make sense of our personal lives and transactions.

SMALL PICTURE STORIES

If we pay attention to our own internal dialogue, we realize that we're telling ourselves stories, adding meaning and interpretation to observable facts much of the time. There are many terms commonly used to describe this natural and necessary human function. We make *assumptions*, *jump to conclusions*, *interpret* other's actions, *infer* meaning or intent. When we are aware of the creative aspect of this activity, we may say we are *guessing* or *speculating*. But if we're not aware, we may believe we are making rational *deductions* or *connecting the dots*.

We fill in the gaps based on our prior knowledge and beliefs. And we do this in order to know how to act and be safe. We drive to the grocery store and decide whether it's too crowded for us to shop based on the traffic in the parking lot. We might decide our friends are not happy to see us if they do not greet us with smiles. We conclude that people are wealthy if we see them driving what we believe is an expensive car. These assumptions happen so quickly that we aren't usually aware of the degree to which we are filling in the blanks. Often, we need our stories—our conclusions can even help keep us safe. For example, when my car breaks down and I am stranded alone on a remote stretch of road, I may need to make a quick intuitive decision about whether the stranger who stops to offer help might be trustworthy or dangerous.

When our interpretations are inaccurate, it is often a function of not seeing or knowing the whole picture. For example, there is a classic story about a group of blind men attempting to describe an elephant. One feels an ear, one the trunk, one the tail, another touches a leg, and they all come up with very different descriptions of the animal.

In this chapter, we will see how our innate ability to add meaning to observable fact enriches and complicates our lives. We'll discover how helpful it is to learn to identify and separate facts, feelings, judgments, and stories. We'll see the value of being open to new information that might change our stories. When we learn to understand our stories, their elements, and our responses to them, we embody an essential skill in the Skills for Change approach to conflict resolution.

STORIES AND EMOTION

When we have strong, uncomfortable emotions in reaction to a situation, it stimulates our story-creating function, often in concert with judgmental pig thoughts we have internalized. When we start to create stories, sometimes with only a bit of emotional charge (just "filling in the blanks"), the stories can stimulate a much bigger emotional charge. Emotions and stories feed each other, and we often confuse them with each other.

People will frequently say, "I feel like…," and what comes next is a story. Usually, we experience in our bodies the actual emotions that come before the story, but we skip over our sensations and emotions and dwell on our explanation of what happened and not how we feel about it. For example, if someone doesn't invite me to a party, when all my friends are going, first I might feel hurt, and then I might make up a story to explain why I wasn't invited. I might think to myself, "Maybe it's because I never have parties or invite people to dinner. I don't make much effort socially, and therefore I'm not included." My story about the event is now perhaps more wounding than the lack of an invitation. Underneath all of those thoughts, there's a fundamental sense of sadness, loneliness, helplessness, and loss.

In the above example, my friend might have thought I wouldn't like this party and decided I was probably too busy anyway. She may have been trying to do me a favor by sparing me the effort of declining her invitation and also avoiding the pain she might experience when I declined her invitation. That's a complicated nest of stories. It takes commitment to unravel interlocking stories and come back to connection and love.

THE CHALLENGES OF STORIES

Prejudice and fears including racism, ageism, imagism, sexism, homophobia, and xenophobia are examples of cultural stories held on a societal level. These stories tend to get internalized, and even elevated to the status of belief. When a stranger is running toward us on the road, our response could be influenced by our beliefs about appearance. If the person is a well-dressed, middle-aged woman, we will likely have a very different response than if it is a young man with a shaved head and tattoos. And on the intimate or personal level, we often go right to believing our own intuitive-interpretive stories about another's confusing or upsetting actions based on our own history, values, and prejudice without knowing their actual motivation or intentions.

Our stories, and even our observations and memories of "facts," may not be the same as those of another person observing the same event. In college, in an abnormal psychology class, I read of psychological studies where participants were shown films of very shocking or confusing events.[1] When the subjects were asked to recount what they saw, their reports differed from the actual events on the film. The differences between their reports and the film increased with the emotional impact of what was seen and also as time passed. Eyewitness testimony of dramatic events like crimes and airplane crashes is not always accurate. We can misremember, create our own story about what happened, and totally believe it.

It is impossible to achieve perfect awareness of when we are "in our stories." But the pursuit of story awareness can be very fruitful. It helps us understand our relationships in the world—our place in intimate, work, and community relationships and our place in the culture. With practice, we can get better and better at identifying when what we are thinking is a story. We want to differentiate the story, any judgments and the simple "facts," and to remember that even those facts may look different to others, especially in hindsight. I love the bumper sticker, "Don't believe everything you think!" The anecdote that opened this chapter about jumping to conclusions when my wife entered the kitchen, grumbling and dropping grocery bags on the floor, is a good example of a story that, while based on observable facts, may be very different from what is actually happening for the other person. If I had realized I was taking a leap from my emotions to a story, I could have been open to learning what was actually going on, rather than preparing for a fight. The reality was that Julia was upset by an encounter she'd had at the grocery store, and her anger had nothing to do with me or the chore I hadn't completed.

Consider, for another example, when one person in a cooperative group frequently arrives later than the agreed start time. The others might have thoughts such as these: "He's lazy and disorganized." "He doesn't care about this project." "He doesn't respect me and how hard I work to get here on time." The creative and very possibly judgmental stories we can tell ourselves are almost endless. The late person may or may not share our values, "shoulds," or even the same memory of the agreed start time! Heightened conflict can emerge when we assume our story is true and act angry or blaming. On the other hand, when we cultivate curiosity about our own stories and other people's experiences and motivations, we create fantastic opportunities for change and growth in our relationships.

THE VALUE OF STORIES AND THE ROLE OF INTUITION

Sometimes we discount our stories because they seem too wild, paranoid, unreasonable, or irrational, or we just don't want to believe they could be true. For example, with my wife, Julia, sometimes after I try to defend or explain myself in response to real or imagined criticism, she says in exasperation, "You're so perfect—you're just a saint, aren't you!" I then feel terrible and remember a recurring story I have about her, "If that's what she thinks, how could she love me—I wonder if she *ever* cared for me." I know rationally that my thoughts aren't true. It *is* probably true that, in the moment, Julia feels less caring for me or my emotions and more hurt about my defensiveness. In fact, she is probably trying to get me to see something about the situation because she *does* care about me and my motivations.

In Skills for Change coaching, we believe that our stories, even obviously erroneous stories, are valuable clues from our intuition. We define intuition as nonrational knowing: what we know when we get clues from all our senses and past and current experiences to make explanatory connections. Our intuitive sense of what is going on is related to something accurate even when the whole story is not.[2]

Whether our stories seem believable or wild, they virtually always contain some intuitive kernel of truth. We are not crazy, even though our stories might be incorrect, embellished, or farfetched. And we are not crazy when we come up with believable but inaccurate guesses about what happened. It is simply a natural function of our minds to "fill in the blanks." When we compassionately ask ourselves why we might come up with a particular story, we understand better what is going on with us. But to know what's actually going on with others, we need to hear from them directly. Innumerable conflicts and struggles, from the interpersonal to major political strife, can be traced to our belief that our stories about others are the "truth." In Skills for Change coaching, we seek to understand others' experiences and points of view as they express them and include their viewpoints in our story of what happened.

VALIDATING STORIES

When we ask a person or group to listen and acknowledge what is true about our story, and they do it well, the experience can provide surprising relief both emotionally and physically. Upon hearing other people's reasons for what they did, I have felt a relaxation of neck and shoulder muscles and a letting go in my gut, prompting me to sigh with relief. Someone *validates* our story when she says what's true about it first, before she says what's not true. When the truth in the story is validated, it becomes easier to drop our attachment to the rest of the story that is inaccurate. Another person's validation of what's true about our story, and our ability to let go of what's not true, leads us to greater understanding and compassion for each other and thus increases our ability to act with love and cooperation. This greater intimacy is the big benefit to sharing and validating stories.

We call the effort to say what's true "finding a kernel of truth" and the process of validation "clearing." It is a skill to listen to a person's sometimes-wild story and look for what is true about it first, rather than immediately saying what's not true, defending ourselves, or reacting in horror that someone thinks that about us. Going back to those "you're just a saint" incidents with Julia, when we later cleared my story, it was relieving to hear her validate the truth that, in the moment, she was angry and didn't care about my feelings because she was hurt by something I had said. She also reminded me that she cares about me and my feelings most of the time and that she loves me even when she's angry.

Occasionally, our cooperative partner in clearing stories will entirely validate our story, even when we do not want to believe we could be right. In these cases, the truth can be upsetting and even painful, but at the same time, relieving. After I ended a romantic living-together partnership with a woman, I experienced this painful type of relief. A few months after we broke up, we were trying to see each other socially as friends. At maybe our second visit, I asked if she was dating. She indicated that she was not, but in some way her answer bothered me. I wanted to believe her, but I couldn't shake the suspicion that she *was* seeing somebody. At a later time, I told her of my remaining attachment to her and of my painful suspicion that she had been seeing someone. She told me that she actually *had* been. She hadn't wanted to tell me the truth because she thought that I was still hopeful we might get back together, and she didn't want to hurt me. It was painful to hear my story validated, but mostly I felt relief.

From Kernel to Cornfield: Getting at the Truth

JULIA CAROL

Sometimes, there's a kernel of truth in the story shared when clearing a held story; sometimes, there's a cob of truth, and sometimes, there's a whole cornfield. All forms of corn aside, the purpose of looking hard for some truth in a story presented to us during a clearing is to reassure others that we understand how they could come to have the stories they have. The importance of this step cannot be overemphasized. When we search for validation of some part of the story we are hearing, we are finding some empathy, and it can aid us in releasing some defensiveness. And more importantly, by beginning with "what's true" and validating some aspect of the story, we are reassuring our clearing partner that we know she is not crazy. When we share a held story, we aren't always aware of having a crazy pig message about ourselves, but it's usually there—and we feel an immediate tension and tightening in our bodies if after sharing a held story, we are told that it's just not true. Conversely, when our story is validated, even if only partially, we are able to feel our bodies relax, and we are open to hearing what might not be true and what else is true. Sharing what's true and what's not true and adding anything new to the story helps heighten the color and complexity necessary to fight duality and gets us out of pig-filled right-and-wrong thinking.

This example again shows how stories can interlock. My ex's story about me (partially correct—I was still somewhat attached but not hopeful of getting back together) caused her to act in a way that led to my story that she wasn't being truthful about dating. Here, and as seen in the previous "you're just a saint" example, one story often leads to another! They are like the Russian folk dolls, one after another hidden inside each other. We call them nesting stories.

Sometimes, it is not possible to get stories validated by their subjects because they are unavailable, or we don't feel safe to ask them to do so. In some cases, in order to achieve some degree of inner peace and relief from the story, we can find an alternate version of events that helps us to drop the story and move on from the associated emotions. Alternatively, in a case of significant danger, we might need to tell ourselves the worst story so that we take care of ourselves, even if the worst story isn't true. For example, if someone's ex-husband says he wishes she were dead, and he also owns guns, it's probably a good idea for her to take action to protect herself, even if his words were said only in anger. Otherwise, when there's no threat of physical danger, why not make up a story that makes us feel better? Our best story allows us to act with love and compassion. After all, we are in charge of own story making, so why not invent a smart, helpful story?

CHANGING OUR STORIES

Our stories shape our world, bodies, relationships, and lives. What we tell ourselves, and what our culture tells us to believe, dictates how we think and act. Many stories are harmful—cultural prejudices and personal internalized oppression, for example. But when we become aware enough and make space around our feelings and stories, we can gain power to change them. We then may choose what stories we tell ourselves or even whether we tell a story at all. Sometimes this can be challenging. For example, many women have negative stories about how they look because of the cultural stories about how they *should* look. For

Conscious Personal Cosmology:
Stories Underneath Life

....

NANCY SHANTEAU

Truth is not a fixed unit. The truth we see changes based on
our viewpoint. When we cultivate the dialectical, nondual adult
consciousness, we learn that our perspective gives us *one* truth but
not *the* truth. Our unique cosmology, our personal belief about the
world and how we fit in it, is the story at the root of the truth we
perceive. An atheist might view an event such as a flood in terms
of unseasonable weather, ground saturation, and county flood
planning. A more religious person might see the same event as a
symbol of a holy plan. Many of us inherited a cosmology we did not
choose for ourselves, and sometimes it takes us decades before we
begin our conscious investigation of whether our inherited belief
system is right for us.

The process of selecting a new cosmology is like trying on
different hats. A cowboy hat is very different from a fedora or a
baseball cap. Examples of cosmology include atheism, religion,
mysticism, animism, humanism, anthroposophy, nihilism,
spirituality, and so on. Our cosmology reveals our values about
the world and, ultimately, is constructed of our values. I know an
avowed atheist who believes strongly in the value of helping others.
He gives back as a volunteer and seeks opportunities to help those
in his community. His atheism does not make him disinterested in
the world. Rather, he is focused on making his life as profoundly
impactful as possible. He is one of the wisest, most compassionate
people I know, and his beliefs shape his choices every day of his life.

Often, in order to truly experience the liberation of a
compassionate adult consciousness, we must align our daily stories
with a greater story (*cosmology*) about our purpose and belonging

on the planet. For example, I have always had a vague belief in the interconnectedness of all beings. I liked the idea of reincarnation and believed people have a soul. However, my actions as a coach were only distantly linked with my belief systems. It wasn't until I heard the story of the bodhisattva, a being who returns lifetime after lifetime to help all beings achieve enlightenment, that I found my current cosmology. The bodhisattva story sounded exactly like what I do as a Skills for Change coach. I help people love themselves, and in the development of that self-love, make plans to cultivate a beautiful life. I help my clients unwind the patterns of self-loathing that keep them stuck and to upgrade their stories about themselves and others so that they are happier, more fulfilled, and satisfied at work, in their relationships, and in their lives. I choose to have an upgradable cosmology: in other words, I have a vision for the life I want for myself, and I will upgrade my story about the world and my place in it if a better story comes along.

Once, when I was helping someone fight her pig, and we were having difficulty getting her unstuck, I asked about her belief system because I guessed pig had lodged in her worldview. When we explored her story about why we were on the planet, it turned out she'd internalized oppressive beliefs from her lineage that she had to earn her salvation with hard work, and that belief was what she was defending in her pig fight. Once we'd challenged the underlying belief, the pig fight went much more easily. We ended up chuckling over the way she'd twisted herself into an intellectual pretzel over a belief system that wasn't really hers. Our cosmology is the springboard from which we design our actions and practices, and it supports or undermines us as we attempt to make changes in our lives. When we are struggling to make changes, a thorough exploration of our cosmology can help us do what we need to do to change.

another example, if we think people generally don't like us, perhaps we walk with our eyes downcast to avoid seeing their rejection. People interpret our lack of eye contact as a desire to be left alone, and they don't approach us. We don't see smiles or curiosity directed our way, and our story that we are disliked gets reinforced and confirmed.

It might be too hard to shift from our negative, pig-fueled stories straight to positive stories of looking great in the first example or of connection and being valued by others in the second. Those affirmations may sound wonderful, but the dissonance they create can send us back to the old negative stories rather than helping us shift toward the hopeful future we desire. It's sometimes helpful to incrementally change our personal values and to fight the cultural big-picture stories repeatedly over time, listening to the positive ripple of our belief as we collect evidence that our new stories are also true.

And, if we can then just *notice* the sensations and feelings associated with the events in our lives, without telling a story, such story-free living can be very liberating. Ultimately, as we learn to identify the memories and values that give rise to our stories, we can begin to make choices about what we believe and what we let influence us.

BELIEFS AND STORIES

Let's look at an example of how beliefs and stories interact to affect our relationships and our lives. My wife occasionally asks me to tell her about my own beliefs. She wants to understand me and make sense of my actions. For example, I believe we are all part of some huge, unknowable universe in a spiritual sense and that the arts, and maybe especially music, can be a profound way to connect to that larger realm. I play the trumpet, and I practice virtually every day in my studio next to our house. Sometimes my wife gets frustrated and wishes my trumpet practice required less diligent effort on my part. I identify myself as a musician. It is one of my ways to contribute to society and connect with our universe. Also, I have worked and struggled to be the best trumpet player I can be. In the process, I have learned more about myself and life than in any other pursuit. When I explain all this to my wife, she feels better about my choice to be a musician. She tells me she loves the part of me that plays music with a larger purpose in mind. Our stories shape every interaction, and when we remind ourselves and others of the stories that give our lives meaning, we often end up feeling more connected to each other as well.

The world is still full of war, famine, disease, and oppression. A positive belief system doesn't make difficulty go away, nor loss. But my own life-affirming story helps me handle what I face, accept what I'm powerless to change, and do what I can to improve things. I hope my story helps me act compassionately, generously, and wisely. When we consciously choose, and choose well, we gain enormous power over our experience.

Fifteen • The Power to Trust

Marybeth Paul and Nancy Shanteau

We were sitting in a circle of about thirty people on the first day of a three-day coaching alumni workshop on a sunny day in May. It was an open discussion period, and an older gentleman with graying temples mentioned he was working on a book about trust, who grants it and earns it, and why trust is an important part of a company's culture. He asked our teacher what he thought about how trust worked. They were having a thoughtful and interesting conversation, discussing promises and breakdowns, and how to communicate requests and needs, and my alarm bells were going off. There was an underlying, unspoken assumption in the conversation that people who withhold trust are disloyal, disruptive, or anti-team in some way. Finally, when I [Nancy] couldn't stand my own feelings of internal dissonance a moment longer, I raised my hand and added to the conversation, "I just want to remind us all that in situations where there is tyranny, it isn't safe to trust the tyrant, governmental or otherwise. If we are students at Kent State, the government might kill us when we protest. There really isn't a possibility for trust when life or death is at stake. When employees withhold trust, it makes sense in the context of power dynamics when the leaders can and do fire anyone who disagrees with them. Ultimately, it takes enormous power to *grant* trust because we have to be able to assure our own safety in the face of someone disagreeing with us or disliking what we have to say. Otherwise, it's safer to stay silent and keep secrets."

At my words, an African American woman said, "Thank you!" in a powerful voice. She continued on to say that she was often silent in groups where she felt a big difference among participants in the amount of historical privilege each person carried and that such an experience often occurred for her in our classroom setting. She said, "It takes a lot for me to trust that you will be interested in what I have to say and put aside your privilege to listen." Our teacher asked if she needed anything. She said she needed to trust that each person would listen to her. She stopped speaking and looked around the room, making eye contact with each and every one of us. Trust wasn't something she would or could grant to us as a group; it was an individual transaction and required our presence and connection, commitment to be honest with one another, and care for the relationship.

TRUST AND POWER

Often in relationship, the giving of trust and withdrawing of trust is a use of power. Our assumptions about who trusts whom might be full of pig, stereotypes, and generalities that do not include the complex reality of being human. When we evaluate the context, contradictions, and specifics of whom we trust to do what and when, we use the word *trust* more skillfully and compassionately. In one analysis we have found helpful in Skills for Change, we begin by considering if the person is *reliable* or regularly able to keep promises and fulfill agreements, *competent* in her skills at doing the promised task, and *sincere* or heartfelt in his willingness and desire to do what he says he will do.

There are two further key distinctions that help us understand how trust works. One is *context*: under what specific circumstances was trust broken, can it be repaired, and how? And the second, does the person have *enough power* to grant trust to the other person? In other words, does she have enough power to protect herself if she trusts, thus making herself vulnerable to the other person's behavior and choices?

We so often are taught in this culture to distrust our intuition, instead labeling ourselves crazy, stupid, or confused, when in fact our intuition is giving us important and useful information. When we work through the trust analysis to understand the situation, identify everyone's relative power and the specific domain where trust is faltering, and determine how to proceed, we increase our trust in ourselves and others.

TRUST IN CONTEXT

Let's look at how context impacts trust when there's equal power in the relationship and a mutual willingness to be vulnerable. "I trust her with my life!" "I trust him 100%," or "I wouldn't trust her as far as I can throw her." Although these statements appear to be absolute and clear, there is an important component missing. Before we can make a statement qualifying our level of trust, we need to define the domain of life in which the trust is required.

My sister, Bev, and I [Marybeth] share a high level of trust. We know we love one another and that we each have the other's best interest at heart. She has a fear of flying that has increased over the years. Several years ago, even though she was uncertain about her willingness to fly, we made a plan for her to come for a visit. Since I had small children, and she was alone, it was a choice that made sense to both of us. We agreed to share the cost of her flight and the expenses of her coming to see me for a week. When she got to the airport, she felt overcome with fear and chose to cancel the visit. We both felt great disappointment and sadness around her change of plans. I also felt angry that I had arranged my life around a visit that never took place. A year later, she cancelled another planned visit, which caused me to question whether she would ever follow through with travel plans. When the topic arose of yet another visit, and I voiced my doubt and skepticism about whether she would actually arrive, she felt hurt and angry that I didn't trust her.

We used the following process to sort through the complexities that were present, and within a matter of hours we regained stable footing in our relationship. First, we needed to define the context in which the trust had been broken. Initially, it looked like my distrust was about Bev not keeping agreements, but after reviewing many agreements she had kept, it was clear that story was not accurate. She does keep agreements. When we hit on the topic of agreements in regard to travel plans, we knew we were onto it because we both breathed a sigh of relief.

Then we considered the three categories into which trust is divided: (1) sincerity, (2) competency, and (3) reliability. We could easily see that she was sincere in planning the visits. We also agreed that she was competent in making the plans. She had never experienced the level

Inequality and Distrust

NANCY SHANTEAU

In a gathering or group, when the power of the parties is substantially different, where one party is one up and one party is one down due to privilege and oppression, the trust analysis can help us understand and reframe the difficulty the one-up party has in earning the trust of the one-down party.

When we walk into a room where there are significant historic power differences between the parties present, it is likely that the person with the greatest difference will not just distrust the rest of the group, that person may also be highly suspicious of the skills and motivations of everyone there. Will they take care of me? Will they understand me? Will they listen? Will they marginalize me? Will they pretend they know who I am or what I experience? Examples include a woman in a group of men, a person of color in a group of whites, a disabled person in a group of able-bodied, a person with different gender identity and/or sexual preference in a of anxiety she felt the day she was to fly, and up until that moment, she had been competent in making travel plans that she had followed through with. When we discussed her reliability, she didn't feel the same ease she had felt in the two previous categories. Her discomfort was a clue that we were approaching a topic with a higher emotional charge, and we needed to proceed with caution and compassion.

Her pig was telling her that she was bad and stupid for not keeping her plan. "Everyone else you know travels by plane with no fear at all. You are so stupid to be thinking of cancelling this trip! You never do what you say you'll do. There you go changing plans again. There is something seriously wrong with you." After she bought into that erroneous concept, she went on to believe that this must be true 100% of the time. As we talked and were both gradually able to recall other times when she *had* been reliable,

group of heterosexual, cisgendered[1] folks, a person who speaks a different language of origin in a group of English speakers.[2]

If we want things to be different and want to wake up to our privilege, then one-up group members must begin to note, name, and define the differences and speak to make more safety and space for the one-down members with less structural, historic power. In fact, this is the only route to trust that I know in such a context. Doing nothing, feeling ashamed or guilty, or pretending that power is equal and everything's all right are completely normal and understandable responses to power differences when one is privileged or one up; they just aren't particularly useful responses and tend not to produce change. In my experience, people begin to relax and build trust with each other when power is discussed, when space and listening is offered to someone who has a different experience, and when everyone has equal rights to be heard, to control our own circumstances, and to choose how we spend our time, energy, and resources. Ultimately, people do what works, and our compassion for the choices we make is a first empowering step toward trust and change.

her pig began to retreat. She described in detail the anxiety she experienced when she arrived at the airport. Her fear was so great that she was trembling, she felt hot and sweaty, she had diarrhea, and she couldn't think clearly. As she followed the cues her body was giving her and decided not to get on the plane, her body relaxed enough that she felt profound relief.

As I listened, I imagined how hard that must have been for her. Bev is fiercely independent, prides herself on being a competent traveler, and believes she has proven this by having spent fifteen years traveling alone all across the United States for her business, both by plane and towing a twenty-four-foot travel trailer with her van. Unexpectedly, the idea of getting on an airplane was so terrifying that her body wouldn't go along with it. In that moment, the most sensible thing to do was to go home and not get on the plane. When we both considered other factors operating in her life (overwhelming financial concerns and serious health issues), her experience began to make more sense. By specifying the particulars and acknowledging the unusually high stress she'd been under, her choice not to fly was normalized, and her pig was unable to hold its ground with the general sweeping statement, "You're bad and stupid to not fly." Bev has a fear of flying that motivates her to use other modes of transportation when she travels, *and* she is reliable to get there when she's not traveling by plane. If I had stayed in my feelings of disappointment, anger, and sadness, and she continued feeling defensive and scared, we couldn't have come to our current understanding. The hope and expectation of experiencing greater intimacy is what motivated each of us to expose our fears and insecurities to each other.

We use the trust analysis to help us understand when trust is breaking down, to make requests for 100% of what we want 100% of the time, and to design solutions that reflect our power and influence, or our degree of true powerlessness. After all, trust is about connection, and whether we are building or eroding connection with our choices and behavior. And when we understand trust, we may choose to gain the skills to change, so we can build even more trust with ourselves, communities, and the people we love.

Sixteen • Cooperative Communication: The Relief of Clearing Held Feelings and Stories

Paula Elliott

Before I learned about the tenets and tools of cooperative communication, my attempts to resolve conflict with intimate partners, as well as with family members and friends, were often fruitless and filled with anger and pig. The incidents left me with a feeling of hopelessness that got worse after each abortive attempt to work on a problem with a loved one. After several years of work with Julia Kelliher on learning the Skills for Change principles, and many hours of practice in mediating conflict with intimates, mostly with my husband, I slowly gained a sense of hopefulness in the process. It was a practice filled with a lot of hard work, but the movement over time was in a positive direction, which added energy and incentive to continue the process.

Julia taught us that cooperative communication involved emotional literacy skills we might not have developed yet in our lives.[1] She taught us that emotional literacy requires that we be able to distinguish between the specific observable facts—what anyone observing the situation might see—and our feelings and stories about the observable facts. Our emotions are like primary colors, at root—there aren't too many of them. Some primary emotions are fear, sadness, anger, happiness, and love. Additional helpful emotions to consider include powerlessness, shame, anxiety, irritation, confusion, loneliness, and hopelessness. It is additionally helpful to consider our sensations, bodily feelings of movement (streaming, tingling, pulsing), temperature (warming, cooling), and pressure (heaviness, lightness, tension, relaxation, emptiness, fullness). Our held feelings are composed of a combination of emotions and sensations. Our stories about what has happened usually combine memories of past events with conjecture about another person's intentions.

When we hold on to our feelings and stories without sharing them with others, we start to build up a complicated version of events that takes over our emotional landscape. We no longer see what happens as an isolated event, but as a confirmation of our past story about the other person. These stories are like a clog in the drain—sometimes they get so thick there's no room for anything new. The process of emptying out and clearing our feelings and stories requires sharing what we feel and think with other people and listening to their version of what is true, not true, and also true about our story. It is necessary emotional and relationship maintenance that seems unpleasant when we start but is a huge relief by the time we are finished. As my husband and I developed emotional literacy skills, our conversations got less heated and defensive, more practical and loving, and ultimately forced us to face our differences.

At one point, I approached my husband wishing to discuss a held feeling about housework. Using the cooperative communication framework Julia taught us, I told him I felt irritated when he sat down after dinner to read the newspaper. The story in my mind was that he did not even think about the dishes that needed washing, and he left them to me. He responded with what was true about my story—that he, in that moment, was not thinking about the dishes; he wanted a moment to read, but he was open to a discussion about who would do the dishes and when. We were able to discuss how we would deal with this issue in the future and made agreements regarding the chore. As we used the newly learned steps to communicate, we gained trust, along with an increasingly strong commitment not to verbally hurt each other in order to be heard. It was truly exciting!

FACING CONFLICT

Conflict is hard for most people to face. We communicate about our conflicts for the sake of love; the motivating factor for most people is the desire to improve the relationship. When we are successful, we have identified and clearly stated our differences, fought our internalized judgments for ourselves and each other, and then feel better about the relationship and our love. From a place of more harmony, our work to clarify issues, negotiate agreements, and learn interpersonal skills is much smoother. Everyone must want to communicate their differences—reluctant participants are unlikely to do the work without resentment and are more likely to be dissatisfied with the process.

COOPERATIVE COMMUNICATION AND PROBLEM-SOLVING

I came to coaching with Julia Kelliher to understand my part of the dynamic in my relationship, reclaim my power, and make changes to improve my marriage. Julia recounts the story of an early session we had wherein she asked me about my marriage, and I replied, "He is a wonderful man, kind, a good father and provider, and I can't think of one thing I like about him." After we had a big laugh, Julia pointed out to me that Harvey and I were deep into the rescue triangle and started to teach me about the three roles of rescuer, victim, and persecutor.

We started to dissect the ways in which Harvey and I were playing all three roles with each other at different times, and how gender roles played into the rescue dynamic. Harvey was also learning alongside me, and we eventually decided to mediate to improve our communication, attempt to get ourselves out of the rescue triangle, and equalize our power dynamic. Our family system, evolved along fairly traditional lines, was as I discovered, actually a good model for safely raising young children. As a pharmacist, a predominantly male profession in those days, Harvey made three times the amount of money I did as a nurse, a traditionally female profession. Therefore, when we had children, it made sense for me to stop working for a while to raise them.

Mothering young children involves rescue by definition; we are in charge of the well-being of small people who cannot care for themselves and depend on adults for their very physical and emotional survival. These circumstances compelled me to ignore a lot of my own needs. Harvey was raised a traditional man. He was eleven years older than me and liked being in charge of financial affairs and making decisions about our money, and I was too overwhelmed and tired to take part in much of those matters for many years. As the kids got older, I worked part time as a social worker at our local hospice, still making much less money than Harvey. I felt powerless, deferred to him in major decision making, and found my heart hardening to him as we sank deeper into our rescue dynamic. He was also rescuing me at the same time in many ways, doing more of the decision making than he wanted to, for example. After twenty years of marriage, our patterns were thick and sticky. We needed help.

Julia Kelliher gave us a series of steps we could follow when we were feeling bad about something that happened between us. When we were first learning the steps, we didn't even try and practice at home because we just ended up yelling at each other. Eventually, we got to the point where we could do the steps on our own and only brought thorny problems to our sessions with Julia. Here are the steps we followed to clear our difficult feelings and stories about each other and our circumstances.

1. One of us would say we had something to clear, and we'd set a time and place to do the clearing based on how long we thought it would take.

2. Both of us would prepare ahead of time by writing down our goals for the clearing, specific examples of upsetting events, our feelings during and after the events, and our stories about what happened.

3. At the appointed time, we got together with our notebooks, and the person who asked for the meeting would start. Usually it was Harvey. We would read each other our goals.

4. Then Harvey would read me his first held feeling and story. I would respond by telling him what was true and not true about his story. When he was satisfied that he understood what had happened, it was my turn.

5. We kept taking turns until we felt complete.

6. We would each say 100% of what we wanted to change and then make new agreements based on our deeper understanding of each other's needs and wants.

7. We would end by telling each other what we appreciated about each other, and often we would be so happy that we would hug.

FACILITATED MEDIATION

Julia Kelliher facilitated our first mediation session, and since I had requested the session, I went first. My first held feeling for Harvey went like this:

"When you came home with a new car without consulting me about it, I was shocked, angry, and afraid." After a pause to let him register the sentence and the feelings alone, I asked him if he wanted to hear my story about the held feeling. When he assented, I told him, "I thought you took too much power in buying this car alone. I am more ecologically minded than you are, and I was upset that you bought a large, four-wheel-drive gas-guzzler, completely unnecessary in Los Angeles. I imagined you wanted to do this alone and have all the power over the decision and did not want to relinquish control. I imagined you did not care what I thought, that maybe you thought I wasn't smart enough." This was my story about the incident.

The recipient should answer first by saying what is true about the giver's story. There is always a kernel of truth in the stories we hear. Intuitions result from something real in our interactions, even if it is only a momentary truth. As humans, we naturally make up stories when we do not understand something. Only by airing what is true can the recipient go on to reassure the giver about any part of the suspicion that is not true.

Harvey answered by saying that it was true that in the moment he did make the decision alone and wanted to do so, and he reminded me that I had told him that he could go car shopping without me, as I was exhausted with our two small children, and it seemed like just another big errand I needed to do. He also said that it was not true that he did not care what I thought. He said that he thought I was very smart and could handle the process. It was true that he did not think about the carbon footprint involved with buying this car. So, the kernel of truth in the moment was validated, but he assured me that he did care in general about what I thought and wanted.

I answered that I did feel relieved and complete with this held feeling. Harvey gave the second held feeling:

"When you are late in sending out our household bills, I feel anxious, irritated, and fearful." After another pause, as I took in his feelings without a story attached, he asked if I wanted to hear his story. I agreed, and he told me that keeping his credit score excellent was very important to him, as he observed much financial strife in his parents' marriage. He had many fights over money with his ex-wife as they were divorcing. It took him a long time to restore his credit after his divorce, and he wanted to keep it that way. He thought that I didn't care about this desire and that maybe I was even persecuting him a little by paying the bills late. He said it was a rescue in the first place to let me take on the job because he wanted control over the process, but he thought, as I did at the time, that this was a way to share more of the financial power, as well as to free up his limited time.

I first validated the kernels of truth in Harvey's story. I realized for the first time that I had been persecuting him by paying the bills late; we were very deeply into the rescue triangle in many ways during this period. This may have been why I had overlooked his need for financial security and order. It wasn't true, in a larger view, that I wanted him to suffer. I shared that it had been a rescue for me to take on paying the bills because I really didn't want to do it. I said that I was looking forward now to making new agreements on power sharing and managing our financial life.

We kept trading off held feelings during the session until we had gotten to all the core issues and were starting to feel very open with each other, expanded in our hearts, and energetic about forging ahead with new understandings, agreements, and a commitment to work on getting out of the rescue triangle, asking for 100% of what we wanted and negotiating for it. As the process unfolded, Julia highlighted the gender issues related to power, and provisions were made in our ensuing agreements to take them into account. When it came time for negotiation, Harvey and I made a contract to give him back the bill-paying job. We set up a weekly financial meeting to discuss purchases, do a budget, and balance the checkbook.

Harvey and I spoke our gratitude for the hard work done, the openness we crafted, and the commitment to our relationship. We acknowledged each other as great learning partners in the process. We gave strokes to Julia for her wisdom, her skill at guiding the process, and her obvious care for us both.[2]

The High Cost of Sexism

....

PAULA ELLIOTT

I grew up in a household with four children, two girls and two boys. My father was a university dean and professor; my mother quit her career in microbiology, after earning her master's degree, to become a wife and mother, and she never worked outside the home again. My brothers were encouraged to achieve in their advanced education and to reach for degrees that put them in the tops of their fields. They both have PhDs. I was also encouraged to reach for the highest position available to me: because I was a girl, this was nurse and social worker. If I had been a boy, it is likely my father would have encouraged me to be a doctor.

I did a comparison of my lifetime income as a nurse, as opposed to what it would have been as a doctor. Here are my findings:

• Annual full-time nursing income: $50,000
• Annual full-time physician income: $170,000
• Nurse's lifetime income with time off to raise children:
    20 years x $50,000 = $1,000,000
• Nurse's lifetime income without time off:
    40 years x $50,000 = $2,000,000
• Physician's lifetime income without time off:
    40 years x $170,000 = $6,800,000

If I had become a doctor instead of a nurse, I would have earned three times more than a nurse who didn't take time off to raise children, and six times more than I have as a nurse who took time off for childrearing! What I've learned in Skills for Change is that genuine oppression can always be enumerated and monetized. There is a financial cost to oppression, and it adds up over generations.

GETTING CLEAR IN THE BODY

Feeling complete with the cooperative communication process is not just an intellectual or emotional understanding. There is a relaxation and spaciousness in our physical bodies when we feel complete and satisfied with the conversation. Eugene Gendlin, in his book *Focusing*, suggests, "You can actually feel change happening in your body. It is a well-defined physical sensation of something moving or shifting. It is invariably a pleasant sensation; a feeling of something coming unstuck or uncramped." It can feel like an "aha" moment or a bodily "phew." Tension eases, and a release occurs in the belly or chest or as an all-over feeling in the body.

If participants do not experience relief, questions seeking more information or held feelings can lead to further uncovering. When I finished successful conversations, I felt a lightness and ease in my body and more energy flowing freely. Harvey and I both felt positive and hopeful after our first session.

WHEN COOPERATIVE COMMUNICATION FAILS

Of course, cooperative conversations don't always end well. When one or both partners have enormous anger and internalized judgments, they may be unable to work within the model. Some people were taught from childhood that anger and conflict are bad and that they shouldn't feel negative emotions. Our feelings of powerlessness may be triggered, and perhaps we feel like nothing will help. Sometimes, one person accepts all the blame and feels at fault for everything and needs to take her power in order to communicate with greater equality.

A major impediment to cooperative communication is the unequal power of the participants. U.S. citizens mostly live in a coercive society disguised as a democracy. For example, our law enforcement community coerces "proper" behavior from the citizenry, based on laws written by legislators. The institutional power of police is greater than our personal power as citizens. We do what authority figures tell us to do, or we suffer painful consequences.

Historically, husbands have been one up to wives, mothers to children, teachers to students, bosses to employees. "I will spank you if you don't be quiet." Or "What do you do around here all day? Can't you have the house cleaned up by the time I get home?" Or "If you don't work the weekend, your job will be in jeopardy." The speech of those in hierarchical power is often laden with threats. The difference in power takes away our opportunity for true intimacy; we cannot be open to each other, or even see each other clearly, in these situations when no mechanisms are built into the system for power sharing. The one-up person consciously or unconsciously wields power in a way that discounts the thoughts, feelings, needs, and desires of the one-down person. The one-down person is often afraid to air feelings that might challenge the power and control of the other and result in punishment.

NEGOTIATING INEQUALITY

If all participants discuss and understand the inherent structural inequities in the relationship, and negotiate agreements in the relationship accordingly, such agreements can go a long way toward enhancing communication. As we name the oppression and privilege in an unequal relationship, and make attempts to even out the inherent power balance, we facilitate hybrid models of communication. For example, in a mediation session between a child and parent, first we have separate conversations to make sure both parties will be safe in the session. We get reassurance that there won't be punishment later. We might suggest the one-down person speak first, give the first held feeling, and perhaps take more of the available time to speak. We agree at the beginning that if the person who is one down needs support from the facilitator, the person who is one up will leave the room. If power imbalances come up during the mediation, we generate creative solutions. Ignoring such differences in power can undermine the entire cooperative conversation from the start.

Historic sources of oppression, such as race, gender, differing mental and physical abilities, class, and so on, are often invisible to the one-up member of the dynamic. This is the second impediment to cooperative communication in work and personal relationships. Often in mediating conflict between a man and a woman, structural inequities need to be named, discussed, and accounted for. Women tend to undervalue their skills due to sexism and go one down to men in negotiations; one-down people often lose their voices by sharing too little or obscure their meaning by saying too much. Women can sometimes

The Twenty-First-Century Hybrid

PAULA ELLIOTT

Many work and personal relationships in twenty-first-century America are a *hybrid* of the hierarchical and cooperative models. Our institutions are built on the hierarchical model in the interest of expediency and getting things done. Someone is usually in charge and dictates to others what needs to be done, for example, in a business. This hierarchical model streamlines getting the work done, as a boss need not take time to gather everyone's thoughts and goals before a job is started, nor stay up to date with individual changes in perspective as work progresses. Despite the need to work within this reality of modern life, a hybrid model can be used and promoted in some situations if participants have bought into the process. Bosses can cede some power to employees and take their needs and desires into account as the bosses make decisions for the whole. Parents can invite children to participate in the creation of household agreements, including rules, consequences, and meetings to stay up to date with each individual's needs, requests, and goals. Sharing power isn't easy, as having power involves work on the part of all participants.

resort to judging men for being one up and less skilled in emotional and communication realms. Men can react to being in a "learning" position in mediation with obstinacy and, feeling a blow to their power, either look for a way to win or withdraw into silence to protect themselves. All of these reactions are learned behaviors in our sexist culture. When we name these influences in the moment, it helps a heterosexual couple grapple with power and work to improve their relationship. Both participants have equal rights to be heard, even if they do not have equal power.

WHEN COOPERATIVE COMMUNICATION WORKS

The success story of my husband and myself continues to this day. We used cooperative communication tools off and on during our marriage to assist us with communication when it was difficult. We brought our children into Julia's office and had family mediations when there was conflict in our interactions at home, especially during the adolescent years. I believe the work transformed their upbringing; as adults, they are extremely happy and successful and both attribute their skillful navigation of life to our empowering negotiations and the Skills for Change tools they learned throughout childhood. Our now-grown children have taken these skills into their lives and relationships. They know a great deal about power and rescue and often teach their friends the principles.

Skills for Change tools can help make an amicable, respectful, and peaceful parting, which was the path Harvey and I chose. Harvey and I live separately now and are good friends and proud parents and will always be family. We even travel together, and we share family holidays and Sunday meals. Conflict resolution can be cooperative even if the result is separation. We continue to work on communication within our relationship, are usually conscious of rescue when it happens, and talk openly about it, in attempts to forestall the rescue triangle dynamic. The tools we learned prevented a much different and less happy outcome of our marriage and provided a good model for our children in working out differences and managing conflict. We are both deeply grateful for these most useful and results-oriented techniques, and we highly recommend them to all.

In Skills for Change coaching, practitioners work from the foundational principle that all people are inherently good, born with a desire for a harmonious community, and that this desire can be thwarted along the way by internalized and external oppression; scarcity of time, energy, and resources; and negative experiences. Skills for Change coaches dedicate themselves to removing as many of the obstacles as possible to this universal desire to communicate, understand others, and be understood. We want our lives to work, our communities to thrive, and the possibility that conflict can be resolved without violence. The cooperative communication model offers a way to achieve peaceful results, even when we must separate to accomplish that peace. The remarkable thing is, after we've listened to each other and expressed ourselves, we often feel more alive, touched by our humanity and our connection to each other, and open to exciting and creative possibilities.

Seventeen • How to Recognize Depletion and Create a Life of Plenitude

Nancy Shanteau

A couple came into my office for a conflict-resolution session. They'd been struggling in their marriage and were hoping to work through some difficult issues that made them feel distant and unhappy. I started the session as usual, led them through a quiet meditation, and then asked one of them to start by checking in about how they were doing and to share their agenda items for the session. The wife burst into tears. I looked at both their faces and knew this would be a different session than we had planned. They were both depleted, and in their current state, any relationship conversation would likely produce more separation and disconnection.

Depletion is a state of exhaustion caused by "not enough," or scarcity. There's not enough energy, money, resources, time, resilience, intellectual capacity, and so on. In Skills for Change coaching we use a scale of −10 to +10 to identify states of depletion and replenishment. When she burst into tears, I knew the wife of the couple described above was at least at a −5 and more likely at −7 or below on the depletion scale. The husband's face was gray and drawn, and his body slumped in a shape that looked like exhaustion and resignation to me. I guessed he was at least at a −3 and possibly lower.

IDENTIFYING DEPLETION

I handed the wife a tissue and proceeded to explain that depletion usually happens to us when we have some sort of difficulty that is more challenging than usual, or if something has been hard for a long time and has gradually worn us down. The problem with depletion is that when someone is below zero on the scale, normal tasks that usually take minimal effort become extra difficult. The first job of someone who is below zero is to get above zero. When our depletion is simply *energetic* or *physical*, we will replenish through personal self-care. If she gets enough sleep, healthy food, her family's basic needs met, and if possible some exercise or pampering, a healthy person who is slightly depleted will bounce back up into positive repletion numbers.

By the time we finished creating replenishment plans for the couple in my office, they both seemed calmer and more connected with each other. The next time they came in for a session, we made real progress on their relationship patterns, and they both credited their focus on replenishment in the intervening week as one of the main reasons they were able to be less defensive and more compassionate and creative.

Repletion becomes more difficult to attain if the depletion is *systemic*. I call systemic depletion the "hole in the bucket" problem. It's as if the efforts we make to replenish are draining out the other end, just like sand out of a hole in the bottom of a bucket. No matter how much replenishment we put in the bucket, we end up with an empty bucket. Usually, people are systemically depleted by undone tasks weighing them down, conflicts in their relationships, grief and loss, chronic or long-term disease, poverty, accident recovery, mental health challenges, oppression or social injustice, overwhelming

Depletion and Repletion Scale

JULIA KELLIHER

It takes energy to make substantial changes in our lives. We can take appropriate actions more easily when we are aware of where we are on the scale of depletion/repletion. Sometimes, we need to replenish before we begin, or partway through implementing our plans for change.

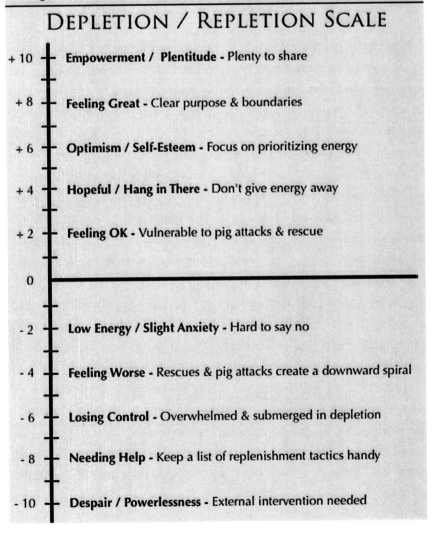

DEPLETION / REPLETION SCALE

+ 10 — **Empowerment / Plentitude** - Plenty to share

+ 8 — **Feeling Great** - Clear purpose & boundaries

+ 6 — **Optimism / Self-Esteem** - Focus on prioritizing energy

+ 4 — **Hopeful / Hang in There** - Don't give energy away

+ 2 — **Feeling OK** - Vulnerable to pig attacks & rescue

0

- 2 — **Low Energy / Slight Anxiety** - Hard to say no

- 4 — **Feeling Worse** - Rescues & pig attacks create a downward spiral

- 6 — **Losing Control** - Overwhelmed & submerged in depletion

- 8 — **Needing Help** - Keep a list of replenishment tactics handy

- 10 — **Despair / Powerlessness** - External intervention needed

paperwork, addiction, legal challenges, job difficulties, or historic trauma. When we are systemically depleted, I find that the most helpful intervention occurs when we make progress toward the resolution of the bigger issue. Self-care practices might help raise our depletion number enough so that we can finally finish paying our taxes or pick up the phone to have that challenging conversation with our boss. And sometimes that impossible task becomes doable when we ask a friend to help us get it done.

MAKE A REPLETION PLAN

When I help people make a repletion plan, I suggest we brainstorm how they can increase their repletion level by four points on the scale. Any more than four points, say from –3 on the depletion scale to zero or +1 on the repletion scale, and people seem to get overwhelmed. Also, when we are at a depletion level of –5, for example, the practices we are actually capable of doing might be very different from what we think would be helpful. Our yoga class that usually relaxes and fills us with energy might actually be depleting when we are overwhelmed and full of emotion. The first day or two, while we're still under zero on the scale, it's helpful to focus on self-care: can we get a full night's sleep, eat healthy food, take a bath, get some exercise? Once we've recovered some energy, perhaps gotten to a +1 or +2 on the repletion scale through doing replenishing activities, it's time to consider less appealing tasks. Perhaps some chores like laundry or cleaning the fridge will make a huge difference in our mood. Or maybe it's a good time to pay bills, enroll in classes, or apply for food stamps. After all, our feelings of being powerless and out of control often further deplete our emotional and energetic energy. Hopefully, the plan itself will start to make us feel better.

At this point, once we are somewhat replenished, it's time to ask ourselves if there's something systemic we'd like to tackle. Maybe we need to face the problems in our relationship that have been nagging at us and disturbing our sleep at night. Or it's finally time to get unstuck and pursue our dreams. This stage of the planning process can be a good time to get help. We often don't see our own blind spots, and our limitations might be obvious to others. It's also important to identify things over which we are powerless and accept the unacceptable. We might be able to directly address, in a face-to-face conversation, the disempowering comment our partner made to us, or a conversation might make the situation worse. When we are depleted below zero, it's not the time to try risky interventions. There's plenty of time to take that risk when we've gotten ourselves above a +3 on the repletion scale and won't be energetically knocked down by disappointment.

THE ORIGIN OF THE DEPLETION SCALE

Julia Kelliher created the depletion and repletion scales to explain why we have trouble doing things that we know are good for us or why we rescue even though we know we shouldn't. Early on in her practice of Radical Therapy, she noticed that Beth Roy would normalize Julia's experience by reminding her that she was depleted. Julia decided to investigate what depletion meant and started writing descriptions of depleted energy states. She realized that she could function effectively at a very low energy level for a long time due to her strategies of "toughing it out" and "figuring out the best way" and because of her personal resilience.

One day in a couples' session, she noticed that the wife was having a very hard time hearing held feelings or validating stories. She said, "Of course, you're struggling; you're depleted!" Then she wrote −10, 0, and +10 on a vertical line and told the client she had probably been functioning in negative numbers for a long time. The client said, "I'm a negative eight!" Her husband said, "I'm a plus two." The session became a discussion of what could be done to help the wife replenish, rather than an exchange of feelings and stories that

Depletion and Repletion Descriptions

JULIA KELLIHER

DEPLETION: Drained of Life Energy

Symptoms: Fatigue, depression, hopelessness, physical weakness, mental confusion, diseases, emptiness, sensitivity, reactivity, edginess, sense of overwhelm, meaninglessness, terror, mania, insomnia

Causes:

1. *External oppression*—Externally oppressive circumstances make us afraid for our survival. Such circumstances require us to do things that are very difficult, cause pain and hardship, go against our will, threaten our dignity, and give us no room to negotiate.

2. *Genuine scarcity*—We do not have enough safety, food, love, appreciation, or rest.

3. *Internalized oppression*—Our minds are filled with beliefs that oppress us and make us think we are bad, ugly, lazy, crazy, weak, stupid and/or worthless (not worthy of being alive). These beliefs trap us into thinking that we have fewer options and cause us to do things just to be safe or loved or to earn our place in society. Our internalized oppression reinforces shame.

4. *Health challenges*—When we suffer pain, discomfort or "disease" in our bodies, fear about the fitness of our bodies, and the resultant fear of suffering and death, we often feel drained and powerless.

5. *Excessive caregiving (rescue)*—We give up our time, health, and sanity for the sake of others, particularly those we love or with whom we share interdependent relationships. Depletion causes rescue, and rescue exacerbates depletion.

6. *Self-neglect*—Our self-care practices lose priority or are forgotten altogether.

7. *Alienation*—The murky combination of external and internal oppression produces a sense of separation from belonging and disconnection to community, nature, a higher power, or our own innate power.

REPLETION: Filled Up with Life Force

Symptoms: Sparkle in the eye, sense of well-being, optimism, generosity, energetic life force, inspiration, compassion, peace, calm, forgiveness, understanding, centeredness, health, connection to source, creativity, balanced appetite, ability to rest and relax

Causes:

1. *Power over our lives*—We feel empowered when our capacity to exert our will and influence over our life circumstances exists without fear of punishment or threats. We make plans and changes that are helpful and significant.

2. *Plenitude*—We have enough money, safety, love, appreciation, and status.

3. *Internal self-regard*—Our beliefs and thoughts nurture our sense of worth and purpose and decrease shame and blame. When we have a balanced and compassionate understanding of what it is to be human, our basic goodness and the flaws, mistakes, blind spots, bad moods, and bad days, we are internally self-loving and have a positive self-regard.

4. *Physical health*—We suffer very little pain or discomfort in our bodies and have a realistic acceptance and appreciation of our bodies' strengths and limits. We get enough sleep.

created more work for her. It turned out that after much negotiation and experimentation, the most replenishing option was for the wife to move into a different housing situation on the property. She lived separately from the family for a year—sharing meals, but having a retreat that allowed her to replenish, take care of herself, and listen to her own needs. In order to replenish, she had to stop rescuing around her standards for the household. She would try (and often fail) to get other people's cooperation, and the constant negotiation of chores exhausted her. She just needed a sanctuary completely under her own control.

This radical intervention, a "break" that actually worked by creating circumstances that met everyone's needs, is a hallmark of how and why Skills for Change works so beautifully. We don't listen to what the culture says about what works or what's needed—we ask people what they want and see if we can create solutions that meet everyone's needs. Neither husband nor wife wanted the marriage to end. They didn't want to fight anymore, either. They wanted

5. *Free of excessive caregiving (rescue)*—How we give to others feels good, and we find ways to share the work of caregiving so that no one does too much. We know our value is not dependent on how much we give.

6. *Replenishing self-care*—We engage in pleasurable activities, baths, walks, time with friends, loving touch, fun, listening to ourselves, creative pursuits, and physical exercise, and we enjoy nourishing food.

7. *Spiritual unity and serenity*—We experience a sense of belonging to life, where we are connected and significant, while also feeling the comfort of knowing how small we are in the scheme of things.

the opportunity for closeness and also spaciousness. Both of them wanted the wife to feel better. No one wanted to split up the family and ferry the children back and forth between households. Voilà—a solution presented itself. Live on the property, in different spaces. Let the common space be ruled by a more relaxed, family-friendly standard of cleanliness. Everyone gets most of what they want. When we are creating radical solutions, we must ignore the culture that says a break means the relationship is over. In fact, breaks work so often that I am amazed more people don't try them. The family survived the year intact, stronger, and more powerful due to their conviction that their needs could be met.

DEPLETION AND RESCUE

Scarcity is one of the great causes of the rescue dynamic. We don't have enough energy to negotiate an agreement—we may not even have enough energy to ask for 100% of what we want or to even investigate what that might be. So we rescue by unilaterally thinking through what would "fix" the problem and then implement it without discussing it with anyone else. We do more than our share of the work, and when our "fix" goes sour, we end up burned out in the victim state or angry and persecutory. We still may not have the energy to ask for 100% of what we want. So out of guilt, we rescue again, losing energy and going down the depletion scale. It's a vicious cycle. Sometimes it's helpful to claim the power of the victim state, let ourselves collapse, and stop doing things to save anyone else. If we know what we need to gain energy, and we do those things for ourselves, we are acting out 100% of what we want, even if we can't ask for it and negotiate to agreement. And sometimes, if we're so depleted that all we can do to make something better is rescue, we can at least be compassionate with ourselves for making that choice.

Sometimes there isn't a nonrescue option, and then it's best to choose the least troublesome rescue. We may need to fight the cultural message that tells us there's always a win-win solution. I've sat with clients who are facing too many win-lose and lose-lose options to think there is always a win-win. In those cases, we just have to choose the least depleting option. And sometimes, when we face a win-lose or a lose-lose choice, all we can do is learn to tolerate our discomfort at being the winner in a win-lose situation.

DON'T MESS WITH ZERO

When we've been depleted for a while, zero can feel exuberant. I call zero a neutral, fragile state. We're not good, but we're not bad. It can be tempting to jump into every hard problem as if we have superhero powers, when in fact, we're vulnerable and easily depleted. It's far wiser to keep making replenishment plans, invest in higher numbers, and leave chronic difficulties for later.

DEPLETION PAR NORMAL

In our puritanical, hardworking, pull-yourself-up-by-your-boot-straps culture, we often get rewarded for being the person who is most exhausted. We trade metaphoric war stories of challenging people and difficult circumstances to see who wins the "biggest vic-tim" badge of honor. In family and community cultures where there is a lot of scarcity, often the person with the most difficulties is the only one who gets any sympathy or help. No wonder we compete to be at the bottom!

We also need to fight other people's pig for us if we actually expe-rience full repletion. Our culture is highly suspicious and judgmental about people who are calm, relaxed, not in overwhelm, and able to make healthy decisions for themselves.

FRUSTRATION AND DEPLETION

Occasionally when I'm coaching, a client will seem very frustrated, as if nothing I say is helping. I used to redouble my efforts, try even harder, and make the situation worse, sometimes even losing the relationship with the client because I pushed too hard. With much earned experience, I now know that most of the time, when someone resists all my efforts to help, they are probably depleted. It's not that they don't want to make the shifts we've discussed in their contract, it's that they can't right now—they just don't have the energy. When we change the subject, redirecting the conversation away from tasks and goals, and we recognize and address their depletion, the whole tone of the coaching conversation changes. Our collective relief is palpable, and we are finally able to come up with a plan that sounds helpful and generates hope.

CHANGE THE RANGE

I often see people who operate in a depletion-repletion range from +2 down to −5. Perhaps in their family of origin it was actually dangerous to be too happy or energized. Their habit of regular depletion became entrenched and subconscious. If we never visit +5 or above, however, we don't know what's even possible from that level of repletion. And being replenished feels so good! Our depletion-repletion range is inherently changeable. What's the difference between a range of zero to +8 versus that lower range of −5 to +2? There's no difference in the value of replenishment versus depletion in our daily lives, but a huge difference in the quality of our experience when we operate at higher numbers. Someone who regularly hangs out at +8 is going to be able to face challenging tasks, recover quickly when difficulties surface, and experience satisfaction with her life. Such a positive lifestyle generates systemic repletion. Just like depletion begets depletion, repletion is self-replicating.

GOING FOR A +10

It is a radical exercise to design a life where we cultivate the confidence and joy of a +10 on the repletion scale. It's unusual in our culture for us to give ourselves permission to be ecstatically energized. If we can't achieve a +10, that number might as well be a million jillion quadrillion—in other words, an unachievable number. But that's not what the scale is designed to describe. The scale describes our best *entirely possible* life, right here on this planet. I often ask clients to take the challenge, imagine what their life would be like if they regularly hung out at a +10, and then we discuss what changes they might make. It's amazing how good our lives feel when we cultivate peace and plenitude on a daily basis.

Eighteen • Loss and Disappointment: The Healing Power of Grief

Julia Kelliher

As much as this book is about the ways to access more power, and hence have more control over our lives, we all eventually experience loss, disappointment, failures, illness, and death. Generally, few people accept these aspects of life. And, personally, I invest most of my time with clients helping them find solutions to problems and create a future that is personally satisfying. But one thing I've learned over and over again is that denying the existence of real suffering and loss doesn't prevent it from happening.

Siddhartha by Hermann Hesse was the first book I ever read that depersonalized suffering. The story follows Siddhartha, a prince in India who realized, despite his wealth and power, that he wasn't happy. He was going to suffer, become old and decrepit, and eventually die. He went searching for some answer to suffering, seeing his fundamental powerlessness over it. Instead, Siddhartha awakened to the inevitability of human suffering. He discovered that "accepting the unacceptable" could lead to personal freedom and equanimity, and hence less suffering.

DENYING LOSS

In the United States, we have learned to fear personal disappointment, failure, and grief. We have been taught that if we aren't happy, something is wrong, and we need to do something about it. Getting over loss and failure quickly, without many tears, so we can get on with productive work is a cultural anthem. "Just do it! Quit whining and get on with it." We have been taught that feeling bad is a waste of time, and we shouldn't feel angry or sad about global warming, the economy, or our personal frustrations if we can't do something to change them.

In short, as U.S. citizens, many of us have become alienated from our genuine experiences of loss and grief. Most of us have internalized the mandate of productivity and success not just in our minds in the form of unquestioned assumptions, but in the very structure of our bodies. We learn we should organize our bodily actions around the principles of direct action leading to successful results. When our actions work, it is wonderful. But if our strategies fail, we lose heart. We then begin to have bodies that reflect a great deal of personal disappointment, low self-esteem, and profound alienation. We long for, and feel powerless to connect with, our birthright of community and love.

The truth is that disappointment is just one inevitable consequence of knowing what we want, hoping to have it, and not actually getting it. We all want to look forward to something. We want to preserve something positive that is happening in the present moment and extend it in some way into the future. In fact, visioning and planning are essential tasks in creating a potential future we want. It is natural then that the more we invest of ourselves into a future dream, the greater the potential for both joy and disappointment.

In our cultural sphere, we generally misunderstand the concept of acceptance. We have been taught that acceptance means we have to give up control. When something unacceptable happens to us, we believe that either we've done something wrong or someone else has done something wrong. We personalize the larger forces of life. When we are faced with disappointment and loss, we can actually take back some power when we start to accept a certain degree of powerlessness.

ACCEPT THE UNACCEPTABLE

The unacceptable truths we face—grief, loss, pain, chronic illness, death—all of these are normal, human conditions of living. They happen to all of us, at one point or another, and we have our reactions to them when they happen. In *On Death and Dying*, Elisabeth Kübler-Ross details the stages of grief and talks about how we may go through many cycles of sadness, denial, bargaining, acceptance, and back again, as we begin to deal with the difficult changes in our lives. I call this work "accepting the unacceptable." We do not have to candy-coat our experience as a "good lesson" or add suffering to our experience by fighting against what is happening. Our internalized oppressive judgments about how we "should" respond become additional, unnecessary burdens we need to address as we begin to heal the wounds of loss. By accepting the unacceptable, we stop struggling with the conditions we are facing. The extraordinary thing is that when we soften our bodies and allow the grief to flow through us, often we begin to see the small things we *can* do to help ourselves process the changes and accept our new reality. Our act of acceptance opens opportunities for changes we can make that ease our path forward. It is the very release of control that allows us to perceive new possibilities.

In the context of love relationships, most of us are passionate about our desires and powerfully attached to getting what we want. We fight for control most ardently. We want to be loved. We want our lovers to act toward us in specific ways. We want appreciation. We want our partners to do the dishes, pay the bills, and still be ready to make love when we are feeling sexual. We want what we want when we want it. Conflict in this domain often brings couples to my office seeking help, and acceptance and patience can be hard to develop.

Breakups between lovers are like little deaths. Bonnie Raitt mournfully sings, "I can't make you love me if you don't. You can't make your heart feel something it won't." My son Jared experienced deep heartbreak in his midtwenties. He thought he had found his life companion, and mother of his potential children, only to have been left by her. I watched him grieve in such a physically emotional way, unable to sleep, eat, or plan a future. My son became a wanderer for a while, giving up his home, putting his possessions in storage, allowing himself to open the closet of his unwept tears. Luckily, he had lots of support and love around him. Instead of feeling alienated and isolated, trapped by internalized individualism, personalizing the abandonment and feeling defective as a human being, he became empowered by shared pain and losses and felt empathy for other people's pain. He realized he wasn't just grieving the loss of a lover and partner; he was grieving many losses over the course of his lifetime, emptying out much of the stored pain he had experienced from childhood to the present moment. I was amazed, watching him do something instinctively that it had taken me years to learn.

The art of accepting the unacceptable is extremely challenging. We naturally fight against losing control of that which makes us feel happy or safe. The power of grief has nothing to do with controlling our environment and everything to do with allowing natural healing processes to kick in. The body knows how to heal when we use our personal power to go along with it, like drinking extra fluids and going to bed when we have the flu. Acceptance of loss is the beginning of grieving and the body's natural way of healing. We can't move on, or create a new dream, until we grieve the loss.

Sometimes with clients, I will recommend they get *The Grief Recovery Handbook* and work through the exercises.[1] When we are alienated from the healing power of grief, we often assign blame for our loss and can get stuck in anger and shame. When we internalize the idea that we are responsible for our grief and loss, we are holding ourselves accountable for something over which we have no power. When we forgive ourselves, we can move on. The acceptance of our circumstances is freeing. Accepting disappointment as a natural part of life can help us flow with the process of grief, reach out for support and empathy, feel connected to life, and see the world fresh again.

Nineteen • The Spacious Adult: Equanimity and Compassion

Julia Carol

The tools in Skills for Change that we've described so far are indeed life-changing, powerful tools. And yet, none of them promises us a life completely devoid of suffering.

Our dog throws up on our new rug, our partner is laid off from work, the car needs new brakes that we can't afford, our daughter is getting bullied at school, a family member has cancer, we have student loans hanging over our heads, we are trying to recover from an affair in our marriage, or we just spilled coffee all over our new interview suit. These and many other problems that are more and less tragic are happening all of the time to everyone on the planet. We have real needs and wants, and while some of them are being met, many are not. As my husband once said to me, "Life is great; life sucks."

When I was first introduced to the concept of the fair witness, equanimity, or nonreactivity, it sounded dry, neutral, and quite frankly, boring. I had no desire to practice nonattachment from my desires and passions. The encouragement to accept suffering as a part of life runs contrary to my essential nature both as a pleasure-seeking hedonist and as an advocate for empowerment and social justice. And the invitation to avoid "taking things personally" seemed like trite nonsense. How could I not take things personally when they were, in fact, happening to me?

I've learned, however, that taking things personally can blind me and limit my choices, whereas cultivating the spacious adult consciousness offers me the ability to see myself from the outside as a part of the whole experience rather than seeing myself as separate and central. Equanimity takes nonduality a few steps further. I see all of the complexity of a given situation, free myself from accepting my story as "the truth," and add compassion in order to accept that, in this moment, this is the way it is. Compassion also helps me open my heart and feel empathy and understanding for the difficulties that I and others experience.

There are many ways to develop spaciousness and the adult observer consciousness. I personally found value in spending time in the present moment, as a way to cleanse my mind, get emotional distance from my thoughts, and become recentered in my body. In 1987, I began a daily meditation practice, only to experience a time-out from my busy mind. I am still benefiting from this practice. (I call it a daily practice, but that doesn't mean I am perfect about meditating daily.) During meditation, my mind is often filled with a beehive of thoughts and feelings about the past and the future, and I count myself lucky to remain completely in the present for brief moments. However, in the last ten years, I've touched more and deeper moments of pleasure and pure love, arising out of surrender and allowing that this is the way things are right now.

When I can embrace all of this moment and say, "Yes, this is how it is," I am free and joyful. Many times the present moment includes my critical thoughts, my agendas, my fears and anxieties, and my pig stories—they also arise in this moment. I am in my adult fair witness when I am able to become the one who is observing my thoughts, sensations, and stories, but not *be* them. When I surround my thoughts and emotions with compassion and kindness and keep bringing my attention to whatever arises in this moment and accepting that too—and that too... and yes, there's some of that—it's pretty spacious.

Once I experienced this peaceful allowing of the way things are during meditation, I was able to begin to incorporate more adult spaciousness into my interactions daily—not always, but more and more often. Julia Kelliher refers to this as "accepting the unacceptable," and she has been superb at reminding me when I forget.

My life might change drastically because of what others have said or done. But it doesn't mean they did what they did on purpose or that their actions were aimed at me at all. When I experience the adult observer, my reactivity is no longer the center of the action. I can choose to respond thoughtfully and with compassion, rather than react from a place of defensive hurt feelings and pride. I am outside of the dualistic good/bad, right/wrong world of absolutes. When I'm feeling equanimity, my internalized judgments and stories fade away. That's real freedom!

We have all experienced a spacious, neutral fair witness at one time or another; we just may not have named it. For example, when we notice we're too cold, we may not like the feeling. And yet, most of the time we don't wallow in the unfairness of the cold (unless it falls in a typically hot month), nor do we believe that it's cold due to nature's hostility directed toward us. The cold isn't right or wrong; it's just cold. It might be quite unpleasant, and we may want to change it, but first, we observe we're cold.

When we cultivate a sense of spaciousness, we become able to avoid much of the suffering caused by making up painful stories about the observable facts. While we're not typically tempted to take it personally when we feel cold, it's often difficult not to take it personally when we interact with other people. And I don't just mean in our relationships. Anything human-made can trigger me to take things personally: like the computerized voice that tells me the importance of my call while I'm holding too long to talk to the phone company, or when I can't find the starting place to grab the plastic wrap on the roll. "The people designing these things are not respecting me. They're idiots who are wasting my precious time!"

Of course, we live in a culture that teaches us to take things personally. Many of us have spent our lives not knowing the difference between observable facts and the meaning we give them. When we are able to separate observable fact from our stories and stop either resisting or grasping the reality of this moment, that's when we need

Buddhism and Skills for Change

JULIA CAROL

Rather than getting depressed and demoralized by life's struggles, Skills for Change teaches us to embrace and employ tools from Buddhist teachings to help us through. I see a delicious alchemy in the blending of Radical Therapy and equanimity, which is part of what makes Skills for Change as powerful a model as it is. I knew about equanimity before I found Skills for Change. I found it much more difficult to take the feelings of nonresistance into my daily life before I had the tools in Skills for Change.

Buddhists use the tools of awareness and compassion for accepting or allowing the way things are. When we understand that a large part of the "way things are" is caused by the social and political systems we're all a part of, and the ways that we have internalized privilege, power, and oppression, then it's much easier to depersonalize our experiences and find equanimity. I love listening to some of the Buddhist teachers in United States, like Pema Chödrön and Tara Brach, and I also find myself wanting to reach our compassionate adult observer. We take a breath and say, "There, there, these feelings and thoughts are all part of being human." A palpable relaxing of the body often follows, and life feels much more pleasant.

And yes, there is much in this world that is really difficult to accept. I still feel heartbroken when I read about war, learn of another rape, or see films showing polar bears drowning because of climate change. I still have strong agendas; I still desire things, I'm still advocating for peace and social justice, and I'm still a hedonistic rebel. And I don't think it's possible to be equanimous and perfectly compassionate at all times. I use meditation to strengthen my adult observer muscles, and I use compassion to regain my inner balance

out to their audience and add the sociopolitical analysis to their equation. The exploration of "what's happening now" is incomplete without the awareness that it's not happening in a vacuum. Our personal troubles are inseparable from the larger context of a culture that may be invisible to us but that is a powerful and often oppressive influence over our sense of well-being.

The tools shared in previous chapters are all a part of becoming aware of how we fit into the larger ocean we're swimming in. Seeing the political as personal, naming the pig messages that plague us, understanding how we react when we get caught in the rescue dynamic, finding our inner adult, acknowledging power and powerlessness, seeing cultural privilege, naming oppression, and separating our stories from observable facts are deeper ways of following the Buddhist practices of inquiry and acceptance of the present moment. For me, this is really big and extremely powerful. I am convinced that not only does Buddhism enhance Skills for Change, but that Skills for Change tools offer key ingredients and add necessary color and depth to Buddhism as it's being taught in Western culture today.

and find that place of peaceful, spacious acceptance. And I am now able to give much less power to the thoughts that things "should not be the way they are." I may want life to be different, and reality may be unpleasant or even heartbreaking and tragic, yet I can allow it to be how it is right in this moment and then strive to make changes in the way it will be in the future.

Twenty • Appreciations

Julia Carol

We humans have long used the method of counting our blessings as a balm to help us cope with daily stress and suffering. I remember taking workshops in the 1970s, where I learned the daily practice of writing my forgiveness, affirmations, and gratitude. In the '90s, Oprah encouraged everyone to keep a gratitude journal and pay attention to what we're grateful for every day. Recently, scientific studies by University of California at San Diego professor Robert Emmons and others validate the concept that feelings of gratitude and appreciation measurably improve mental health.[1] The United States holiday Thanksgiving may have been created after a deadly season in the Plymouth colony; however, it didn't become a national holiday until the Civil War, when Lincoln declared it one. And it was elevated in importance and assigned to the fourth Thursday in November during the height of the Great Depression. It's not hard to imagine why Thanksgiving was highlighted during those periods in our history—people were suffering and needed a lift.

The gratefulness movement itself breaks the mainstream puritanical restriction of appreciations. When we pay attention and focus on gratefulness, we produce change on an individual level; we shift our attitude about our lives. As we give and receive appreciations, we support those around us and strengthen our community.

Claude Steiner, one of the original Radical Therapists, noticed his clients' feelings of self-loathing, isolation, competition, and scarcity. He identified how U.S. belief systems promoted cultural taboos around the giving and receiving of appreciations. He dubbed these taboos the "stroke economy."[2] The rules of the stroke economy create a scarcity of love and affection. We internalize these rules as unspoken injunctions:

- Don't give appreciations.

- Don't ask for appreciations we want or need.

- Don't accept appreciations when they are given. We may even deflect the appreciation by disbelieving the appreciation or verbally diminishing the appreciation or the appreciation giver.

- Don't decline unwelcome appreciations.

- Don't give ourselves appreciations.

My clients nod in recognition as soon as I name our inherited internal taboos against appreciations. Not only is this prohibition against giving or receiving appreciations in our heads, it's also in our bodies. Being on either end of an appreciation can generate physical discomfort. We can either feel too tongue-tied to speak the praise we feel for another person, or overwhelmed when someone heaps too many compliments on us. Those physical prohibitions against giving and receiving appreciations come from our internalized oppression and the pig messages that tell us to be quiet and take up less space.

On the other hand, when we're not appreciated, we may feel invisible and isolated. There were many days when I would have felt better if I could have said, "Hey, I want to appreciate myself for the way I just kept my cool when that guy stole my parking space!"

It's possible to fight against the stroke economy in part because it is a *false* economy. In reality, appreciations are abundant and free. When we are in appreciation scarcity, we are more inclined to see ourselves as isolated, disconnected from our community, and disempowered. When we are appreciated and seen, we feel powerful, and if we are powerful, we are able to disagree with our internalized cultural beliefs and work with others to affect change. The presence of appreciations can help us feel included, valued, engaged, committed, connected, and empowered.

When we give and receive appreciations, we gain many benefits. Stated positively, we fight the scarcity of the stroke economy by adopting new injunctions:

- Give appreciations whenever possible.

- Accept appreciations. Listen to what people say, be willing to take their words seriously, and offer thanks.

- Ask for appreciations when we're in a cooperative environment. Be specific in our requests.

- Decline appreciations we don't want. Perhaps even share why, so that our listeners understand our reasons.

- Give ourselves appreciations in the company of supportive peers.

APPRECIATIONS AS UNITS OF POWER IN GROUPS

Whether a group is made up of family, work colleagues, friends, neighbors, or others, there is an inherent power dynamic to a group, and it gets ever more complicated as the group size increases. Even when we aren't consciously aware of structural, positional, or contractual power, we feel its presence in our bodies. We might ask ourselves, "Am I being seen and heard, and do I matter?" How involved are we in the decision making about the conversation topic, temperature of the room, lighting, formation of chairs, noise, and the rules of engagement? We scan the environment to determine our relative level of safety and comfort, and small changes in our emotions, sensations, and mood might be clues to disruptions in the power dynamic. Our internalized judgments may tell us these are little, unimportant details, but it's natural for us to care about those details: the person designing the details holds a lot of power in the room.

Our ability to skillfully give, receive, ask for, give to ourselves, or decline appreciations while we're in a group can go a long way to easing our discomfort and building our personal power. While it's true that the scarcity of appreciations is a false one, challenging the stroke economy is not easy—it often takes a strong sense of courage and trust in the group. We have to fight our internalized judgments, be willing to surprise others, perhaps trigger an uncomfortable physical reaction in ourselves or other people, and generally confront our social anxiety about what others will think or do. Others who are aware and cooperating toward the same goal make the whole process not just easier, but possible.

I remember back to my first group with Julia Kelliher—I felt awkward and uncomfortable in my body whenever it came time for sharing appreciations. I dislike being told what to do or how to feel, so I initially chalked up my discomfort to an inner rebellion against being told it was time to feel appreciative. Looking back on it, I now believe I was experiencing my internalized oppression around the stroke economy. I was afraid to give or receive appreciations. If I gave an appreciation, would it be valued? Would I be judged if my appreciations weren't insightful enough? Would someone feel left out if I didn't give an appreciation to everyone? What if no one had anything appreciative to say about me, or if it was the same appreciation I was used to getting, or what if I read a backhanded insult into their words? What if there was someone who was getting so much appreciation that I felt competitive?

My body reacted by raising my blood pressure and pushing sweat out of my forehead. All of my stress responses to being in a space where appreciations are being shared are normal reactions to the power inherent in appreciations, given or withheld. As I see more clearly the false scarcity in the stroke economy, I've embraced the liberating aspect of appreciations. The exchange of appreciations increases connection and community, produces a new collective culture with a shared and authentic truth, and energizes people, so they are inspired to make changes in their lives and the world.

Appreciations help different kinds of people in different ways. It helps equalize the power by highlighting someone's otherwise unrecognized contribution. For example, think how empowering it feels for the quiet, shy person to receive an appreciation, voiced to the whole group, about how her presence is important because she holds the space with her compassionate body language or shares great eye contact and has a reassuring smile. For the person who has less experience with whatever the group is gathering about, an appreciation for his courage in trying new things or thanks for his fresh view of the group's project, can make him aware of his value and feel more comfortable.

As a Skills for Change practitioner, I've committed myself to helping the underdog in situations where I notice a hierarchical or unjust power dynamic. When I'm in a group situation, I might notice someone who seems to be feeling one down in power, and I will try to find an authentic appreciation that I imagine would be empowering—then go and give it to her and pay attention to how her energy shifts. She might drink it up and look more energized, or she may get uncomfortable, or she may have both reactions at the same time. I find that searching for and sharing an appreciation with someone helps me stay connected with the group and also often changes the experience of the other person, sometimes with amazing results. It's worth the effort!

APPRECIATIONS AS UNITS OF POWER IN ONE-TO-ONE RELATIONSHIPS

A member of my extended family, I'll call her Kora, is an unusual person. At age fifty-four, she hasn't found a way to bring in enough income to completely support herself. She works part time in a personal service industry. She often loses the checks people use to pay her and gets flustered by ATMs, paperwork, and large institutions.

She came over once and was in the midst of a painful pig attack about money. "I'm no damn good with money. I deserve to be shot." "Dear Kora," I said, "while it may be true that you could use some more skills and luck in earning money and in dealing with financial institutions, I have to disagree with you—there are ways in which you are extremely good with money, better than I am, even better than most people I know!" She looked at me, tears streaming down her face, in pure astonishment. I continued, "You have a knack for living on next to nothing and making a very comfortable life for yourself; you know where to buy the best clothes on consignment, how to hold the most successful yard sale, and how to pick up the best bargains at others' yard sales! Why, look at your house! Your furniture is as lovely as can be and cost you a fraction of what mine cost me! Maybe we can help one another?" She perked up, and since then she's seen herself in a different way. She not only felt better, but stopped losing checks. Her internalized oppressive voices quieted, and it turned out that her pig was the thing that was in the way of managing the money she earns. Not everyone's pig gets fought so easily, but I doubt anyone else had ever tried to reframe Kora's self-image with an appreciation based in specific, observable facts before.

The analogy I use with the couples I coach is that if their relationship were a garden, resentments are the destructive pests, and appreciations the fertilizer. I encourage folks to weave the giving and receiving of appreciations into their daily lives. The receivers of the appreciations get to know that they are seen and heard and that they matter. The givers of the appreciations get a reminder of what they value in their partners, instead of focusing on what they want to change. The giving and receiving of appreciations rebalances the power, sets the stage for hearing each other's wants and needs, and redirects couples out of the rescue dynamic and toward cooperative relationship.

Conversely, a lack of appreciation can cause resentment. I coached one couple where the wife often complained that her husband didn't do his share of the domestic chores (a common complaint, I might add). However, one day she shared how disappointed she was to come home to find him cooking a prime rib in the oven the way she'd cook a pot roast. She was appalled that he ruined such a good piece of meat and let him know it immediately, with her words and body language. I reminded her that the last time we met, she encouraged him to try to make dinner once in a while. He was trying! If all he heard was criticism, he might not try to cook again. When we can remember to do so, it is powerful to give an appreciation of someone's intentions and to ask permission to give feedback, *before* we offer a correction. The shift of our attention from correction to appreciation can go a long way to having someone hear us and want to please us.

When power is unequal, we need to give appreciations with caution. Our attention and choice to speak is powerful, and when we speak, our structural and positional power comes with us. It's important to consider how an appreciation might be received. I still remember being the only woman in a room of twenty-three men at an important meeting of leaders in my days working in public health. I was executive director of an advocacy group, while the others at the meeting were mostly PhDs and lawyers. With the exception of one African American man, we were all white. At a bathroom break, one of the more powerful men in the room came up to me, smiling, and said, "Julia! You were *so* articulate in there!" I imagine he thought he was bestowing a great compliment. He probably didn't realize that I imagined he was surprised a woman, an activist no less, without an advanced degree, could be articulate and that I thought he was revealing his expectation that I would be less articulate than the others. At the next meeting, I approached him at a break and gave him the same compliment he had given me. His response was surprise and confusion, which validated my story that his original appreciation was patronizing. If his original compliment had been genuine, I should have been able to give it back to him and have him receive it with pleasure. Even when they are not patronizing, appreciations can trigger judgments in the receiver. We may not know what the other person's experiences are—what internalized judgments they have for themselves—or how deeply they have internalized scarcity in the stroke economy.

TYPES OF APPRECIATIONS

The type of appreciation we give impacts the way it is received by the listener. There is a big difference between a general good/bad, right/ wrong, dualistic appreciation and one that comes from our nonjudging observer. Appreciations grounded in particulars can't be refuted in the same way as nurturing generalities. This is a significant point: just like clearing a held feeling and story in the cooperative communication model, the more specific we are with our appreciations, the greater their impact. Appreciations are our positive stories about people; they represent our feelings and opinions, not facts. For example, if after I observe a friend dancing, I say, "You are such a good dancer," it makes a different impact than if I say, "I love how fluidly you dance. You move so gracefully through the crowd." When we speak in generalizations, we also risk sounding as if we are designating ourselves as an expert, thus going one up in power. If I say, "I so enjoyed watching you dance. It made me really happy," I am naming only my personal experience. Appreciations given with specifics and "I" statements are the most impactful and tend to be less triggering of other people's pig.

As we play with how the power of appreciations works in our lives, we begin to notice "for the sake of what" we are giving our appreciations. If we are giving an appreciation to help someone stop diminishing herself, the details we share will help the person fight her pig, as my appreciation for Kora's financial power helped her. If we are trying to liberate ourselves from the false scarcity of the stroke economy by expressing the joy others' contributions have given us, we frame our appreciation in terms of how the other people impact our lives.

APPRECIATIONS AS HIDDEN REQUESTS

Sometimes an appreciation has a request motivating it. I recently hosted a guest in our home who found us through a vacation rental website. My guest was a woman of about the same age as I am, and she clearly enjoyed her visit. She gave me appreciations for the art in my home, for the décor, the view, the bird feeders, and for what a gracious, warm hostess I am. I received the first few appreciations with pleasure, as it meant a lot to me to get a good grade in the completion of our rental contract. However, after five or six led to a dozen or more, I began to imagine that her gushing was a request for friendship outside of our contract. Indeed, she soon followed up with an offer that I stay in her home sometime at no charge and that she would be happy to show me around her town. Here the power dynamic was tricky; I was a bit one down in the transaction since I wanted her positive feedback of my guest room on the rental website and did not want to risk offending her with an outright rejection of her overtures. In this example, if she had given me only several compliments, gone home and written a positive review, and then later asked if I was open for friendship with her, I would have felt more comfortable. As it is, I found a way to gently redirect the conversation. I let her comments about my visiting her go unanswered, and before she left, I gave her several warm appreciations about what a great guest she was and that I'd be happy to recommend her to other vacation rental hosts. Our transactional power affects how and when we give and receive appreciations and can increase the success of our offers, requests, and declines.

I've also had experiences where I was gushing about someone and felt them stiffen. Different cultures have different etiquette and interpersonal standards for giving and receiving appreciations. Sometimes people are tired of hearing appreciations for the same thing over and over and feel hurt by what has gone unappreciated. Attractive people want to be seen for more than their looks; smart people want to know they're more than their brains. People might refuse an appreciation if it corresponds to a box they've been put in too many times. Sometimes it's not people's internalized cultural judgments causing them to refuse the appreciation, but their own ability to contend with the stroke economy's admonition against refusing strokes.

THE PAYOFF OF APPRECIATIONS

Don't lose heart—while the underlying power dynamics of appreciations can be complicated, the test for a successful appreciation is how it makes us feel. If we feel satisfied and connected, great job! If we feel confused or disconnected, lost or irritated, we see if we can identify the power in the transaction and try again. In contrast with the disease of stress in our culture, appreciations relieve our minds and ease tension in our bodies. Imagine all the good feelings, hope, energy, and empowerment that go with a world abundant with appreciations. We learn to see ourselves as our friends see us, through the eyes of love, rather than the eyes of "just fix one more thing, and then you'll be okay." More self-love, more love for others, more appreciation, more compassion—that sounds like a world worth creating. We're helping to change the culture as we practice, and if enough of us do the work to embody these types of changes, we'll change our world while we're at it.

In Closing

Julia Carol

This book would never have made it to fruition had it not been for the authors' level of mastery of the very tools we're writing about and our commitment to using them. The complexity of group writing is several orders of magnitude greater than that of a single author. The original vision of the book changed over time, and the goal that members of a group hold a shared vision at any one time, though laudable, is all but impossible. As the writing process took us seven years, it was critical that we each maintain our own "for the sake of what." We had fits and starts, hurt feelings and brilliant insights, our hearts and minds opening and closing, and yet we persisted.

Indeed, we relied on each of the skills and tools and our understanding of the theory in Skills for Change in order to finish writing this book:

- We rescued, felt victimized, and persecuted.

- We cleared our held stories and feelings and negotiated to get out of rescue.

- We acknowledged, even when painful, the power and privilege differences among us.

- We tried with loving hearts to be both pragmatic and compassionate, to remember our equality as human beings while working with each of our strengths and weaknesses and differing skills and styles.

- We fought our internalized judgments valiantly, and with deep determination, until we recentered ourselves in embodied love.

- We advocated for our own perspective and preferences, and we negotiated until we came to agreement.

Through it all, I know we strengthened our shared belief that Skills for Change is an effective and important modality for helping people lessen their suffering and for increasing love, connection, and joy. Each of us has experienced huge benefits by applying the tools in this book to our own lives.

Our appreciation for the work we do in our own lives, and our commitment to empowering others, is what kept us going.

We hope that what we've shared here helps us all understand how we're not crazy, there's nothing wrong with us, we're not alone in experiencing our lives the way we do, and we're not responsible, all on our own, for how things are.

We are not at fault for blaming ourselves and holding ourselves to excessively high standards. Cultural values are strong, but they do not change some fundamental values that are intrinsic to us as human beings. Regardless of what the culture says, some parts of human nature will remain. For example, it's really healthy to want to take care of ourselves. It's healthy and normal to want love, connection, relative physical safety, food, shelter, and some control over how we spend our time and who we spend it with.

The particular dramas, disappointments, heartbreaks, losses, and fears that we experience are different, but the human condition is the human condition. We use the tools in *Access to Power* to communicate more clearly, uncover and empower our more authentic selves, escape and avoid as many rescues as possible, feel less isolation and mystification, and in general, be happier. We value our intuition, listen to our bodies' wisdom, and embrace the practice of not buying all of our thoughts, or our "stories," as true.

Understanding these concepts goes against the cultural grain, so it often takes time for the concepts to become clear. That's okay. That's normal. And once they are applied, progress is often made with baby steps, leading to more progress, with a few setbacks (sometimes large setbacks), and then more progress; that's how most of us learn new behaviors. We did not write this book so others could use it as a sledgehammer to beat themselves up.

I haven't yet met the person who is able to embody and practice all of these concepts all of the time. Recently, I phoned Julia Kelliher and told her I really wanted a time in my life where I wasn't in trouble with some percentage of the people in my life. "Is that possible?" I asked her? "Sure!" she said with false glee. "Just go back to rescuing, and they'll all love you again!" We both laughed, and I reminded myself, yet again, that I'd rather have people mad at me than go back to my old habit of rescuing. This story shows how even a veteran forgets how things work when caught in the turmoil of her own life. It also shows we can make a choice, once we understand some of the basic dynamics. And although we laughed, I do give myself permission to go back to rescuing, if I decide that I'd rather rescue than have people mad at me. I've made that choice before, and I may make it again. The difference is that my understanding of power dynamics means it's a choice; I understand the consequences of rescuing or not rescuing, so I'm not as frustrated.

Skills for Change tools don't make us perfect and don't make our lives perfect. When we apply the tools to our lives, they empower us to experience less mystification and act with more choice. Our relationships are not harmonious at all times. The skills in this book help us find true harmony more often. *Skills for Change* tools don't keep

In Conclusion, a Summary

MARYBETH PAUL

People who apply Skills for Change to their lives endeavor to do the following:

- Learn to define where in our lives we have power by engaging an objective, sound voice of reason via our internal adult.

- Discover a simple method of measuring energy levels to avoid burnout and communication breakdowns, capitalizing on times when our energy is positively abundant.

- Examine cultural beliefs that lead to confusion. Examples include the cultural beliefs that say, "If you get a degree, you'll find a great job," and "If you work hard, you'll get ahead."

- Identify ways to get out of isolation and commune with those who support social justice and personal growth.

- Understand how we internalize oppressive beliefs and then learn to shift from negative and judgmental to more life-affirming stories.

- Clarify our own set of personal values, and decide where we need to shift our habits to reflect our values, rather than the cultural beliefs we've internalized.

- Embrace the complexity of life. Replace right/wrong and good/bad thought patterns with the notion that there are almost certainly multiple competing truths.

- Ask for 100% of what we want and negotiate to agreement instead of unilaterally rescuing to "fix" a problem.

- Become skilled in distinguishing between the objective facts of a transaction, our feelings, and our story about what happened.

us from being angry or having conflict or using power plays or having power plays used on us. They help us recognize what's really happening and why it might be happening, and they help us know what our realistic options are. They also help us find compassion for ourselves and others in our lives. Ultimately, awareness and compassion help us make real change in our lives, and that is no small thing. We are able to see ourselves more clearly, what we can and cannot change by ourselves, and what we can do something about, even if all we can do is just be a little nicer to ourselves about it.

All of us who contributed to this book have better lives because we use these tools. Our sincerest hope is that our collective work to change our lives will create positive change in our shared experience of possibility, culture, and community.

Notes

Acknowledgments

1. From Robert Hall's poem "I Work in the Fields All Day."

2. Beth Roy and Claude Steiner, eds., *Radical Psychiatry: The Second Decade* (Berkeley, CA: Radical Psychiatry Collective, 1994). This book is typically printed with a red cover; thus, we fondly nicknamed it the "Red Book." There is no connection between the nickname and either Carl Jung's journals or any Communist Party documents.

Preface

1. Theodore Roszak was one of the originators of the term "Deep Ecology." I became its passionate student in a college philosophy course called *Rationality, Mysticism, and Ecology*, which was taught by George Sessions. Feminist teachers and leaders—Joanna Macy, Starhawk, and Terry Tempest Williams, to name a few—taught me the consequences of patriarchy and our separation from the feminine, deepening further my understanding of how our civilization and its belief structure affect our entire politics and experience of the world.

Chapter 1: Of Course

1. Coleman Banks, *The Essential Rumi* (New York: HarperCollins, 2010).

2. Nietzsche also wrote, "There are no facts, only interpretations." Walter Kaufmann, ed. and trans., *The Portable Nietzsche* (New York: Penguin, 1954).

3. The person who controls physical space is at the top of the power hierarchy in any given group. This type of control may seem subtle, but when a group cooperates, listens, and tries to meet everyone's needs, sometimes direct conflicts emerge, and novel solutions must be discovered. We can tell we're in a Skills for Change group when we're invited and welcome to ask for 100% of what we want and when our requests are honored and addressed with respect and concern for our comfort.

Chapter 2: Power

1. "Cultural Anthropology/Social Stratification, Power and Conflict," *Wikibooks*, last modified November 18, 2013, http://en.wikibooks.org/wiki/Cultural_Anthropology/Social_Stratification,_Power_and_Conflict.

2. "Power (Social and Political)," *Wikipedia*, last modified April 14, 2014, http://en.wikipedia.org/wiki/Power_%28social_and_political%29.

3. Beth Roy, "Power, Culture, Conflict," in *Re-Centering*, ed. Mary Adams Trujillo et al. (Syracuse University Press, 2008).

4. Eric Berne, *Games People Play* (New York: Random House, 1996); Roy and Steiner, *Radical Psychiatry* (see acknowledgment, note 2).

5. Some mothers have children later in life and maintain some structural and economic power through their affiliation with work. Nonetheless, the job of nurturing children is still unpaid work that requires enormous amounts of time without financial reward.

6. While the division of labor between motherhood and provision for economic needs is still common, particularly in privileged families, many women find themselves working as both economic provider and nurturer. Historically, the privilege of mothers who stay at home with children has been held only by the middle and upper classes.

Chapter 3: Oppression, Alienation, and Empowerment: Loss and Recovery of Power

1. Roy and Steiner, *Radical Psychiatry* (see ack., n. 2).

2. In his classic book *Politics of Experience* (New York: Pantheon, 1967), R. D. Laing described what he calls "normal alienation from experience": "As adults

we have forgotten most of our childhood, not only its contents but its flavor. . . . we retain just sufficient proprioceptive sensations to coordinate our movements and to ensure the minimal requirements for biosocial survival. . . . [our genuine experience is so] shrouded in veils of *mystification* that an intensive discipline of unlearning is necessary for *anyone* before one can begin to experience the world afresh, with innocence, truth, and love" (my italics).

3. In *41 Shots . . . and Counting* (Syracuse University Press, 2009), Beth Roy presents an incisive analysis of the racialization of our legal system. This drug law bias has resulted in the enormous overincarceration of young people of color, changing the face of our culture, law enforcement practices, and future economic opportunity. People with felony convictions carry oppressive injunctions against their future job opportunities, access to resources, ability to vote, and success in everyday transactions. It's dangerous to fight internalized oppression in an environment where one faces external, punishing, oppressive circumstances on a daily basis.

4. Martin Luther King Jr., "Where Do We Go from Here?" Annual Report delivered at the 11th Convention of the Southern Christian Leadership Conference, Atlanta, GA, August 16, 1967.

Chapter 4: Culture Inside and Out

1. My Spanish and French ancestors probably left both countries to escape oppression. They came to the North American continent, and they were part of an immigration wave that committed genocide and oppressed indigenous peoples (while also occasionally loving and marrying them—my great-grandfather was probably half-Navajo). And when the U.S. government annexed New Mexico as a state, my ancestors were oppressed as Spanish speakers with Spanish surnames but still had the privilege of their European ancestry and white skin color. Colonialism, genocide, oppression, privilege, slavery—these atrocities are woven into the fabric of U.S. history, and they shape us, our economics, relationship with the land, and most of all, our ideas and actions toward each other on a day-to-day basis. May we learn to honor each other's history, have sensitivity and care for each other's pain, and listen to each other's stories with open hearts. When I fight for your rights and you fight for mine, we will know greater peace.

2. I use the word *nullify* here because sometimes when I work with immigrants or people whose family of origin has rejected them, I see what seems to be a

vacuum of values that gets created when their original culture and the new culture clash. People seem lost until they form their own culture and choose a new value system.

3. Trujillo, *Re-Centering* (see chap. 2, n. 3).

Chapter 5: The Parent-Adult-Child Model: Understanding How Human Beings Work

1. The term *safety reflex* was coined by Marybeth Paul in the writing of this book.

2. P. D. MacLane, *The Triune Brain* (New York: Springer, 1990).

3. Berne, *Games* (see chap. 2, n. 4).

4. Many books and workshops focus on reconnecting people with their "inner child"; while such work owes its origins to Eric Berne's formulation of ego states, I find that the absence of focus on the adult ego state lends to an elevation of "young" and "playful" behaviors. Perhaps such a process offers an important recovery of one's aliveness. And our connection with our child ego state is just one stage in an evolution that ultimately and hopefully results in the development of a healthy whole self: adult-guided, child-centric.

5. Augusto Boal, *Theatre of the Oppressed* (New York: Theater Communications Group, 1985).

6. Roy and Steiner, *Radical Psychiatry* (see ack., n. 2).

7. Georg Wilhelm Friedrich Hegel, *The Science of Logic* (Cambridge UP, 2010).

Chapter 6: Pig Parent: How We Internalize Oppressive Beliefs

1. From Molly Fisk's Skills for Change Demonstration, Nevada City, CA, January 24, 2014.

2. *Oppression* is defined as "unjust, cruel . . . or excessive exercise of authority or power" and as "a sense of being weighed down in body or mind." *Merriam-Webster OnLine*, s.v. "oppression," accessed February 1, 2009, http://www.merriam-webster.com/dictionary/oppression.

3. *Merriam-Webster OnLine Dictionary*, s.v." shame," accessed January 6, 2009, http://www.merriam-webster.com/dictionary/shame.

4. Roy and Steiner, *Radical Psychiatry* (see ack., n. 2).

5. Alternatives to the jargon word *pig* include *inner critic, voices of judgment, bully, thief, pusher/driver,* and others. What I've found is that the loss of the political language invoked by a reference to the police-nature of the pig can lead us to forget that these internal voices are not an essential part of us. Pig messages are learned and can be unlearned.

6. Roy and Steiner, *Radical Psychiatry* (see ack., n. 2).

7. Claude Steele subsequently wrote a wonderful book called *Whistling Vivaldi* (New York: Norton, 2010) about the stereotype threat experiments and remedies. Most pig messages contain a stereotype we are afraid to confirm, and that stress affects our daily lives.

8. Roy and Steiner, *Radical Psychiatry* (see ack., n. 2).

9. Much of early psychological theory is based on the diagnosis of women's hysteria, a condition that plagued Victorian society. Judith Herman's *Trauma and Recovery* (New York: BasicBooks, 1997) provides an elegant and thoughtful analysis of the development of psychological theory, with a particular focus on the work of Sigmund Freud and his seldom-heard theory that childhood sexual abuse was the primary cause of "hysteria." The senior thinkers of his profession were horrified by his assertion; if the many cases of hysteria were caused by childhood sexual abuse, that meant there were that many perpetrators in society. Freud was forced to retract his theory or lose his ability to work in his chosen profession. Such assertions of social norms in the development of psychological theory have left it rife with inequality and injustice. The book *Re-Centering* (see chap. 2, n. 3) offers many attempts to address this type of normative dissonance in conflict resolution by including writings by people from marginalized communities about their culturally conscious approaches to mediation and conflict resolution.

10. "Luisel Ramos," *Wikipedia*, last modified April 2, 2014, http://en.wikipedia.org/wiki/Luisel_Ramos.

11. Derek Thompson, "The Financial Benefits of Being Beautiful," *The Atlantic*, January 11, 2014.

Chapter 7: Getting Unstuck: From Pig Fight to Plan

1. Not to pig all cultural norms—cultural norms can have benefits, such as keeping people from killing each other in traffic accidents at intersections. Thank goodness for the cultural norm of the stop sign!

2. Wilhelm Reich, *Character Analysis*, trans. Mary Boyd (New York: Farrar, Straus & Giroux, 1933).

3. Many mind/body practitioners are skilled at leading clients through body scan practices to promote relaxation. In addition, there are many recorded resources online, if you are curious and would like to give a guided body scan practice a try.

Chapter 8: Competition and Scarcity

1. Research by Shelley Taylor and others added the "tend and befriend" threat and fear response to the previously identified "fight or flight" response. "Fight or flight" corresponds neatly with competitive instincts and "tend and befriend" with cooperative instincts. Shelley E. Taylor et al., "Biobehavioral Responses to Stress in Females: Tend-and-Befriend, Not Fight-or-Flight." *Psychological Review* 107, no. 3 (2000): 411–29.

2. The Prisoner's Dilemma, a social science experiment from game theory, shows how two individuals might not cooperate even if it appeared in their best interest to do so. Two prisoners are offered less punishment if both cooperate with each other. If one cooperates and the other betrays confidence, the one who betrays confidence is set free, and the one who cooperates is punished more severely. If both betray the other, both receive a more severe sentence than if they both cooperate. A Wikipedia article of the same title explains the Prisoner's Dilemma game theory and many game and real-world tests; most of the time people cooperate more than "rationality" predicts. "Prisoner's Dilemma," *Wikipedia*, last modified March 21, 2014, http://en.wikipedia.org/wiki/Prisoner%E2%80%99s_dilemma.

3. False scarcity has been dubbed "poverty consciousness" in some popular psychology.

4. Research on happiness reveals that we feel more deprived and unhappy even with relative abundance when we perceive that we should or could have more.

5. For more on this topic, read Rob Dietz and Daniel O'Neill's *Enough Is Enough* (San Francisco: Berrett-Koehler, 2012) and Bill McKibben's *Deep Economy* (New York: Macmillan, 2007).

6. See the 2013 UNICEF report that indicates that the child well-being in the United States ranks 26th out of 29 wealthy nations, mostly as a result of the lack of time and attention children receive. The Netherlands ranks first because of the very flexible work schedules of parents, who sometimes are allowed to work three to four days per week for eight hours per day. UNICEF Office of Research, "Child Well-Being in Rich Countries: A Comparative Overview," Innocenti Report Card 11, 2013.

7. For a great article on this topic, read Tim Kreider's "The 'Busy' Trap," a *New York Times* opinion piece, June 30, 2012.

8. Sheryl Sandberg, *Lean In*. (New York: Random House Digital, 2013). Sandberg advocates creating more family-friendly work policies that support women to stay in the workplace throughout their childbearing years—this approach to workplace policy benefits fathers and children as well.

Chapter 9: Theory of Change: Change in Our Personal Lives

1. In Richard Strozzi-Heckler's *Anatomy of Change* (Berkeley, CA: North Atlantic Books, 1993), he offers an intelligent discussion of what he calls our "conditioned tendency"—our automatic, embodied reaction to survival needs.

2. Richard Strozzi-Heckler, "Leadership in Action" (lecture, Strozzi Institute, Petaluma, CA, 2003). For more information on this topic, see www.strozziinstitute.com.

3. George Leonard, *Mastery* (New York: Plume, 1991). Leonard talks about the importance of the "plateau" in the change process and how, even though no change seems to be happening, much restructuring of the nervous system is occurring, and it's important to stay the course and see the change through to embodiment.

Chapter 10: Embodied Change: Body over Matter

1. Julia Kelliher reminds us that tools are an attempt to explain our lived experiences. If a tool does not help you improve your life, by all means let it go.

2. Fourth Way enneagram," *Wikipedia*, last modified February 2, 2014, http://en.wikipedia.org/wiki/Fourth_Way_enneagram.

3. In Steven Johnson's *Mind Wide Open* (New York: Scribner, 2004), he reports on studies of traumatized rats. When a part of the rat's limbic brain is damaged, the rat no longer acts traumatized. Limbic memory replays traumatic scenes with horrifying accuracy both sequentially and with sensory detail. This difference suggests that people suffering from post-traumatic stress memories are experiencing limbic recall, and limbic memories don't fade with time. Limbic memories can be rewritten, with interventions that are physically intense.

4. Richard Schmidt and Timothy Lee, *Motor Control and Learning: A Behavioral Emphasis* (Champagne, IL: Human Kinetics, 2011).

5. Richard Strozzi-Heckler, *The Leadership Dojo* (Berkeley, CA: North Atlantic Books, 2007).

6. Reich's research into body-based change led him ultimately to die in prison, persecuted for his groundbreaking work. Still, Reich left a legacy that shaped the California body/mind therapy movement, gently touching the Radical Therapy Collective's theories, and powerfully underpinning Skills for Change coaching theory and practice.

Chapter 12: Empowered Transactions: Cooperative Negotiation

1. Crazy pig has historically applied to groups of people who are structurally one down in the cultural hierarchy. Women, people of color, people with different mental processing patterns, people who value intuition over rationality, poor people—all these groups get labeled crazy by people in structurally one-up groups. The act of labeling people crazy is a convenient way to ignore their dignified complaints and is ultimately a power play.

2. In Skills for Change coaching, confidentiality and secrets, like many cultural norms, are something we negotiate rather than taking for granted.

Chapter 13: The Rescue Dynamic

1. The rescue triangle originated as the "alchoholic game" in Eric Berne's *Games People Play* (see ch.2, n. 4). The Radical Therapy Collective contributed to the theory by adding their understanding of the loss of power and the way the roles represent an inherent attempt to reclaim power. Julia Kelliher noted the concurrence between depletion and rescue in her clients and developed the theory of the depletion/repletion scale to help clients learn to replenish in order to stay out of rescue.

2. Some Skills for Change practitioners teach, "Ask for 100% of what you want, 100% of the time," to remind us that it is important to ask for what we want all the time and not just during formal negotiations. For some people, the added "100% of the time" feels like pressure and produces the rescue of doing more than they want to do. For others, it is a necessary reminder that even when we aren't negotiating, we need to let people know what we want. Additionally when we ask for what we want "100% of the time", we are more likely to notice that what we want changes from situation to situation. Ultimately we want to include all our competing, contradictory, met and unmet needs in our 100% statement.

3. In *The Seven Principles for Making Marriage Work* (New York: Three Rivers, 1999), John Gottman calls *criticism, contempt, defensiveness,* and *stonewalling* the "Four Horsemen" of relationship communication. In his analysis, these types of interactions are signs that a relationship will end, sooner or later. We differ from Gottman in that we interpret these communication types as nongenerative expressions of powerlessness. If we are willing to commit to ongoing practice, we can begin to express our story-free feelings of vulnerability, accept our powerlessness, and ask for 100% of what we want.

4. Chas August, "Pearls of Wisdom from Stan Dale," *HAI Global*, http://www.hai. org/2826/wisdom-from-stan/.

5. Sometimes the person hearing the held feeling may genuinely feel apologetic and offer an apology, and sometimes the person who holds the feeling might ask for an apology to help let the feeling go. However, a demand for an apology also can be an obstruction to the successful resolution of a topic, as it might represent a rescue or a power play to the parties involved.

Chapter 14: Stories: Filling in the Blanks to Create Meaning

1. Robert Wright discusses these types of studies in *The Moral Animal* (New York: Vintage, 1995).

2. Some Skills for Change practitioners use the term paranoia, as coined by the Radical Psychiatrists, when we refer to an "intuitively based" story. One derivation of the word paranoia means "beyond rational thought." Our redefinition of paranoia is "a radical response to mainstream psychiatry's dismissal of people's inaccurate stories as pathological paranoid beliefs." On a larger scale, like Skills for Change, the school of psychology known as social psychology also

seeks to depathologize human behavior. They assert that "crazy," dysfunctional, delusional, or harmful beliefs and behavior can be attributed to "cognitive dissonance"—attempts to deal with the stress of mysterious, contradictory, and/or traumatic observations. Thomas Steven Szasz, *The Myth of Mental Illness* (New York: HarperCollins, 1974); Richard H. Price, *Abnormal Behavior* (Austin, TX: Holt, Rinehart, and Winston, 1978).

Chapter 15: The Power to Trust

1. *Cisgender* is a term that originates in transgender activism to designate when people identify with their medically determined cultural gender. While most cisgender folks take their gender for granted, a complex cultural transaction takes place by which medical personnel determine a child's gender, particularly in cases when an individual has genital identifiers that could go either way.

2. The opposite formation in a group—when a man is in a group of women, for example—may be uncomfortable for the person of difference, but it is a significantly different formation in that the systemic, historic oppressive forces are against the majority in this case, instead of against the minority member. Oppression can almost always be monetized. Since the man in the group of women has not suffered loss of income due to his status in the group, the formation of the group is just potentially uncomfortable—in other words, there is no such thing as "reverse" oppression. The women may hold a stereotype of men, or he may have an internalized stereotype of himself that produces increased bodily stress. He might use the pig fighting techniques to help him face his difference as a learning opportunity if it aligns with his goals for the future. Claude Steele's writings on stereotype threat in *Whistling Vivaldi* may be particularly useful in such a situation (see chap. 6, n. 7).

Chapter 16: Cooperative Communication: The Relief of Clearing Held Feelings and Stories

1. Claude Steiner, *Emotional Literacy* (Fawnskin, CA: Personhood Press, 2003). Steiner also wrote a story about "strokes" called "A Warm Fuzzy Tale." He makes it available free online on his website at www.claudesteiner.com. Steiner ran a Radical Therapy group called Stroke City to help people learn new ways to be more appreciative. One of the reasons Radical Therapists call appreciations "strokes" is that they want to highlight the way humans have been alienated from touch as a means of healing.

2. Steiner, *Emotional Literacy* (see chap. 16, n. 1).

Chapter 18: Loss and Disappointment: The Healing Power of Grief

1. John W. James and Russell Friedman, *The Grief Recovery Handbook* (New York: HarperCollins, 2009).

Chapter 20: Appreciations

1. Robert Emmons, *Thanks!* (New York: Houghton Mifflin, 2008).

2. Steiner, *Emotional Literacy* (see chap. 16, n. 1).

Sidebar List

Julia Kelliher, Julia Carol, Paula Elliott, Marybeth Paul, Glenn Smith, and Nancy Shanteau live in Nevada County in Northern California. To find out more about them and their work, visit Skills for Change on the web at http://www.skillsforchangecoaching.com.

CPSIA information can be obtained
at www.ICGtesting.com
Printed in the USA
FSOW02n1200061014
3195FS